# www.wadsworth.com

*wadsworth.com* is the World Wide Web site for Wadsworth and is your direct source to dozens of online resources.

At *wadsworth.com* you can find out about supplements, demonstration software, and student resources. You can also send email to many of our authors and preview new publications and exciting new technologies.

**wadsworth.com**
Changing the way the world learns®

# Explorations in Counseling and Spirituality

## PHILOSOPHICAL, PRACTICAL, AND PERSONAL REFLECTIONS

**CHRISTOPHER FAIVER**
*John Carroll University*

**R. ELLIOTT INGERSOLL**
*Cleveland State University*

**EUGENE O'BRIEN**
*St. Elizabeth Health Center*

**CHRISTOPHER MCNALLY**
*Doctoral Student*
*The University of Akron*

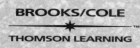

**BROOKS/COLE**

**THOMSON LEARNING**™

Australia • Canada • Mexico • Singapore • Spain • United Kingdom • United States

**BROOKS/COLE**

──────✳──────™

**THOMSON LEARNING**

Counseling and Human Services Editor:
  Julie Martinez
Editorial Assistant: Marin Plank
Marketing Manager: Caroline Concilla
Project Editor: Dianne Jensis Toop
Print Buyer: Robert King
Permissions Editor: Robert Kauser
Production Service: Vicki Moran

Copy Editor: Patterson Lamb
Cover Designer: Stanton Design
Cover Image: Digital Imagery © 2000
  PhotoDisc, Inc.
Cover Printer: Webcom Limited
Compositor: Publishers' Design and Production
  Services, Inc.
Printer: Webcom Limited

**Wadsworth/Thomson Learning**
**10 Davis Drive**
**Belmont, CA 94002-3098**
**USA**

For information about our products, contact us:
**Thomson Learning Academic Resource Center**
**1-800-423-0563**
http://www.wadsworth.com

**International Headquarters**
Thomson Learning
International Division
290 Harbor Drive, 2nd Floor
Stamford, CT 06902-7477
USA

**UK/Europe/Middle East/South Africa**
Thomson Learning
Berkshire House
168-173 High Holborn
London WC1V 7AA
United Kingdom

**Asia**
Thomson Learning
60 Albert Street, #15-01
Albert Complex
Singapore 189969

**Canada**
Nelson Thomson Learning
1120 Birchmount Road
Toronto, Ontario M1K 5G4
Canada

**Library of Congress Cataloging-in-Publication Data**
  Explorations in counseling and spirituality : philosophical, practical,
  and personal reflections / Christopher Faiver . . . [et al.].
      p. cm.
  Includes bibliographical references and index.
  ISBN 0-534-57582-X
    1. Counseling. 2. Counseling—Religious aspects. 3. Psychology
  and religion. 4. Spirituality. I. Faiver, Christopher, 1947–
  BF637.C6 E95 2000
  158'.3—dc21
                                            00-062119

# Contents

## *Chapter 4*

### *The Story of Job and Human Suffering*    **62**

## *Chapter 5*

### *Guilt and Mental Health*    **74**

## *Chapter 6*

### *Discernment to Epiphany: Inclusion of Religion and Spirituality in the Assessment Process*    **90**

## Chapter 7

### Interventions    117

## Chapter 8

### The Spirituality of the Twelve Steps    130

## Chapter 9

### Counselor Belief System Self-Assessment    151

## Chapter 10

## The Journey Continues: Some Final Thoughts    162

## Appendix A

## *Mantras and Meditations for Counselors and Other Therapists    167*

## Appendix B

## *The Twelve Steps and Twelve Traditions of Alcoholics Anonymous    174*

## Appendix C

## *Client Assessment Form    176*

## Appendix D

## *Spiritual Competencies of the Association for Spiritual, Ethical, and Religious Values in Counseling    178*

## Appendix E

## *Counselor Self-Assessment Exercise    181*

*Appendix F*

**Related Web Sites      183**

*Appendix G*

**The Spiritual Wellness Inventory      185**

# *Preface*

## WHY WE WROTE THIS TEXT

In the late 1960s, undergraduates at Hiram College, a small, midwestern liberal arts school, could witness a long-standing tradition of the "last lecture." Naïve, impressionistic undergraduates paid close attention as their instructors summed up the many lessons of their own individual experience. Instructions to the professor were simple: Imagine that you were to give the very last lecture of your career. What would you say?

Following in the footsteps of those who modeled this exercise for us, we endeavor here to present a particular variation of this "last lecture" motif. When we consider counseling and spirituality, what, as authors, do we most want to share with readers? This question led to our exploration of counseling and spirituality. In this book we seek to provide a basic foundation, from which the reader may draw practical and personal conclusions regarding the interface of counseling and spirituality. We have made a conscious attempt to fill the gaps not addressed by similar books. To accomplish this objective, we have divided the book into three domains: the philosophical, the practical, and the personal. It is our contention that a holistic model of counseling and spirituality must integrate the scholarly and philosophical with the practical and personal. We admit that our contributions are limited and, as such, provide a jumping off point for further exploration rather than academic conclusions.

Working as mental health professionals, we remain extremely hesitant to divorce client spirituality or client religious belief from our clients themselves. In an attempt to explore and explain this position, we may frame a question in the manner of the Hiram lecturer: "What lessons would we share with those in the field of counseling and therapy?" Lessons arrive in the form of a journey, involving exploration of ancient and emotionally laden concepts such as evil, guilt, and suffering as well as love, compassion, and forgiveness. As such, this text offers a unique opportunity for both didactic and experiential investigation of spiritual and religious beliefs in relation to the counseling process. While, as authors, we have diverse experiences in various spiritual practices, we recognize that we have all been imprinted by Judeo-Christian culture. This imprint is undoubtedly reflected in the lessons that we offer here.

## FOR WHOM IS THE TEXT INTENDED?

We wrote this book primarily for counselors in practice, counseling students, and counselor educators who are integrating spirituality into their counseling work or who are interested in doing so. We also feel that the book will be of interest to those who are exploring their spiritual selves in counseling relationships. We trust that those who have taken only their first steps—as students or practitioners—will reflect and pause as they read this book, while working toward personal and professional wholeness. For those who are well along in their personal or professional journeys, it is our hope that this text may provide an impetus to assess and value unique and individual paths to the source, however conceptualized. We ourselves have found this process to be one of balancing two inherent parts: the Scientist, who skeptically demands tangible and verifiable evidence; and the Artist, who accepts life intuitively, spiritually, and with a child's sense of awe and wonder. Our life journeys lead us on convergent, yet distinct, paths—one, the secular, and another, the sacred. A primary goal of our book is to *reconcile these two paths within a field that has traditionally kept them more or less separate.*

## HOW DOES OUR BOOK ADDRESS THIS GOAL?

In Chapter 1 we offer supports for integrating counseling and spirituality, an integration that has been so much a part of our own journeys. Chapter 2 was inspired by ways in which our journeys are interwoven with threads that run throughout the world's great religions and various spiritual movements. These interweavings have had a sizable impact on the field of counseling. In Chapters 3, 4, and 5 we address evil, suffering, and guilt, recognizing that this shadow side is an important component in both our own and our clients' directing of spiritual energies. Chapter 7 provides a summary of spirituality-linked counseling interventions. Chapter 8 gives an overview of twelve-step spirituality, which we see as a useful complement to counseling for a significant number of clients. In the context of a thorough assessment of both spirituality and religious belief, we ask readers to consider the processes of client assessment and counselor self-assessment in Chapters 6 and 9. Finally, in Chapter 10 we sum up where we've been and where we're headed. Our appendices take the form of instruments, competencies, sources, and professional and personal forms and exercises.

For the student or practitioner who is interested in coming to terms with the role that spirituality and/or religious belief may play within the counseling dynamic, this text provides one possible justification in unique, user-friendly form. In a world increasingly dominated by "the secular mind" (Coles, 1999), our personal and professional attempts to grapple with the issues elucidated here have become increasingly important. It is our hope that this text will provide relevant guidance as a classroom resource, while also functioning as a model for related individual inquiry.

Coles, R. (1999). *The secular mind.* Princeton, NJ: Princeton University Press.

## ACKNOWLEDGMENTS

This book would not have been possible without the inspiration of Craig Barth. We also appreciate the encouragement and support of Annie Bertreche, Caroline Concilla, and Mike Daniels. A number of students and colleagues contributed valuable assistance during the writing of this book. They include Geriann Cahill, Sheri Eisengart, Dale Galgozy, Rhonda Harrison, Kathy MacCluskie, Valerie Moyer, Susan Previts, Susan Vesely, and Liz Welfel.

The staff at Brooks/Cole was enormously helpful. We would particularly like to thank Julie Martinez, Lisa Gebo, and Eileen Murphy for their help in completing the project.

We would like to thank the following people who reviewed early drafts of the manuscript and contributed valuable observations and suggestions: Dr. Marsha Wiggens Frame; Professor Mary Fukuyama, University of Florida; Professor Harold Hackney, Syracuse University; Professor Pamela Highlen, Ohio State University; Associate Professor Janice Holden, University of North Texas; Dr. Patricia Hudson, The George Washington University; Dr. Judy Miranti, Our Lady of Holy Cross College; Professor Kathleen Ritter, California State University-Bakersfield; and Professor Scott Young, Mississippi State University.

## DEDICATIONS

Ingersoll: To my wife Jennifer and my family who are always with me and to Will Brewster, my first spiritual mentor who always made time when it would have been easier not to, and who always listened when it would have been easier to instruct.

Faiver: To Alberta and Howard Faiver, Uncle Chris Clark, my sisters Carolyn L. Faiver and Susan Faiver Noday, and my dear family; to my mentors Dr. H. Carl Brunson and Dr. David W. Cliness; to my healers Dr. Thomas Cutolo and Dr. Jody N. Telfair; to my spiritual director, the Reverend Thomas L. Schubeck, S.J.; to the Reverend Ernest F. Edmunds, who influenced my early religious training; and to loyal and trusted friends Dr. Roger G. Baldwin, Dr. David J. Weber, Dr. Eugene M. O'Brien, and David P. McElwain, ACSW.

McNally: To those who have guided me on a shared path of spiritual and religious growth, most notably my trusted friend Marie Lipka and the Reverend Dennis T. Dillon, S.J.

O'Brien: To Patrick and Alice O'Brien, my sister Pat and all my wonderful family; to my partner Edward R. Stride, for his support and understanding; to Sister Mary Maud and Father B.J. Wernert, S.J., who helped set me on a spiritual path many years ago; and to my faithful and hard-working friend Chris Faiver.

# INTRODUCTION

*I know there's no Easter bunny; and I know that there is no Santa Claus.
As for God, I'll have to think about that.*

—Cory, age 8

*A seeker after truth must shun no science, scorn no book, nor cling fanatically
to a single creed.*

—Muslim (Islamic) Proverb

*Every concept grasped by the mind becomes an obstacle in the quest to those
who search.*

—Gregory of Nyssa

Belief, faith, life. All are a struggle, both for us who counsel and those whom we counsel. Some find answers through spirituality. There are many ways to describe spirituality although there is no real agreement on any one definition (Maher & Hunt, 1993). For the purpose of this book, let us begin by describing spirituality as "magical" in that it has the power to transform. Whatever is spiritual touches us deeply and can transform suffering into learning, enmity into collaboration, and indifference into love.

So that we may approach the subject from a common stance, this chapter defines spirituality versus religion and explores its intrinsic and extrinsic expressions. Counterarguments are then made for separating spirituality and religion from counseling, followed by reasons to consider a holistic stance. From this base we can then offer philosophical, practical, and personal reflections in subsequent chapters. In this examination we invite the reader to approach the counseling process with a holy regard.

# SPIRITUALITY VERSUS RELIGION

Spirituality may be described as a deep sense of wholeness, connectedness, and openness to the infinite (or the magical, if you prefer) (Shafranske & Gorsuch, 1984). The Fourteenth Dalai Lama of Tibet has described spirituality as concerned with the qualities of the human spirit that bring happiness to oneself and others—qualities such as love, compassion, patience, tolerance, forgiveness, contentment, and a sense of harmony and responsibility (Gyatso, Dalai Lama XIV, 1999). We believe spirituality is an innate human quality. Not only is it our vital life force, but at the same time it is also our experience of that vital life force. Although this life force is deeply part of us, it also transcends us. It is what connects us to other people, nature, and the source of life. The experience of spirituality is greater than ourselves and helps us transcend and embrace life situations. This initial description is purposely broad so as to encompass many different expressions, such as one person's commitment to serving humanity, another person's cultivating an artistic talent, and another's focus on raising a family.

Across the world's diverse cultures there are many people who find their answers through religion—the social vehicle to nurture and express spirituality. From another view, as an essential aspect of humanity, spirituality may be channeled through the vehicles of the world's various religions (Ingersoll, 1994). If one agrees with our notion that spirituality is an innate human quality that may be channeled through the practice of a religion, the distinction between religion and spirituality becomes somewhat easier to make. Otherwise, as some writers have noted, there may be difficulty in conceptually separating the two (Fukuyama & Sevig, 1999; Richards & Bergin, 1997). As with many topics in counseling and spirituality, each person must arrive at his or her own conclusions.

# EXOTERIC VERSUS ESOTERIC EXPRESSIONS

Two other terms may add clarity to our thinking about spirituality and religion: *exoteric* and *esoteric*. The exoteric is the outward, public, and more conventional form of a religious or spiritual impulse. This may include creeds, rituals, and stated beliefs. Such forms provide channels for the spiritual impulse and facilitate the teaching of a religious or spiritual path. A primary purpose of exoteric religion or spirituality is to instruct, to teach, to prepare us metaphorically as the vessel to receive an actual spiritual experience. In the exoteric forms there may be more emphasis on belief than experience. This makes the exoteric useful for people initiating their spiritual journey or beginning a new phase of it. It is the heart of organized or institutionalized spirituality.

The exoteric is also profoundly influenced by a person's culture. Its channels are sculpted by culture and responded to by the individual. Thus, when you as a counselor learn about the impact of a client's cultural background on his or her spiritual or religious path, you are learning about the taught cultural exoteric forms.

The esoteric is the inward, subjective experience of the spiritual/religious impulse, typically embodied in the mystical sects of the world's religions. The esoteric may be directed through the culturally shaped channels of the exoteric, but this is not essential. Developmentally, a person might initially practice an exoteric form of spirituality and then progress to an esoteric experience. This may be the case in only some instances, however.

Frequently the esoteric is a "secret" teaching. This is not so much to shut people out as to prevent people who are not developmentally ready for a direct spiritual experience from misinterpreting it in harmful ways (Armstrong, 1993). In many cases, the esoteric may clash with the exoteric, depending on the cultural circumstances. The esoteric is the heart of the sacred consciousness that experiences God as the center of the universe (Bache, 1990; Smith, 1976). In fact, the esoteric may lead to experiences that transcend the exoteric and its cultural influences.

More recently, the philosopher Ken Wilber (1999) has referred to these poles as *translation* and *transformation*. Translation refers more to the exoteric, transformation to the esoteric. In translation, a person is given a creed, doctrine, or belief that provides a new way to think about life. Wilber noted that this is a widespread and shared exoteric function. On the other hand, the self who makes choices in the realm of translation may quite literally be transformed. This transformation is a radical shift in identity, a death and rebirth from believer to the knower behind the believer. For Wilber, transformation is the force behind what has been termed *enlightenment*. Perhaps transformation is the same force that facilitates the process of conversion in its many cultural forms. Wilber maintained that in a developmental context, translation is essential to transformation, but only a minority of people, for whatever reason, experience transformation.

## NONTHEISTIC STANCES AND SPIRITUALITY

While many seek their answers in exoteric and esoteric religious and spiritual practices, still others develop a nonpersonal, nontheistic stance for understanding reality (what the theologian Paul Tillich referred to as that which we "bump into" from time to time). For many reasons, these people may resist using the labels of religious and spiritual traditions for their experiences. For them, there is an awareness that even as they "work on their lives" for answers, their lives "work on them." They may accept or reject a spiritual worldview.

Can such a person be considered spiritual? We believe so. Even those who reject the spiritual must first think about its possibility in order to dismiss it (The sixteenth-century Anglican theologian Richard Hooker [1836] identified two types of atheists—those who didn't believe in a God and those who acted as if God didn't exist.) Others of us waver back and forth on beliefs, dependent upon our life circumstances, influenced by others' opinions, or, perhaps, by how far along we are developmentally. Yes, we all struggle to make sense of belief, faith, and life.

## COUNSELING AND SPIRITUALITY: A PART OF EACH OTHER OR APART FROM EACH OTHER?

In this chapter we introduce our struggle to make sense of how counseling and spirituality are both convergent and separate. We begin by addressing the notion that spirituality and counseling should be kept separate. We then offer defenses of understanding spirituality as experientially and conceptually related to counseling. Our defenses include (1) the psychological fact of interest itself, (2) the mind/body problem, (3) postmodern and multicultural considerations, (4) existential considerations, (5) the experience of evil, (6) transpersonal considerations, and (7) the commitment to truth. Because of their import, these defenses merit separate consideration.

> It is not appropriate to see as separate things, things which cannot be distinguished.
>
> —Albert Einstein

Despite Einstein's advice, many Westerners are quick to conceptually break wholes down into parts. Since we feel that spirituality is innate to the human experience, we logically also believe that it is a dimension of the human experience that merits therapeutic consideration. The idea that a person's beliefs can be separated from that person is based on the Western philosophical bias that breaks wholes down into parts and categorizes the parts.

As counselors, we are no strangers to trying to break wholes into parts. We may find ourselves trying to understand a case saying "this client is ruled by her feelings" or "this client's thought processes are his worst enemy." The Western approach of factual thinking seeks to understand things by differentiating them for the purpose of examination. This is useful for some purposes, such as differentiating the body from invading bacteria it is temporarily hosting. In other endeavors it is less useful, as in differentiating mind/body/spirit or thinking/feeling/behaving. In closely examining elements like mind, body, and spirit, we find that they all work together, informing each other in a manner that defies the simplistic categories imposed on them. These elements are akin to ground coffee beans, water, cream, sweetener, and a coffee mug that, taken in the proper combination, are a cup of coffee. Yet, we really can't describe "cup of coffee" through reference to any one of these elements alone.

Occasionally we meet colleagues who believe spirituality should be separated from counseling clients. To us, this would be like telling a client, "We're sorry, you are experiencing irrational thoughts and in our practice we only deal with feelings" or like ordering a cup of coffee without the water. Spirituality is as much a part of the human experience as thoughts and feelings. Obviously there are clients who have no particular interest in spirituality or any issues related to spirituality and religion. In those cases the counselor need not bother with consideration of the spiritual domain.

Whenever we differentiate and organize elements we create models or, as linguist Alfred Korzybski (1933) noted, "maps" of reality. These maps are not reality itself. As a Zen saying goes, "A symbol is a finger pointing at the moon and he is a fool who mistakes the finger for the moon." This may sound obvious but it is amazing how quickly we can forget it. We can become passionately attached to our "maps" whether they be counseling theories or concepts of God. As a species we have gone to war to defend the maps of reality we have created.

Many people (Korzybski included) have bemoaned the human tendency to confuse the map with the reality. Most of us treat paper and metal money as if it were real wealth rather than a symbol used to trade for things of real wealth. In the United States, people debate the burning of the flag often more passionately than the maltreatment of citizens whom the symbol of the flag represents. As Korzybski wrote, confusing the map with the reality is akin to trying to eat the menu in a restaurant rather than the food, which the menu points to. It is certainly not a practice that leads to a nourishing diet!

Historically, people across cultures have confused models of the spiritual with the spiritual itself. Often this has been done with representations of God, confusing the words or images used to *describe* that ineffable reality with the reality itself (Armstong, 1993). How did we get in this situation? Some theorists like philosopher Ken Wilber (1981, 1995) note that as our species has become more self-conscious, this self-consciousness has led to experiencing the world as if we were separate from it. This trend, paired with the Western tendency to break wholes into parts, fueled the positivist modus operandi of Western science, which, although an ideal tool for some jobs, is altogether inadequate for others.

In earlier times, Western contributors to the scientific method also had strong spiritual leanings. Granted, these "leanings" were maintained under great pressure from the Western Christian church, but the mingling of the spiritual with the scientific is something we have lost in recent centuries. It is Descartes' philosophy, rather than his theology, that students learn today—an illustration of one unfortunate result of scientific thinking: to negate much that is intangible, including the soul. The same dynamic was at work when Freud's writings were being translated from German to English. Freud made extensive use of the metaphor of the "soul" but this has been deleted in translation (Bettleheim, 1983).

Experimental design has greatly contributed to our understanding of many phenomena; and many advances in science, medicine, and other disciplines, including counseling, have come about through this way of confirming reality. However, the scientific method, with its emphasis on objective differentiation of what is being studied, is only complementary to the subjective, phenomenological experiences that make up the primary content of our lives, our spiritual experiences, and our counseling sessions. This point is worth noting, because the subjective experience is a powerful component of both the counseling process and the spiritual journey.

The scientific method appears less useful in the subjective realm. Applying a strict scientific method to evaluate the subjective experience of another is akin to analyzing a Beethoven sonata through the physics of sound. To plumb the depths of the subjective experience that is so integral to counseling and the spiritual journey, we must consider other modes of confirmation.

Just imagine the possibility of other models of confirmation of meaning, of reality, of existence. These models open a universe of immeasurable intangibles, inspiring a childlike awe and wonder. Think of the possibility of black holes, wormholes, and a vast, expansive universe. Different models of confirmation do not have to be mutually exclusive of scientific methodology but can be complementary to it—just as it is possible to be both spiritual and yet a believer in Darwin's theory of evolution.

Other modes of confirmation can certainly include consensus. Wilber (1999) has noted that every school of esoteric spiritual practices includes teachers or guides who help students determine their progress. These guides or teachers use the consensus of a practicing community to determine whether the student is progressing spiritually. In such instances the consensus of those comparing their subjective experiences serves as an alternative model of confirmation.

Most counselors know that there is virtually no way to chart or to measure the "unconscious," a central concept of Freud, the father of modern psychiatry and psychotherapy. Freud himself could not measure it, but he had the utmost respect for these vast reaches of inner space.

As counselors and therapists, we must cultivate the same respect for the uncharted mysteries of each individual. Just as we must use clinical skills and objective measures to assess clients initially, we must also rely on our subjective experience of clients as they share their stories with us. In some ways this process of meaning making can be a spiritual practice in itself. We must heed Milton Erickson's essential advice: to follow the client and to stay out of the way. That is, all that we do in therapy should be tailored to this unique individual, including his or her subjective experience that we cannot measure, but which we can begin to learn through experiencing the client in the sacred space of the counseling session. The implications of this approach affect every aspect of the counseling relationship—choice of theory, choice of therapy, choice of technique, type of client, type of concern, personality type, time constraints, amount of psychic pain, impact of significant others, agency and managed care constraints—with all carrying their own permutations.

Among the numerous subjective experiences that clients bring into the therapy room are their belief systems. The client's belief system cannot be separated from the client's essential self. We accept that some systems of belief may be dysfunctional to a client, causing excessive guilt, anxiety, or negative thinking. Other belief systems, however, are sustaining and comforting and perhaps link clients to their own vital life force. We are acutely aware that the counselor also brings his or her own belief system into the consulting room. Sometimes belief systems conflict, and countertransference can result, necessitating a referral. Sometimes systems conflict, then converge, and both parties grow as a result. Most certainly, we are not in the therapy situation to preach or proselytize. However, we are in the business of assessment, treatment, referral (as necessary), and follow-up (if possible). Any good assessment, treatment, referral, and follow-up *recognizes* (and, concomitantly, does not discount or demean) what the client presents us with, including a spiritual or religious belief system, as well as the possibility of none.

Scholar Karen Armstong (1993) reminds us that every generation and culture must define its spirituality, including secular expressions. Western society in many ways has become dominated by the scientific worldview. Counseling and psychotherapy may be one way we can address losing touch with the mythic, subjective, magical world of inner experience. In earlier times, clerics were the helpers in this realm; counselors now engage in confessionlike dialogues and assist in the provision of lay absolutions. Perhaps we are, as psychologist Perry London (1986) has suggested, lay priests or (in a non-Christian sense) "healers" of the soul.

Certainly, the history of the helping professions has its early roots in the ministrations of diverse spiritual groups. To a large degree, any lay priest or folk healer analogy is dependent on the type and quality of the therapeutic relationship. As Erich Fromm (1950) noted, there is therapy that aims simply at social adjustment and therapy that aims at a "cure of the soul." Shortcomings of delivering mental health services under an emerging system of managed care have been well documented in recent literature (Cummings, Budman, & Thomas, 1998; Dana, 1998; Small & Barnhill, 1998). Fromm's distinction may be applied when comparing the worst aspects of this managed care (often seeking only to adjust an individual quickly to a sometimes equally sick surrounding society) with a more rewarding psychotherapy—focusing instead on profound, intrapersonal change. It is this latter type of therapy that we feel enters the domain of the spiritual.

# REASONS TO INTEGRATE COUNSELING AND SPIRITUALITY

*The spiritual dimensions of counseling require a counselor's dedication to quality care with a sense of purpose and mission.*

—David Powell

There is still debate over the appropriateness of mixing spirituality and counseling, defining a relationship between spirituality and religion, and the status of the church-state separation in the United States. One may therefore ask, "How can counselors support the integration of counseling and spirituality?" We feel this question deserves a response. Our response can also serve as a justification for counselors who are appropriately integrating the two in their practices currently—and perhaps being criticized for it.

There are many ways to respond to the above question. As Scott Peck (1997) would suggest, the answer is "over-determined," meaning that there are many reasons working in concert and the whole may be greater than the sum of the parts. We believe integrating spirituality and counseling is supported by the following elements: (1) the psychological fact of interest, (2) mind/body issues, (3) postmodern/multicultural considerations, (4) existential issues, (5) the experience of evil, (6) transpersonal considerations, and (7) the central place in counseling and spirituality of a commitment to truth. Let us now examine these in some detail.

## THE PSYCHOLOGICAL FACT OF INTEREST

All human cultures have a psychological sense of the spiritual. In this sense the spiritual exists universally as a psychological fact of interest. Jung (1933) stated:

> Among all my patients in the second half of life—that is to say, over thirty-five—there has not been one whose problem in the last resort was not that of finding a religious outlook on life. It is safe to say that every one of them feels ill because he lost that which the living religions of every age have given to their followers, and none of them have been really healed who did not regain his religious outlook. (p. 264) (See Chapter 8 for a discussion of how Jung's views on spiritual experience influenced the development of Alcoholics Anonymous.)

In his many writings, Carl Jung pointed to the "psychological fact" of religious and spiritual explanations, noting that they do occur across cultures. Jung's analytical psychology took the concept of God very seriously. Armstrong (1993) has noted that Jung's God was akin to that of the mystics, "a psychological fact, subjectively experienced by each individual" (p. 357). This fact of interest is indeed cross-cultural, even trans-cultural. Armstrong also noted that peoples of all places and times have sought spiritual understandings of life

and were not coerced to do so. Currently, in American polls, a clear major-
ity of respondents endorse religious/spiritual beliefs and/or experiences
(Caplow, Bahr, Chadwick, & Hoover, 1983; Gallup & Castelli, 1989; Gallup
Poll Monthly, 1993).

The way spiritual interests are expressed seems to fluctuate on a continuum, from those with institutional sponsorship to more individualistic models
(Armstrong, 1993). Sociologist Robert Bellah and his colleagues (Bellah, 1970;
Bellah et al., 1985) have observed that since colonial times Americans have
moved steadily toward an individualized spirituality. Although in the last decade
of the twentieth century, 93% of Americans identified with a religious group—
typically Christian (Hoge, 1996; Kosmin & Lachman, 1993)—they still pre-
ferred to label themselves "spiritual" rather than "religious" (Hoge, 1996).
Americans in the twenty-first century seem to prefer to express their spirituality individualistically. Even so, this may be under the auspices of a larger religion
or organization.

We seem to be in a situation reminiscent of that of sixteenth-century Christians. At that time, people were demoralized by the Catholic/Protestant violence, the proliferation of sects, and the arguing of unprovable and divergent
views. They felt paralyzed by the sheer number of theological choices (Armstrong, 1993). Twenty-first-century Americans, dissatisfied with their experience in organized religion, have no shortage of options in a free-market culture
that offers anything that will sell. And spirituality sells. This is not necessarily
good or bad but, rather, illustrative of the psychological fact of interest in the
spiritual.

## QUESTIONS FROM THE MIND/BODY PROBLEM

Can the spiritual, which has been designated a psychological fact of interest,
be reduced to a "side effect" of the way the human brain and mind work?
As much as scientific method has brought our culture, it has not yielded a great
deal in explaining what the mind is or how it works, thus leaving this question
unanswerable. Trying to define the conceptual "mind" and explore its relationship to the physical brain has been an ongoing challenge. Many practitioners,
some brave enough to write eloquently on the topic of their own battles with
psychiatric illness, have wrestled with this distinction between "mind" and
"brain" functioning in both their personal lives and their professional efforts
toward assisting clients (Jamison, 1995). This important distinction relates
directly to spirituality since in many societies the "mind" was thought to be related to the "soul." Perhaps the spiritual or religious impulse is simply an
epiphenomenon of the brain. This hypothesis would be easier to address if we
understood more of how the brain works, but we don't (Churchland, 1986).

All of this uncertainty has contributed to the mind/body problem encountered in the helping professions (Gabbard, 1994). Theorists like philosopher

Patricia Churchland (1986; Churchland & Sejnowski, 1992) have posited elaborate information-processing models in defense of the position that the mind is an epiphenomenon of the brain. Others, like psychiatrist Stanislav Grof (1985), posit that the mind (and soul/spirit) is to the brain as TV transmissions are to a television receiver. This is more of a dual substance theory—the mind and soul are essentially separate from the brain and body.

We do know that mental events (spiritually inspired or not) exert an influence on the structure of the brain. Neurologist Roger Sperry (1988) referred to this as the mentalist paradigm and noted that it increases the complexity of trying to differentiate the mind and the brain. Ultimate truths aside, this knowledge raises the question of what effects a spiritual outlook may have on the brain. Could it be that aside from the ultimate reality of a spiritual worldview, holding a spiritual outlook is advantageous to one's survival and happiness? Until we learn more about the nature of the mind and the brain, such questions will elude answer. Armstrong (1993) notes that throughout recorded history spirituality has been important to people of all cultures in dealing with crises. She also states that when a religion or spirituality ceases to fulfill a function (such as making meaning in times of crisis), it dies out. Clearly we are biased in the direction of accepting the ultimate reality of a spiritual worldview. However, even if there were no such ultimate reality, that worldview might serve a powerful explanatory function for clients, meriting our attention as a result.

## POSTMODERN/MULTICULTURAL CONSIDERATIONS

Interpretations, spiritual or otherwise, must hold explanatory power for clients in order to be useful (Yalom, 1995). Both the postmodern and multicultural movements have supported such thinking by encouraging a multiplicity of perspectives. There are "hard" and "soft" schools in both movements. Adherents to the "hard" schools maintain that all of reality is socially or culturally constructed, while adherents to the "soft" schools claim that only some elements of reality are socially/culturally constructed.

Both movements have their origin in what we call the end of the modern era. The postmodern era recognizes the limitations in humanism and logical positivism. The modern Western era was typified by the Western belief that human progress was endless and human reason and technology would continually be put toward that progress. That notion was shattered by the Jewish holocaust of World War II. Although massacre was nothing new to the human species, this was the first time in history that all the mechanizations of a "civilized" country had been systematically geared toward the destruction of groups of people.

Postmoderns seem to understand that both reason and technology are akin to a surgeon's scalpel and can be used for healing or destroying. The modern Western era understood science to be a linear progression in which constant laws served to explicate the phenomena of nature. The advent of quantum theory diffused this understanding when the traditional methods seemed to turn up more questions than could possibly be answered, as well as to show particles acting in strange ways that contradicted "constant" laws. Stanislav Grof (1975, 1980) also noted that the systematic exploration of consciousness through psychedelic states (beginning in the 1940s) altered and supplemented the psychodynamic "hydraulic" map of the mind in much the same way that quantum theory added to Newtonian physics.

In addition to the shift from the modern to the postmodern, increasing awareness of the cultural diversity in U.S. citizenry is fostering changes in metacognition. For the first time, counselors (and citizens in general) are encouraged to expand their awareness of their cultural "software." This software may differ from culture to culture. Rather than seeing cultural differences as a threat needing to be stamped out, the multicultural movement posits the value of different cultural worldviews existing side by side. In one sense this has represented a resurfacing of the value placed on human subjectivity. Our multicultural directions as a nation blend quite well with the postmodern encouragement of different perspectives. Whereas the modern era encouraged conformity in the interpretation of experiences, the postmodern era attempts a cautious approach toward understanding the multiple perspectives involved in experiencing reality. Spirituality is a distinct part of this reality.

Fukuyama and Sevig (1997, 1999) have stated that spirituality is greatly about cultural differences. In their work, some of the richest exploration of spirituality in the counseling session emerges in relation to the cultural trappings of the client's spirituality. For other theorists, spirituality is a human universal channeled through culture, shaped by culture, and responded to uniquely by each individual (Speight et al., 1991). Note that we do not focus this text on issues of cultural diversity. Entire books have been dedicated to exploring the cultural aspects of counseling and spirituality (Fukuyama & Sevig, 1999) and we refer the reader to these works.

## EXISTENTIAL CONSIDERATIONS

*Do we not stray, as though through an infinite nothingness?*
—Friedrich Nietzsche

Existential considerations focus on the relationship between counseling, spirituality, and the existential givens of life. Existential givens include aging, disease, death, pain, injustice, and the uniquely human need for meaning. These constants seem to call on us to both transcend them and succumb to them. Across cultures, the paradox of these existential universals has inspired a spiritual interpretation and response. As in our discussion of the mind/body problem (or soul/body), whether a particular spiritual interpretation is ultimately and totally true is not the question. As counselors, our questions focus on the role that such interpretations play in the client's struggle with the existential givens of life. Certainly all spiritual impulses could be written off as responses to fear (as the philosophers Lucretius and Bertrand Russell [1957] believed), yearnings for a parent figure (as Freud [1953] asserted), or as life-affirming responses to the mystery of existence (as mystics of all cultures and ages have implied). Whatever the underlying dynamic, spiritual impulses exist and help our clients make meaning of their lives. As such, these spiritual impulses deserve our fullest respect.

As much as a sense of God figures into any person's spiritual impulse, there is an additional existential given that should be considered. This affirmation is found time and time again in all the world religions and suggests that God, being such as God is, cannot be an object of human knowledge any more than one can kiss one's own lips or see one's own eye directly with the same eye. Although this assertion is not universally accepted (what assertion is?), it may help the atheist or agnostic counselor reframe the client's belief in God.

## THE EXPERIENCE OF EVIL

*Life lives on life—it is cruel, but it is God's will.*

—Antonie van Leeuwenhoek

Undoubtedly, the universal experiences of those things called "evil" have contributed to and fueled the spiritual outlook. While we read news stories about the violence in our inner cities, shootings in our schools, and injustices suffered by many people worldwide, we also are struck by stories of how spirituality has helped people in these situations. Counselors cannot discount the spiritual outlook so long as clients use the construct of evil and seek a spiritual response to it.

*Evil* may be understood as metaphysical, natural, or human. In general, the term is used to describe those things that are harmful, disintegrating, injurious, morally repugnant, and influential in the suffering of our clients. Perhaps those things called evil are nothing more than the existential constants discussed above. Perhaps the spiritual impulse is nothing more than a rationalization, allowing us to coexist with evil in an imperfect universe. In either case—as we learn in Chapter 3—the construct calls forth a spiritual response in many people, and such a response deserves respect in the counseling session.

## TRANSPERSONAL CONSIDERATIONS

The integration of counseling and spirituality receives support from a related field: transpersonal psychology. The first documented use of the term *transpersonal* is by William James in 1905 (Vich, 1988). The term was also used by

Jung's translators for the German *ueberpersonlich* (Chinen, 1996). Transpersonal refers to developmental levels or types of human experience (including spiritual experiences) that transcend and include the ego levels. Just as the structure of the oak tree transcends and includes the acorn, transpersonal levels of development transcend and include what we normally think of as healthy ego functioning. Transpersonal psychology, a recently developed branch of psychology, got its start when Anthony Sutich "began gathering like-minded individuals in his California home for informal discussions on 'transhumanistic' topics: issues that seemed to go beyond humanistic psychology" (Scotton, 1996, p. 10). The label for this "fourth force" in psychology was influenced by Stanislav Grof, Viktor Frankl, and Abraham Maslow (Scotton, 1996).

Transpersonal psychology embraces what writer/philosopher Aldous Huxley (1945) called the "perennial philosophy." This philosophy holds the following premises:

- The world as we know it is an expression of a Divine ground of being.
- Humans can know about the Divine ground of being from inference and from direct intuition.
- All human beings possess a dual nature of phenomenal ego and eternal Self.
- Each person can identify with either the phenomenal ego or the eternal Self and each person's life on earth is a means to the end of identifying with the eternal Self.

Transpersonal psychology includes in its mission a facilitation of human development toward these transpersonal goals, as embodied in the perennial philosophy. As such, it becomes a valuable resource for counselors who seek to integrate spirituality into their practice.

## THE COMMITMENT TO TRUTH

In defending the integration of spirituality into counseling practice we note that a commitment to the truth intimately links the spiritual journey and the counseling relationship. Our use of the word *truth* deserves more exploration at this point. One Hebrew definition of truth is "that which is real" (Hays, 1990). Counseling, like a healthy spirituality, is a commitment to truth (Naparstek, 1991), or to that which is real. A healthy commitment to truth, a healthy counseling relationship, or a healthy spirituality, helps a person say "yes" to life as it is. To say "yes" is to live with what Peck (1978) called a dedication to truth. This is not so easy as it may sound. Truth is not static but ever unfolding (Polanyi, 1946). Much of our suffering (and our clients' suffering) is due to our saying "no" to what has unfolded as true or real. Buddhist scholar Reginald Ray (1993) has noted, "When reality will not be what we want and we try to make it be, we suffer" (Bercholz & Kohn, 1993, p. 305). As counselors we try to help our clients say "yes" to reality as it is (which includes its ever-unfolding nature). Ideally we help clients become more proficient in the art of living a human life. Bear in mind (as Scott Peck, 1997, has observed) that this does not necessarily mean a person will be happier. The same is true of a healthy spirituality—it may not make a person happier, but it will improve her or his ability to live a human life, to say "yes" to life, to live with a commitment to truth, and to cope with or accept what cannot be changed.

Our counseling training teaches us to be committed to truth generally; however, there are many specific levels or types of truth. Too often, our training omits the deeper mystery of spiritual truths (Ingersoll, 1994; Pate & High, 1995; Richards & Bergin, 1997; Shafranske, 1996). One reason for this omission (noted earlier in the chapter) is that the counseling profession aspires to (and often falls short of) the scientific method used by older, similar professions like psychology (Burke et al., 1999). In a society in which fiscal concerns are valued at least as much as therapeutic concerns, that which is quantitative (measurable) may be overemphasized while less measurable constructs like spirituality are underemphasized.

Since the invention of the microscope and telescope, we have known that truth—that reality—exists on different levels. When physician Ignaz Semmelweis, in the 1840s, tried to convince his medical colleagues that washing their hands of invisible germs could decrease cases of puerperal fever, he was denounced and ridiculed. We now know that microscopic germs can and do infect healthy organisms, and that when doctors wash their hands before examining patients, the incidence of infections diminishes. It is harder for many in a scientifically oriented age to consider a level of truth that transcends and includes all known levels. What are we to make of a client who says God healed her? There are no scientific instruments to measure such a claim and yet, across cultures, people make such claims with regularity.

## CONCLUSION

Belief, faith, life—all are a struggle, both for us who counsel and those whom we counsel. As clinicians, we have spent years examining and questioning the spiritual nature of our counseling work. As authors, we now hope to share our conclusions (thus far) regarding this. We have sought our answers in various spiritual traditions as well as in our own counseling, psychotherapy, and spiritual direction. In our experiences we have learned that the scientific method has its place but only goes so far in guiding our actions. Although there are numerous defenses for integrating counseling and spirituality, we have learned that we must not only find our own answers to numerous questions but that definitive conclusions remain elusive because of the nature of the topics involved. We agree that the honoring of clients includes acknowledgment of and respect for the uncharted mysteries all clients harbor, including their belief systems.

With that said, we invite you to the next step in our journey—a more detailed look at the themes uniting counseling and spirituality.

## QUESTIONS FOR REFLECTION

1. What issues are you struggling with currently? Is there a spiritual or religious component to these struggles? How might you go about resolving these issues?
2. What struggles plague your clients? Are there spiritual or religious components to these struggles? How might you assist clients?
3. How do you perceive your understanding of the exoteric/esoteric dichotomy? Are there certain aspects of these types of expression that result in either comfort or discomfort for you? How might this apply to your counseling approach?
4. Gauge your own confirmation of meaning, reality, and existence. To what degree do you balance the personal nature of this confirmation with scientific methodology? Do you have specific expectations of your clients in this regard?
5. Have you witnessed a spiritual worldview actively benefiting a client? In your experience, to what extent have the particular characteristics of postmodern society and culture affected the possibility of this occurrence?
6. Do you agree or disagree with our notion of spirituality as an innate human quality? Why or why not?
7. If someone were to challenge you, claiming that counseling and spirituality should be kept separate, do you feel that the defenses given in Chapter 1 are adequate? Why or why not? What is your position on the question?

## REFERENCES

Armstrong, K. (1993). *A history of God: The 4000–year quest of Judaism, Christianity, and Islam*. New York: Alfred A. Knopf.

Bache, C. M. (1990). *Lifecycles: Reincarnation and the web of life*. New York: Paragon House.

Bellah, R. (1970). *Beyond belief: Essays on religion in a post-traditionalist world*. Berkeley: University of California.

Bellah, R. N., Madsen, R., Sullivan, W. M., Swidler, A., & Tipton, S. M. (1985). *Habits of the heart: Individualism and commitment in American life*. New York: Harper & Row.

Bercholz, S., & Kohn, S. C. (Eds.). (1993). *An introduction to the Buddha and his teachings*. New York: Barnes and Noble Books.

Bettleheim, B. (1983). *Freud and man's soul*. New York: Alfred A. Knopf.

Burke, M. T., Hackney, H., Hudson, P., Miranti, J., Watts, G. A., & Epp, L. (1999). Spirituality, religion, and CACREP curriculum standards. *Journal of Counseling and Development, 77*, 251–257.

Caplow, T., Bahr, H. M., Chadwick, B. A., & Hoover, D. W. (1983). *All faithful people: Change and continuity in Middletown's religion*. Minneapolis: University of Minnesota Press.

Chinen, A. B. (1996). The emergence of transpersonal psychiatry. In B. W. Scotton, A. B. Chinen, & J. R. Battista (Eds.), *Textbook of transpersonal psychiatry and psychology* (pp. 9–20). New York: Basic Books.

Churchland, P. S. (1986). *Neurophilosophy: Toward a unified science of the mind/brain*. Cambridge, MA: MIT Press.

Churchland, P. S., & Sejnowski, T. (1992). *The computational brain: Computational neuroscience*. Cambridge, MA: MIT Press.

Cummings, N. A., Budman, S. H., & Thomas, J. L. (1998). Efficient psychotherapy as a viable response to scarce resources and rationing of treatment. *Professional Psychology: Research & Practice, 29*(5), 460–469.

Dana, R. H. (1998). Problems with managed mental health care for multicultural populations. *Psychological Reports, 83*(1), 283–294.

Freud, S. (1953). *The future of an illusion*. New York: Doubleday.

Fromm, E. (1950). *Psychoanalysis and religion*. New York: Bantam.

Fukuyama, M., & Sevig, T. (1997). Spiritual issues in counseling: A new course. *Counselor Education and Supervision, 36*, 224–232.

Fukuyama, M., & Sevig, T. (1999). *Integrating spirituality into multicultural counseling*. London: Sage.

Gabbard, G. O. (1994). Mind and brain in psychiatric treatment. In G. O. Gabbard (Ed.), *Treatments of psychiatric disorders* (Vol. 1, pp. 21–34). Washington, DC: American Psychiatric Press.

Gallup Poll Monthly. (1993). *Report on trends, 331*(4), 36–38.

Gallup, G., & Castelli, J. (1989). *The people's religion: American faith in the 90's*. New York: Macmillan.

Grof, S. (1975). *Realms of the human unconscious: Observations from LSD research*. New York: Viking Press.

Grof, S. (1980). *LSD psychotherapy: Exploring the frontiers of the hidden mind*. Alameda, CA: Hunter House.

Grof, S. (1985). *Beyond the brain: Birth, death, and transcendence in psychotherapy*. Albany: State University of New York Press.

Gyatso, T., Dalai Lama XIV. (1999). *Ethics for the new millennium*. New York: Riverhead Books.

Hays, E. (1990). *In pursuit of the great white rabbit: Reflections on practical spirituality*. Kansas: Forest of Peace Books.

Hoge, D. R. (1996). Religion in America: The demographics of belief and affiliation. In E. P. Shafranske (Ed.), *Religion and the clinical practice of psychology* (pp. 21–42). Washington, DC: American Psychological Association.

Hooker, R. (1836). *Laws of ecclesiastical polity*. London: Church & Paget.

Huxley, A. (1945). *The perennial philosophy*. London: Harper and Brothers.

Ingersoll, R. E. (1994). Spirituality, religion, and counseling: Dimensions and relationships. *Counseling and Values, 38,*(2), 98–112.

Jamison, K. R. (1995). *An unquiet mind: A memoir of moods and madness*. New York: Random House.

Jung, C. G. (1933). *Modern man in search of a soul*. New York: Harcourt, Brace.

Korzybski, A. (1933). *Science and sanity: An introduction to non-Aristotelian systems and general semantics*. Lakeville, CN: International Non-Aristotelian Library Publishing Co.

Kosmin, B., & Lachman, S. (1993). *One nation under God: Religion in contemporary American society*. New York: Crown.

London, P. (1986). *The modes and morals of psychotherapy* (2nd ed.). New York: Holt, Rinehart, and Winston.

Maher, M. F., & Hunt, T. K. (1993). Spirituality reconsidered. *Counseling and Values, 38,* 21–28.

Naparstek, B. (1991). *Counseling and spirituality.* Unpublished lecture given at the University of Akron.

Pate, R. H., & High, H. J. (1995). The importance of client religious beliefs and practices in the education of counselors in CACREP-accredited programs. *Counseling and Values, 40,* 2–5.

Peck, M. S. (1978). *The road less traveled: A new psychology of love, traditional values, and spiritual growth.* New York: Simon & Schuster.

Peck, M. S. (1997). *The road less traveled and beyond: Spiritual growth in an age of anxiety.* New York: Simon & Schuster.

Polanyi, M. (1946). *Science, faith and society.* Chicago: University of Chicago Press.

Ray, R. (1993). Rebirth in the Buddhist tradition. In S. Bercholz & S. C. Kohn (Eds.), *An introduction to the Buddha and his teachings* (pp. 301–311). New York: Barnes and Noble Books.

Richards, P. S., & Bergin, A. E. (1997). *A spiritual strategy for counseling and psychotherapy.* Washington, DC: American Psychological Association.

Russell, B. (1957). *Why I am not a Christian: And other essays on religion and related subjects.* New York: George Allan & Unwin Ltd.

Scotton, B. W. (1996). Introduction and definition of transpersonal psychiatry. In B. W. Scotton, A. B. Chinen, & J. R. Battista (Eds.), *Textbook of transpersonal psychiatry and psychology* (pp. 3–8). New York: Basic Books.

Shafranske, E. P., & Gorsuch, R. L. (1984). Factors associated with the perception of spirituality in psychotherapy. *Journal of Transpersonal Psychology, 16,* 231–241.

Shafranske, E. P. (Ed.). (1996). *Religion and the clinical practice of psychology.* Washington, DC: American Psychological Association.

Small, R. F., & Barnhill, L. R. (Eds.). (1998). *Practicing in the new mental health marketplace: Ethical, legal, and moral issues.* Washington, DC: American Psychological Association.

Smith, H. (1976). *Forgotten truth: The common vision of the world's religions.* San Francisco: Harper.

Speight, S. K., Meyers, L. J., Cox, C. I., & Highlen, P. S. (1991). A redefinition of multicultural counseling. *Journal of Counseling and Development, 70,* 29–36.

Sperry, R. W. (1988). Psychology's mentalist paradigm and the religion/science tension. *American Psychologist, 43,* 607–613.

Vich, M. A. (1988). Some historical sources for the term "transpersonal." *Journal of Transpersonal Psychology, 20,* 107–110.

Wilber, K. (1981). *Up from Eden: A transpersonal view of human evolution.* Boston: Shambhala.

Wilber, K. (1995). *Sex, ecology, spirituality: The spirit of evolution.* Boston: Shambhala.

Wilber, K. (1999). *One taste: The journals of Ken Wilber.* Boston: Shambhala.

Yalom, I. (1995). *The theory and practice of group psychotherapy* (4th ed.). New York: Basic Books.

# ARCHETHEMES THAT UNITE COUNSELING AND SPIRITUALITY

## *The Pilgrim's Journey*

In this chapter, we share some of the common themes in the human experience that unite counseling and spirituality. These include hope, virtue, sacred ground, polarities, facing oneself, compassion, love, meaning, and transcendence. These common themes emerge in the stories of our lives, whether being told through spiritual traditions or within the counseling session itself. The mythologist Joseph Campbell (1949) was acutely aware of how the same themes run through the world's mythologies, the life stories explored in the psychoanalytic session, and the dreams we have at night. These themes are interconnected threads in the tapestry of the human drama that, when explored, allow us to tap into the spiritual dimension of human experience.

## WHAT IS AN ARCHETHEME?

We have created the word *archethemes* as a label for these interconnected threads. The prefix "arch" (the root of "arche" and "archi") is borrowed from the Greek language and means "chief" or "foremost." Archethemes can be thought of as principal themes in the unfolding human drama.

Jung's archetypes were primordial themes with universal images (Jung, 1959); archethemes are ever-developing, transcultural themes, universal to human existence. Archethemes provide patterns or templates through which we experience the truths of the human story. While not retaining rigid form themselves, archethemes help give structure to our understanding of life. They do this much as color, being formless, gives definition to form. Whether the vehicle for a human journey is one of the world's diverse religious or spiritual systems or a counseling relationship, archethemes are present. Sometimes exploring an archetheme in a client's narrative provides an entrance into the spiritual dimension of the client's life. Counselors familiar with these archethemes have a conceptual tool with which to view the grandeur of the human story in the most "normal" of circumstances, to address spiritual issues with clients, and to cultivate a sense of counseling practice as a spiritual discipline.

## COUNSELING PRACTICE AS A SPIRITUAL DISCIPLINE

In Chapter 1 we described spirituality broadly to encompass many different expressions. One such expression can be doing counseling work. In this chapter, in addition to the archethemes uniting counseling and spirituality, we introduce the idea that counseling can be approached with a spiritual attitude and even constitute a spiritual activity. This depends to a large degree on the attitude and intent of the counselor. The counselor may in fact be engaging in a type of spiritual practice when he or she enters the counseling relationship aiming toward a deep sense of wholeness; a connectedness with the client and perhaps God; and seeking to practice spiritual qualities like love, compassion, patience, and forgiveness. When such attitudes and intentions are applied in one's counseling work, the resulting counseling practice may be a spiritual work of sorts or at least a vehicle for spiritual development.

Obviously, conducting counseling with this type of sacred reverence can be something the counselor never needs to share with the client. Most counselors we know who consider their work a spiritual practice also have personal spiritual practices that fulfill their personal spiritual needs and energize them for their counseling practice. We state this so that the reader does not confuse approaching counseling work as a spiritual practice with countertransference (doing the work solely to meet one's perceived spiritual needs).

This chapter is by no means a comprehensive list of all themes uniting counseling and spirituality or the final word on how counseling may constitute a spiritual practice. It is a list drawn from our personal and clinical experiences and, as such, is a work in progress. Wherever possible, we have tried to give the reader enough background to understand the archethemes, their history, and how they are manifested in clients' stories. We have also tried to offer examples of how interventions can be crafted when these themes emerge in a client's narrative. These interventions are explored separately in Chapter 7.

To explore the archethemes uniting counseling and spirituality in this chapter, we will present the client's journey through counseling as a variation on the hero's journey, a mythological motif developed by Joseph Campbell (1949).

## THE HERO'S JOURNEY

The hero's journey is a motif found across cultures in the world's mythologies. Although the word *hero* is often associated with maleness, the precise definition includes the notion of *any person* (male or female) who has heroic qualities or is associated with a model or ideal. The hero, of course, is all of us—the hero's journey is our journey. Campbell noted that the journey typically has three stages—departure, initiation, and return. In departure, the person is missing something in life; he or she feels incomplete in some way. Whether by choice or through the influence of life circumstances, the person leaves or is somehow cut off from this former life. Thus begins the initiation stage. In this stage the hero encounters strange lands, trials, and often a guide or helping figure that assists the hero in overcoming trials. In passing through the initiation stage the hero is transformed. At this point the hero returns to the daily world but as a whole (holy) person.

## Common Archethemes in the Stages of the Hero's Journey

Here we introduce the major archethemes within the context of the hero's journey motif and describe how a version of this motif may emerge within the counseling relationship. Remember, the hero is all of us, including our clients, so in this section we consider the client as a hero embarking on a sacred journey. In the departure phase of the hero's journey we examine the archethemes of hope, virtue, and sacred ground. In the initiation phase of the hero's journey we examine the archethemes of polarity, facing oneself, compassion, and love. Finally, in the return phase of the hero's journey we explore the archethemes of meaning and transcendence. Figure 2.1 illustrates the archethemes linking the counseling session with the hero's journey at each of the three stages.

### Departure: What Is the Hero Seeking?

What are heroes seeking from their journey? What is the hero as client seeking from the counseling relationship? On one hand, the answer to this is as varied as the individual problems that clients present to us in the counseling session.

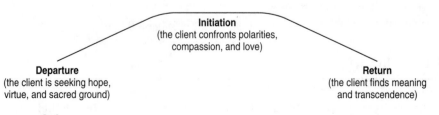

**Initiation**
(the client confronts polarities,
compassion, and love)

**Departure**
(the client is seeking hope,
virtue, and sacred ground)

**Return**
(the client finds meaning
and transcendence)

FIGURE **2.1**

The client's journey in counseling seen as the pilgrim's journey and the themes at each state linking the counseling and spiritual journeys.

Certainly, they are seeking some type of transformation—of symptoms, of situations, of themselves. On the other hand, to achieve transformation clients will have to confront their fears, their desires, and themselves. The archethemes of hope and virtue may help them in this task.

## Hope: The Psyche's Pick

*Hope is indispensable to human health.*

—Huston Smith (1976, p. 118)

Huston Smith (1976), an expert on world religions, has noted that in a world of polarities where we are subject to the vicissitudes of life, hope is our prime resource. "Ascending a sheer-faced cliff, a mountaineer can lodge his pick in an overhead crevice and, chinning himself on it, advance. Hope is the psyche's pick" (p. 118). In this sense hope is also "the hero's pick" as it pulls her further on her journey toward transformation. As an archetheme, hope works in concert with many variables (we have heard it said that clients finally seek therapy due to the push of despair and the pull of hope).

Hope has also been widely accepted as a powerful contributor to human action and achievement (Stotland, 1969). Hope can be thought of in a linear, psychological sense as the expectation of attaining some desired goal, object, or situation. In a deeper, existential and spiritual sense, hope is the experience that one's suffering is not in vain or everlasting. In whatever form, the archetheme of hope always involves a possible future (Fox, 1996). Hope is expressed by the client as faith that there is some reality to life that allows her to endure experiences of suffering. This reality may be a god who intervenes in history to end suffering, a faith in counseling or the counselor, a faith in science, a faith in the goodness of human nature, or any combination of these.

Hope is optimism about life—what Kivly (1988) called "positive outlook"—and, as such, is consonant with the counselor's values. Some academicians have written that we should not advocate values to our clients. We assert that there *are* some universal values we hope our clients will adopt, such as optimism about life (expressed as hope). If we have a client who finds something wrong with everything, we would not write in our case notes, "This client is truly living up to her or his potential as a pessimist." Of course not. We would aim to explore the client's pessimism and assess the appropriateness of introducing her or him to a more optimistic or hopeful perspective.

It has been suggested that for the spiritual or religious person, a loss of hope is actually a loss of faith in God (Sasonkin, 1995). We often see clients who have either lost hope or remained curiously adamant in their insistence of their own hopelessness. For these clients who profess a belief in God, this is almost akin to claiming omniscience in that they believe they know without a doubt what is going to happen forever and ever—and it is all bad! These clients become their own prosecutor, judge, and jury. At this point, the counselor may try guiding the client through these irrational thoughts. Sometimes the counselor can dispute irrational thoughts. When guiding and disputing is appropriately seasoned with humor (in the manner of Ellis), these clients can gain more distance from overwhelming emotions and begin to construct the foundation for a hopeful outlook.

Certainly the existential givens of life (aging, suffering, death, injustice) challenge even the most hopeful among us. Despite this, as Frankl (1946) has claimed, the last human freedom is the freedom to choose the attitude we are going to take toward any situation. We have seen many elderly residents in nursing homes continue to live healthy, vibrant lives, while others lose all hope—sometimes to the point of considering suicide. We know that about six out of ten elderly people say they would rather die than enter a nursing home (Nussbaum, 1998). Still, despite this, many nursing home residents radiate hope.

*One client, Ethel, was suffering hemiplegia due to a stroke. She said, "Life works even if my parts don't." Ethel said "yes" to a remarkable pilgrimage and experienced a transformation in her identity. She had a remarkable identification with life that transcended her bodily self, connecting her to something greater—something she simply called* life *for lack of a better term. Another client, a devout Jehovah's Witness confined to a wheelchair after suffering a stroke, stated repeatedly that it was only her religious convictions that prevented her from committing suicide.*

In both cases, these clients were on a spiritual journey, a hero's journey, living a commitment to truth that included a sense that suffering had meaning and that existence remained worthy of hope. For the first client, hope was evident in a living sense of spirituality. For the second, anticipation of a better world to come brought hope. The more skeptical reader may propose that both clients were simply good at fooling themselves. However, we posit that such a proposition is without substance. The world is religiously ambiguous (Smith, 1996) and religious propositions and a subjective sense of the spiritual do not lend themselves to empirical analysis, so this question remains open. As the surgeon Bernie Siegel has written in many of his publications, for the pilgrim on a journey toward transformation there is no such thing as false hope—there is only false "no hope."

## Virtue: The Pilgrim's Power

Part of our client's pilgrimage is a journey to claim or reclaim his or her virtue or power. The Latin root for the word *virtue* actually refers to "power." It is this sense that we intend to convey here, when referring to virtue as an archetheme. Virtue is a word that has suffered diverse interpretations through the centuries, ranging from "manliness" to "female chastity." With regard to "power," we are referring to a type of power that allows one to live as genuine a life as possible. This power is the fuel of Maslow's "self-actualization" and Jung's "individuation." This power is the "bliss" that Joseph Campbell (1988) meant, a force that whispers to be followed. This power may be the animating substance of life that expresses itself uniquely in each person. Fox (1996) clarified "being virtuous" as about "being in touch with one's own power, one's own strength; about being empowered and acting out of that power" (p. 216).

For each client to be able to live out her or his uniqueness, unfettered by the distortions of neuroses or mental/emotional disorders, is one meta-goal of the counseling relationship. It is also at the heart of various spiritual traditions. The theologian Martin Buber wrote that upon his death, God would not ask him why he wasn't more like God, but why he wasn't more like Martin Buber. This notion of virtue as power is at the heart of genuineness and is directly related to living with a commitment to truth.

Peck (1978) offers caution when considering power. Whereas political power is the ability to coerce others to do what one wants, spiritual power (spiritual virtue) is the capacity to make decisions with maximum consciousness. Frequently, clients have lost touch with parts of themselves, thereby making life decisions with minimal consciousness. When any of us make decisions in this manner for too long, problems are bound to arise.

*One client, Al, had studied psychology as an undergraduate and had told himself for years that he must go to graduate school in psychology in a program accredited by the American Psychological Association (APA). Over and over he told himself that the quality of the program was all that mattered. He was quite dejected when he was not accepted to a graduate school immediately after he received his undergraduate degree. This was a hard blow, but he resolved to get a master's degree in counseling, to work for a few years, and then to pursue his dream. After doing well in both his master's degree and his work experience, Al did eventually get accepted into an APA-accredited doctoral program in psychology. This program was, for him, in an unappealing area of the country, far from his family and friends, and with faculty he did not feel particularly connected to. As the time grew closer to relocate and begin school, he became more and more depressed. Al had visited the school several times, had lined up housing, and was three weeks from beginning the fall semester when he became so depressed and anxious that he thought he was going to have a total breakdown. He ended up canceling his plans. He could neither function properly nor attend to his daily affairs. It was at this point that his pilgrimage landed him in a therapeutic relationship with one of our colleagues. For weeks, this counselor just listened while Al talked about how he had failed himself and his family, how he had "blown" his dream. At the end of Al's third session his counselor commented, "You've told me all the reasons you should have moved away and begun school but you haven't told me one reason why you didn't." Over the next few months it became clear to Al that he valued family, friends, and the life that he had built more than he valued attending a particular graduate program. Al's counselor pointed out that his attachment to loved ones, in addition to being a virtue, was a gift—even a blessing. Rather than a blessing, Al had been addressing this sense of closeness as a curse. Accepting the transformation of a curse into a blessing became a "virtuous" experience for Al—he had acted from his power, overcoming an impersonal idea that he had picked up along the way. With newfound awareness, Al had honored what was most important to him.*

## The Hero Journeys to Sacred Ground

> *The present contains all that there is. It is holy ground.*
> —Alfred North Whitehead

In the religion of Islam, every Muslim is expected, if possible, to make a pilgrimage to the holy city of Mecca. This pilgrimage, called the *Hajj*, is one of the sacred pillars of Islam. Designed to purify the Muslim's soul, it is a reminder of human equality intended to heighten the pilgrim's devotion to God and to God's will, revealed within the sacred ground of the holy city of Mecca (Smith, 1991, p. 247). Humanistic psychologist Stephen Schoen (1991) has referred to the counseling session as sacred ground, signifying the counselor's concern with the free flight of a client's soul.

Sacred ground is set off from everyday ground. Religious scholar Mircea Eliade (1957, 1958) saw sacred ground or sacred spaces as existing in opposition to secular ground. Like Islam, all spiritual traditions have sacred spaces and behaviors (rituals) that individuals may enter into or enact, so as to be transported out of the secular and into the sacred realm. Whether counselor or client, we spend most of our time in the secular world. For the client who has sought out the sacred ground of the counseling relationship, the secular may seem to be a disenchanted wasteland. One function of the sacred ground of the counseling session is to guide clients in transforming their sense of this secular "wasteland."

In the sacred ground of the counseling session, the counselor not only offers her clinical tools to help the client, but also offers her life energy—her very self—as a therapeutic tool. We agree with Schoen's (1991) view that the counseling session constitutes sacred ground for both client and counselor, while the client seeking transformation by journeying onto such ground has made the first strides toward gaining hope and reclaiming his virtue.

### The Place of Mystery Within the Sacred

No discussion of the sacred would be complete without a note on "mystery." Mystery is an integral part of all things sacred. Many attempts to describe spirituality or the sacred allude to mystery or ambiguity. Scott Peck (1993) calls mystery a "taste for the spiritual." Pilgrims in the counseling session often find this to be an acquired taste. Many therapists are aware that if clients begin the process of counseling fully prepared to change their lives, we would have easy work. Of course, the reality is that clients will resist our efforts and their own growth. They will often cling to the painful familiar, while fearing the ambiguous unfamiliar. Perhaps this would not occur were counselors able to discuss the future with some degree of certainty, but this is not the case. In sacred realms we are at the boundary of the ineffable and the mysterious.

Mystery and a taste for mystery are a part of all spiritual traditions, as well as a powerful aspect of the counseling relationship. As counselors we simply do not know how things are going to turn out for clients (let alone ourselves!). We must have respect for the uncharted mysteries of these pilgrims who become our clients, as well as a respect for the mystery of what course their lives will take. When we meet a new client, regardless of previous history, diagnosis, or presenting problem, we are on entirely new ground. We must merely be receptive to the mystery of this person, allowing the fruits of counseling interventions to grow from undifferentiated ground that is receptive to mystery.

Westerners are often reinforced for being active; the other side of the coin is that they may find dwelling in mystery or ambiguity inherently uncomfortable. However, dwelling in mystery or ambiguity is necessary if we are to experience the sacred. Experiencing the sacred ground of the counseling session increases the client's chance of experiencing the transformation she seeks.

### The Place of Ritual in Cultivating the Sacred

Certainly, one way we increase the probability of being touched by the sacred is through the use of ritual. In all spiritual traditions, ritual is used to invite the sacred into one's life. According to scholar Karen Armstrong (1993), "A ritual presentation of events that would be unendurable in daily life can redeem and transform them into something pure and even pleasurable" (p. 37). In our daily lives, we all have special rituals; if they don't invite the sacred experience, they at least provide a degree of comfort. The counseling relationship also includes rituals to facilitate the transformation referred to earlier in this chapter. From intake to termination, the counseling relationship relies on small rituals and, in and of itself, comprises a transformation ritual.

The phases of this transformation ritual include three stages similar to those in the hero's journey (Merriman, 1992). The first is an initial state of distress and ambiguity, wherein the client seeks out the counselor and initiates the therapeutic relationship. Next, in the liminal state, the client leaves the ordinary, profane realm and begins the healing journey with the counselor. In this second stage, neither the client nor the counselor knows just what will happen, but they both become comfortable dwelling in the mystery, receptive to what gradually arises. Ideally, the final stage is one of healing, renewal, and reintegration for both the client and the counselor. The client reenters the profane, daily life, touched by the sacred and more whole (holy) as a person. All of these possibilities are available, though not guaranteed, for the pilgrim on sacred ground.

## Initiation: The Pilgrim and Polarities

I once saw the devil and thinking it odd,
Asked if he still could hold counsel with God.
He said they could meet, whenever he'd want
Since he was God's back and God's back was his front.

—Anonymous

*Just as all energy proceeds from opposition, so the psyche too possesses its inner polarity . . . polarity is inherent in all living things.*

—Carl Jung, 1961, p. 346

*Man has not been able to acquire even his oldest and simplest conceptions otherwise than in contrast with their opposite; he only gradually learnt to separate the two sides of the antithesis and think of the one without conscious comparison with the other.*

—Carl Abel

Hot and cold, male and female, up and down: These polarities are common enough in our daily experiences. Good and evil, transcendence and immanence, the rational Apollonian and the irrational Dionysian: These are perhaps less pondered polarities but still an important part of our daily lives. In many of the world's mythologies, polarity is described as two related but opposing forces. However, these forces frequently turn out be one and the same force, playing both opposing roles. A polarity is more than opposition. It is a pair of opposites working in complementary fashion (Woldt & Ingersoll, 1990).

The main characteristic of polarities is that one cannot exist without the other. This conundrum has plagued spiritual pilgrims and counselors for years, and yet, the paradox remains. Each aspect of a polarity is necessary to the existence of the other. However, this necessity is often the source of many problems that clients hope finally to resolve in counseling. Many of us think we want to be happy, but of course happy moments are sandwiched between unhappy moments. Many of us think that we should strive for continual success, forgetting that at the boundaries of all our successes lie our failures. As the Buddha noted, there is a middle way between the extremes of polarities. It is often in this middle way that we direct our clients on their hero's journey through the counseling relationship.

## Some Background on Polarities

Eastern and Western spiritual paths concur that the game of life is a game of polarities. As such, to learn the "rules" of polarities is to learn to play the game. Our clients may be halted in their journeys because they have either not learned these rules or have learned them and resist them. In Eastern literature, polarity is expressed in notions like *dvandva* and *samsara*. Dvandva (pronounced "voondvah") is a Sanskrit word referring to the pairs of opposites that are transcended or held in creative tension in yoga practice. Dvandva includes common opposites like hot and cold, as well as cosmic opposites like good and evil (Coward, 1985). While we will return to the lessons of dvandva in Chapter 3, we should note here that life often requires us to learn to "hold" opposites in creative tension, even though we would prefer focusing on one of the two. To learn to hold opposites in creative tension is one way of saying "yes" to life.

As an example, consider the frustrations we have all felt in relation to the quest for financial security. We finally get some savings and the car needs repairing. We think we can afford the car repair and the landlord increases the rent. Ad infinitum. To attain security we must first learn how to accept this cycle of ups and downs. Otherwise we will find ourselves clinging to the "up" periods and dreading the "down" periods. In this manner we will only exacerbate our suffering.

In the West, philosophers like Heraclitus (with his philosophy of flux) and theologians like Clement of Rome (with his writing of the two hands of God) have also addressed polarity. The polarity of God and Satan is prominent (although interpreted differently) in Judaism, Islam, and Christianity. The complementary nature of God and Satan is indicated in the name "Lucifer," which means bearer of light. In the case of Christianity, rather than a figure of deliberate malice, Lucifer has been noted as a symbol of the necessary dark side of life, against which the redemptive deeds of Christ may be seen clearly (Watts, 1953).

## The Polarity of Activity and Receptivity

A specific polarity we can examine as an example is the polarity of activity and receptivity. This polarity poses a common trial for people in the dominant American culture. Our society is fast-paced and, in the opinion of many, obsessed with activity. Historian Ronald Takaki (1993) has noted that this obsession seems to be built into our national myths of constant progress. Though unending activity may seem desirable, it goes against the grain of our organisms, which require balance between polarities. Many clients learn this when they develop mental and/or physical symptoms as a result of too much activity.

All people have access to two modes of awareness that have been labeled "active" and "receptive" (Deikmann, 1971, 1976). The active mode, which is quite popular in Western cultures, is used to organize, manipulate, and act on the environment. Our active mode involves attention that is akin to a spotlight focusing narrowly on its subject (Watts, 1963). Our receptive mode, which is more popular in many non-Western cultures, is demonstrated when we are vulnerable or receptive to rather than manipulative of our environment. The receptive mode involves attention more like a floodlight that throws a diffuse beam, capturing as much of the target as possible (Watts, 1963).

Many clients exacerbate their suffering through their obsession with activity. In some cases, nonstop activity seems to be the very source of the client's symptoms. *We recall one man, Luis, who was part owner of a religious publishing company. For Luis, receptivity was practically as foreign as eating ball bearings. While his activity had brought him much success, his inability to be receptive seemed to be correlated with migraine headaches, marital problems, and stomach ulcers. He associated receptivity with weakness and vulnerability. Luis's greatest challenge in counseling was first accepting the existential given of polarities. In his case, this involved accepting that all of his activity needed to be complemented by receptivity.*

Psychiatrist Arthur Deikmann (1971) reviewed and conducted research concerning meditation and concluded that meditative and contemplative practice can cultivate the receptive mode. From this information, he developed the theory that mystical experience—by which he meant awareness of the presence of God—becomes possible when we move out of the active mode and into the receptive mode. He called this process of movement from active to receptive "de-automazation." The term *automazation* comes from society's teaching us how to think and encouraging us to focus in the active mode automatically. To balance this activity we need to learn a practice that helps us cultivate receptivity. Such a practice would be a style of de-automazation.

For Luis, learning a practice of de-automazation enabled him to realize his style of receptivity. The resulting counseling strategy was aimed at supporting him on his current religious path and encouraging him to try more receptive styles of daily prayer, congruent with his path. Setting this practice as a goal appealed to his active orientation and also served to heighten his awareness of how he might be "receptive" in prayer. With this heightened awareness, Luis learned to generalize of this receptivity within his marriage.

## Polarity and Counseling Tools

While polarities may be related to client problems, they just as often provide useful tools for the counselor. The notion of polarity plays an important role in many therapeutic approaches, particularly Jung's analytical psychology and Perls' Gestalt therapy. Jung's (1923) theory of personality types is based on the complementarity of attitudes (introversion and extraversion), style of perception (sensing or intuiting), and style of judging (thinking or feeling). A primary goal in Gestalt therapy is to recognize polarities in oneself and to experience contact with each aspect of these polarities (Perls, Hefferline, & Goodman, 1951; Polster & Polster, 1973). In each of these approaches the middle way is practiced, with the pilgrim guided toward contact with both aspects of the polarity in question, disowning neither and solely ruled by neither.

## The Polarity of Mythic and Factual Language as a Tool in the Counseling Session

Both spiritual traditions and counseling interventions make use of the polarity of mythic and factual language. Factual language (scientific language) is designed to refer as precisely as possible to specific aspects of reality. Mythic language (simile, metaphor, and allegory) is used to immerse the reader/listener in an experience. Whereas factual language describes things in terms of a detached observer, mythic language attempts to convey the psychophysical involvement of the reader/listener. We use factual language to describe reality (as we know it) to clients: *Mr. Brown, your symptoms seem to indicate that you are suffering from a disorder called Major Depression.* This is quite different from saying to a depressed religious client, *Mr. Brown, you're wrestling with a demon we call depression.* Depending on the client, both statements may communicate the diagnosis of depression. Still, for counselors who may resist religious imagery, it is important to consider this polarity.

As Ingersoll (1994) and Bullis (1996) have noted, a client's religious language is a window to that client's perception of the infinite. As such, this language can provide valuable metaphors for the counseling relationship. In the world's religious and spiritual texts, mythic and factual language both have their place. Both the parable and the step-by-step instruction in meditation serve important ends that are complementary. Milton Erickson and his followers were great proponents of the use of metaphor in therapy (Erickson & Rossi, 1976). More recently, narrative therapists (somewhat influenced by Erickson) offer a metaphoric approach as well.

One such metaphor, common to the stories told in spiritual traditions and in the counseling session, is the story of lost and found. "The story of lost and found, of death and resurrection, of self-forgetting and self-discovery, is perhaps the most common theme of mythological and religious symbolism" (Watts, 1950, p. 132). The story of lost and found is also a common polarity in counseling and psychotherapy. Our clients may have either lost touch with some aspect of themselves or their lives or are feeling lost in a world that seems a disenchanted wasteland. If the work goes well, we assist the client in movement toward a realization of wholeness. As noted, this may not necessarily make the client happier. However, it will enhance the client's ability to say "yes" to life as it is. Both the mythic hero who has fallen from paradise and the client suffering complicated grief struggle to regain this lost state. When they realize that there is no way back, they must say "yes," moving forward and embracing life. It is the counselor's privilege to assist in this process. With this background, we now turn to a polarity that serves as a trial for many who are on a pilgrimage in counseling relationships.

### Initiation: Facing Oneself

*The only journey is the journey within*

—Rainer Maria Rilke

In living with maximum awareness in a commitment to the truth, the archetheme of facing oneself is inevitable. This can be one of the greatest trials for clients and heroes in the initiation phase of the hero's journey. If the client/hero continues in the therapeutic relationship, this confrontation is inevitable.

Most of us are familiar with Carl Jung's notion of the "shadow" as the element of our psyche containing all aspects of ourselves that we do not accept. According to Jung, to protect ourselves from awareness of these disowned elements, we project them onto others. This projection results in our seeing our own worst aspects of ourselves in others, rather than in ourselves. Part of Jungian analysis is to bring these "shadow" elements to awareness and to integrate them.

The idea of facing oneself is well developed in both Eastern and Western spiritual traditions. Various Buddhist traditions are geared toward helping the initiate face his or her true nature. To some degree, Judaism, Islam, and

Christianity are all deeply concerned with each person's tapping his or her true nature and freeing this nature for expression in daily life. Are we seeking anything less in counseling or psychotherapy?

*We recall a client named Maria who suffered from involvement in a string of unhealthy relationships. She had been raised by a verbally abusive father and a passive mother. Maria had great hostility toward her parents and although she vowed she would not reenact their faults, she found herself becoming passive time and again in relationships with verbally abusive men. Maria's pilgrimage was a difficult journey into the repressed pain of her childhood and the emerging awareness that she had been reenacting the very things she most disliked about her parents' relationship. In facing herself, Maria learned to see that the faults she condemned in her parents were very much a part of the person she had become. However, this same awareness freed her to change the patterns that had been at the root of her unhappy relationships.*

## Initiation: Tools of the Healer

Earlier in this chapter we mentioned that the hero in his journey often encounters a healer, helper, or guide in the initiation stage. In the client's heroic journey in counseling this healer/helper/guide is the counselor. While the counselor uses numerous tools to help the client on her or his journey, two of these stand out as prominent archethemes uniting counseling and spirituality: compassion and love.

### Tools for Initiation: Compassion

> *What happens to another, whether it be a joy or a sorrow, happens to you.*
> —Meister Eckhart

> *In the beginner's mind there are many possibilities; in the expert's mind there are few . . . the beginner's mind is the mind of compassion.*
> —Shunryu Suzuki

> *Great compassion is the root of all forms of worship.*
> —His Holiness the Fourteenth Dalai Lama of Tibet

It is hard to imagine even entering a field like counseling without a sense of compassion. Compassion is a primary tool in the counseling relationship and the spiritual journey. Matthew Fox (1979, 1996), founder of the Institute in Culture and Creation Spirituality, noted that the true meaning of compassion seems to have been lost in Western culture and religion. Compassion is defined by Webster as "a feeling of deep sympathy or sorrow for another who is stricken by suffering, accompanied by a strong desire to remove the pain or remove its cause." This interpretation, derived from Greek sources and undoubtedly well intended, sounds closer to pity and countertransference than anything appropriate or healing. We agree with Fox that this understanding of compassion falls short of the mark.

Where pity (from the Latin *pietas*) has come to imply condescension or looking down on another, compassion implies equality, a suffering with and sharing of solidarity with another (from the Latin *cum patior*) (Fox, 1979). The latter meaning is far more developed in Jewish traditions. Fox noted that Fritz Perls, cofounder of Gestalt therapy, was acutely aware of this difference when he wrote that pity emphasizes the differences between the pitied and the one offering pity. As we suffer and struggle in solidarity with our clients, we recognize, as Jung (1958) did, that the counselor must be a fellow-sufferer with the client. In being a fellow-sufferer the counselor/healer is joined together with the client/pilgrim. Conversely, if the separateness of client and counselor is emphasized, a perceived condemnation of the client may emerge. As Jung emphasized, this perception oppresses rather than liberates. Clearly, compassion involves an acceptance of our interconnection with others, working "from a strength born of weakness" (Fox, 1979, p. 2).

If compassion is rooted in interconnection, does this make the line between passionate involvement and countertransference too thin? Some may say "yes" and prefer to emphasize the distance between client and counselor. We believe that the recognition of interconnection and, hence, the experience of compassion is unavoidable if one is committed to truth. With compassion comes an awesome responsibility to seek ongoing supervision and to consistently discern the bases for one's actions within the counseling relationship.

## Compassion and Justice

Compassion in the Jewish tradition is justice. The Western mystic Meister Eckhart wrote that "those who follow compassion find life and justice and glory. . . . Compassion is just to the extent that it gives each one what is his. . . . What is compassion, is also justice" (Fox, 1980, pp. 434–435). In this sense, injustice is antithetical to compassion. What may counselors glean from an understanding of compassion as justice? Certainly one possibility may be the work of counselors as advocates for those who are unable—either temporarily or otherwise—to be advocates for themselves. This understanding is reflected in the very best intentions of the cultural diversity movement in counseling. The Fourteenth Dalai Lama of Tibet wrote that "compassion can be put into practice if one recognizes the fact that every human being is a member of humanity and the human family regardless of differences in religion, culture, color, and creed" (Gyatso, the Dalai Lama, 1989, p. 20). Perhaps the difference between compassion and a more specific social justice is that the former is realized through experience while the latter is a doctrine followed strictly on principle. Social justice is potentially most effective when resulting from compassion rather than principle.

## Compassion and Forgiveness

If compassion is an egalitarian empathy moving us to strive together toward justice, it also must encompass forgiveness. Forgiveness is a willful process, engaged in from the perspectives of both giving and receiving. It is also a process requiring a great deal of time. This notion, like the notion of receptivity, is rather antithetical to the norms of American society. There is a tendency to want a "quick fix" in many areas, with forgiveness numbered among them. We see this in everyday life—a pill for all ills, the instant denouements of television programs, and so forth.

*Another client, Dana, lived with an abusive alcoholic man for years before mustering up the courage, energy, and resources finally to leave. She spent a lot of time reading new-age literature and tried to follow prescribed dictates in order to forgive her ex-spouse. This simply seemed like the best thing, but the speed with which Dana was trying to accomplish this task left no time for an experience of her anger, a grieving of her loss, or an integration of her experience into who she was as a person.* We agree with Doris Donnelly (1993), who wrote, "Forgiveness is difficult. Ignoring that it involves struggle makes forgiveness a fanciful, silly, and weak activity" (p. 130). Perhaps the therapeutic benefit to engaging in forgiveness is that forgiving is not forgetting, it is just not remembering. To forgive an act does not mean to pretend it never existed. Instead, forgiveness involves preventing the act from controlling one's every waking moment. Akin to a transference reaction, when we resist forgiveness we experience a greater chance of remembering the original hurtful situation in subsequent similar circumstances.

Many people imagine that there are things they could never forgive. *A related story concerns a woman who had spent many years in a concentration camp during World War II. Ruth was finally released during the Allied liberation. Following this experience, she made ministry her full-time occupation. She met with success in this work and was eventually highly sought after as a speaker on the topic of the Holocaust. During one of her talks, a man who had actually been one of her tormentors in the Nazi prison camp approached her in tears, asking for her forgiveness. It is reported that Ruth, after overcoming her initial surprise, said to him, "I cannot forgive what you have done—only God can do that—but I will pray with you that you may be forgiven."* This story illustrates the strength of Ruth's compassion as she worked to engage in the process of forgiveness.

### Tools of the Healer: Love

> *Compassion and love are precious things in life. They are not complicated. They are simple, but difficult to practice.*
>
> *Love is the center of human life.*
>
> —His Holiness the Fourteenth Dalai Lama of Tibet

We should say at the outset of this passage that trying to define or describe love is difficult. Love so transcends descriptive categories that we can only point toward it with signs and symbols. Perhaps elements that have truly transcendent qualities can be fully understood only within the depths of experience.

Like justice or time, we know what love is when we feel it, and yet, when we try to describe it, we struggle. Sometimes we resort to saying what love is not (describing it *via negativa*). We know as counseling professionals that when infants are not loved, they fail to thrive. We know that when adults do not have love, they are more likely to fall into meaninglessness and hopelessness or to develop various forms of sociopathy. Spong (1998) stated, "Love is the essential power that deepens our relationships and simultaneously expands our humanity" (p. 66). Scott Peck (1978) wrote that, "love is too large, too deep ever to be truly understood or measured or limited within the framework of words" (p. 81). Peck has also described love as "the will to extend one's self for the purpose of nurturing one's own or another's spiritual growth" (p. 81). This particular understanding of love describes an optimal relationship between counselor and client.

## What Love Is Not

It is important not to confuse love with charitable or "loving" acts. Such acts are ideally an outgrowth of love, but these acts can be performed even when love is lacking (May, 1982). As psychiatrist Gerald May has pointed out, charitable acts are often performed because of our desire to maintain a selfless image or because they are the easy choice. For those of middle- and upper-level income, it essentially costs nothing to give a dollar to a homeless person. Is this dollar given because the giver does not want to feel pangs of conscience for the rest of the day, or because he or she feels genuinely moved out of love or compassion?

In graduate school, students in the helping professions frequently say they have chosen our profession because of their desire to offer assistance to others. Ideally, this may be true. However, a certain selfish image may also emerge. Students may find themselves enjoying the image they project as they profess their desire to help. In such cases, one may be motivated more by pity than by love or compassion. One student said, "Well, someone needs to help destitute people and since I'm aware of the problem, I guess it is me that has to help." This student's actions were grounded more in logical pragmatism than a sense of love or compassion. She had a difficult time with empathy and often reported feeling exhausted with "those people" during her internship experience. As May has noted, charitable acts inevitably backfire if the giver feels superior to the recipient.

## What Love Is in the Counseling Session

Dare we speak of love between client and counselor? Ours is a time in which a majority of ethical violations reviewed by state boards of counseling and psychology have to do with inappropriate and often sexual relationships between counselor and client. Ours is also a time in which, at least in colloquial thinking, love is still often associated with sexuality (what has been called "erotic love"). It is indeed difficult to speak of love in a manner that transcends the scandals and misinterpretations of the day. Still, we must try, for love is a core tool for many counselors working successfully in the field. You won't typically see large numbers of papers on the topic of love being published in refereed journals, for love is a "sloppy" construct. It eludes operational definitions. Most likely, we will not see "love in the counseling session" as a major conference theme any time soon. Essentially, working lovingly is easier to model than to teach.

If we return to a definition of love that is the willingness to extend oneself for the spiritual growth of oneself or another, we begin to appreciate parallels to the way counselors render themselves vulnerable to the humanity of each client. As counselors allow this humanity to touch and inspire them within the counseling relationship, a therapeutic intervention develops in and of itself. Each client offers a new opportunity for the counselor to extend herself or himself. This extension requires will and intent on the part of the counselor, as well as patience. The counselor must be fully present with the client.

The payoff in this case is perhaps as intangible as love itself. If we manage to extend ourselves lovingly to each client, rendering ourselves vulnerable to their humanity and saying "yes" to their life, our initial reward may involve facing our own countertransference issues. In order to extend ourselves lovingly, we must be willing to reflect constantly. Increasingly personal work seems to be one reward for loving. We cannot afford the luxury of unexamined lives if we intend to extend ourselves lovingly to clients. In one sense, living every day with the intent to love is like walking off a cliff—every single day. There are no certainties, no consistently familiar crevices in which to secure a foothold. We must have a trust in life, believing that even our own issues may be faced, both for our clients and for ourselves.

## Return: Treasures of the Pilgrimage

With what treasures do clients take leave of the counseling relationship and return to living their lives? Again, there are as many treasures as there are clients and—as the old saying goes—one person's trash is another's treasure. (Many a graduate student has noted that one person's trash is another's dissertation!) Again, we have no exhaustive list of the treasures that clients may take from their counseling experience. However, we would like to elaborate on two archethemes that fall into this category—the archethemes of transcendence and meaning.

### Transcendence: Where Hope and Virtue May Lead

> *Religion and spirituality are grounded in an affirmation of transcendence.*
> —Eugene Kelly

> *Transcendence and development are synonymous.*
> —Stanislav Grof

What is the hero's journey if not a journey beyond one's own limits? Transcendence describes the quality or state of going beyond ordinary limits. It is a surpassing or exceeding of what has already been or what currently is. Transcendence might refer to anything from a person overcoming test anxiety to a person experiencing a metaphysical realization.

In counseling research, transcendence has been consistently included as a dimension of spiritual wellness (Westgate, 1996). We do not believe it is our place to judge the qualities that various experiences deserving of this label might contain. Rather, we would like to simply outline transcendence as an archetheme in counseling and spirituality. In our personal and clinical experience we have found that utilizing hope and finding one's power often facilitate transcendence. In this section, we discuss transcendence generally, offer some case examples, and finally touch on two specific manifestations of transcendence—humor and play.

Human development is a common link between spirituality and counseling. Some authors have simply viewed spiritual transcendence as the farther reaches of human development (Alexander & Langer, 1990; Wilber, 1995). These authors see human development proceeding by differentiation and integration. Differentiation allows new elements to unfold, while integration includes and transcends these new elements, allowing them to be differentiated. This certainly may be the client's experience in the counseling relationship. In many schools of counseling, we help clients develop an observing ego, with which they may later transcend (and include) problematic elements.

*A client named Andrew, deeply troubled by obsessions about going to hell, entered Christian counseling. Andrew came from a conservative religious background and was engaged to be married. In developing his observing ego, he learned that his obsessions arose whenever he entertained sexual fantasies. His fantasies themselves seemed normal, but Andrew's reaction to them seemed excessive. Psychodynamic work with Andrew turned up a history of negative imprinting regarding sex, all stemming from Andrew's family of origin. Once he gained insight into these issues and realized that his religion did allow for appropriate sexual expression within marriage, Andrew used his newly developed observing ego in therapy, finally including and transcending the negative "tapes" received from his family. Andrew's pilgrimage required differentiating and transcending both his early messages about sexuality and his appropriate sexual impulses.*

Transcendence in the form of growth is always healthy. If it is not healthy, it is not transcendence but, rather, "dissociation." Wilber (1995, 1997) explains that to attempt to transcend something that has not been either adequately developed or differentiated in its function may result in dissociation from that thing, or possibly a developmental fixation. This same theme is familiar to counseling and spirituality.

*Gabe was a client who was suffering from recurrent Major Depression and who was quite astute in the practice of Hatha yoga. He had a deep understanding of yoga philosophy and a genuine yearning for spiritual growth. Gabe clearly saw himself as being actively on a spiritual pilgrimage. Yet, what was also apparent was his distaste for the tasks of daily living. At the time of Gabe's treatment, he was residing in a group home, following a lengthy hospitalization. He consistently failed to complete his share of the housework, yard work, or grocery shopping. He was always "too busy" with his yoga practice. This much was true. However, Gabe failed to realize that he had numerous issues to deal with regarding ego functioning. His pilgrimage required a great deal of confrontation during counseling sessions. This confrontation helped Gabe to develop necessary ego strength that he could attend to the mundane tasks of daily living. He was fixated in the realm of personal issues and until he finally dealt with these issues adequately, it remained unlikely that he would attain his long-sought realization.*

## Transcendence as Humor

> *The angels fly because they take themselves lightly.*
>
> —G. K. Chesterton

Perhaps the most common experience of transcendence is the experience of humor. Someone has said that the highest form of humor is to laugh at oneself. This is, in fact, a variation of the observing ego. How many times have we all looked back on a painful memory and said, "But I can laugh about it now"? Is such a response merely a rationalization of the frightening nature of living in our universe, where we have little control? Or is this something more? We feel this response to be an example of integration and transcendence. A person who is capable of making such a statement will be better able to endure future difficulty. Many people suffering from psychological and existential problems share a grim outlook on life. This has been called "depressive reality." Interestingly, people with a "depressive reality" worldview have frequently shown themselves to be very accurate judges of interpersonal dynamics and attributions. Still, this accuracy seems a high price to pay for an existence that is largely humorless.

*One pastoral counselor related a story of a client who was suffering from an unrelenting depression and an overwhelming guilt regarding his anger at God. The counselor described this client as "one of those folks who is a procession unto themselves—very serious." The client was not improving and the pastoral counselor was getting increasingly frustrated. One day after a long tirade about how unjust life was, the client said dramatically, "and Pastor, the worst of it is that in the past year, much to my dishonor, I've gone away from God." The pastor who had just given a sermon on God's omnipresence said, "Where the hell did you go?" As this statement left his mouth, the pastor regretted having uttered it, but later recounted that after a moment of silence, the client laughed for the first time in six sessions. At that moment he and the client seemed to transcend their "stuckness." From this point on, the counseling relationship became more productive. This particular client was called on in his pilgrimage to be less serious and more sincere.*

## Transcendence as Play

Another common experience of transcendence is contained in one's capacity for play—for experiencing life as "safe." (Similar to the client in the last case example, we may all suffer from too much seriousness and not enough sincerity, or from too much work and too little play. Even as we wrote this chapter we were aware of the overt seriousness of such terms as *archetheme*.) Play is best described by Fox's (1981) notion of "natural ecstasies." In forgetting themselves in play (which can include sexual play), individuals give themselves over to something greater than themselves. Here, there is giving that is simultaneously pleasurable. To play for a purpose (such as winning a game or using one's sexuality to control) is not play at all. In fact, these manipulations are the antithesis of play.

Why include play under the archetheme of transcendence? American culture typically places precious little value on quality leisure. Activity is frequently valued while receptivity is often neglected or denigrated. Play is by nature active. Yet, play may also cultivate receptivity and balance seriousness with sincerity. Can one play while on a pilgrimage? We certainly hope so! Again, we only risk noting the obvious due to our society's tendency to look down on play. Think of some of the colloquial descriptions of someone who enjoys play: "light-hearted," "easy-going," "laughter-loving," "merry," "care-free," and "frivolous." Many of these descriptions are used pejoratively in our "workaholic" American society. In fact, what is many times referred to as "play" may actually be aggression masquerading as play (for example, violent sports or an extreme focus on "winning").

The client's journey through the counseling relationship can certainly be marked with very serious encounters, but it can just as often refresh through playful moments. In the first reviews of this book, one reviewer pointed out the nature of the word *recreation*, noting that the word may be broken down as re-creation. Ideally recreation does help us re-create ourselves and in this re-creation there may be elements of transcendence. *We recall one client noting that transcendence wasn't any huge metaphysical realization, but instead an everyday experience wherein she was "re-born" for the purpose of a new moment. This client made it clear that her weekend soccer league had far more transcendental value than any organized religious service she had ever attended. For her, these moments took on a meaning that eluded verbal description but had a powerful impact on her day-to-day life.*

## Meaning and the Sense of Purpose

> *Man is by nature a philosopher, and cannot be otherwise. . . . A philosopher can assert that the universe is without any objective meaning, seemingly unaware of the fact that his very idea, as part of that universe, must also be without meaning.*
>
> —Alan Watts

> *How could I endure to be a man, if man were not also poet and reader of riddles . . . a way to new dreams?*
>
> —Friedrich Nietzsche

As the client takes leave of the counselor, we hope for his or her sense of peace with the question of meaning. *Meaning* is an archetheme that permeates philosophy, theology, and counseling. All three disciplines take as their charge an aiding of humanity in the "meaning-making" enterprise. Meaning has been defined as a sense of what makes a life worth living (Frankl, 1946, 1958). Viktor Frankl (1955) noted that the problem of meaning (apt to arise more frequently, though not exclusively, in times of crisis) can truly overwhelm a person. Frankl also noted that human beings have an innate will to meaning, which manifests itself as a search for ultimate meaning in the individual life. Although no counseling relationship can provide such ultimate meaning, it can point a client (as well as a counselor) in this same direction.

"Is life worth living?" The answer one gives to this simple question is usually supported by a sense of meaning. It is important to note that many would answer a resounding "yes" to this question, without a real cognizance of "why." Many of us have had clients who spent more time at the self-help shelf in the local bookstore than in bed sleeping! These people were on a frantic search for meaning that could be grasped or explained. The intensity of their search became more telling than the supposed lack of meaning in their lives. Thus, meaning can be an inherent sense unaccompanied by logical explication. (Or, as Thomas à Kempis said about contrition, "I would rather feel it than be able to define it.") One client, a mother of three, said that the birth of each of her children was meaningful, although she could not begin to describe why. Accepting this is perhaps a bit easier for counselors, since we are taught to value the client's subjective sense of life rather than to rely strictly on observation alone. Any such inclusion of the phenomenological calls for more than good reasoning ability. Receptivity and some element of trust are required as well. In the end, it is the client who must define meaning, while the counselor must trust that what has been offered to the client has truly enhanced this process.

## Conclusion

In this chapter on archethemes and the client's/hero's journey, we have explored the transcultural themes that unite spiritual and counseling journeys. We have attempted also to place the counseling relationship in a mythic context, permitting the reader to see the grandness of the human story inherent in the very ordinariness of the counseling relationship. In the chapter that follows we investigate the problem of evil and its relationship to counseling and spirituality.

## Questions for Reflection

1. How would you describe your personal and professional journey? Where and when did it begin? Where are you, the hero, headed? What changes must you make to get there?

2. How might the archethemes described in this chapter relate to Jungian archetypes? How might they differ?
3. What additional archethemes do you see uniting counseling and spirituality?
4. Reflect on a life event that is captured by one of the archethemes in Chapter 2. Which archetheme was it related to? What was the outcome? What significant others (if any) helped you through the experience?
5. What are your best hopes? Do your hopes inspire or enliven your work?
6. Polarities are important in psychotherapy as well as in the spiritual realm. How do you see polarities operating in your own life and in your work?

## REFERENCES

Alexander, C. N., & Langer, E. (1990). *Higher stages of human development*. New York: Oxford University Press.

Armstrong, K. (1993). *A history of God: The 4000-year quest of Judaism, Christianity, and Islam*. New York: Alfred A. Knopf.

Bullis, R. K. (1996). *Spirituality in social work practice*. Washington, DC: Taylor and Francis.

Campbell, J. (1949). *The hero with a thousand faces*. Princton, NJ: Bollingen.

Campbell, J. (1988). *The power of myth*. New York: Doubleday.

Coward, H. (1985). *Jung and Eastern thought*. Albany: State University of New York Press.

Deikmann, A. (1971). Bimodal consciousness. *Archives of General Psychiatry, 25,* 481–489.

Deikmann, A. (1976). *Personal freedom: On finding your way to the real world*. New York: Viking Press.

Donnelly, D. (1993). *Spiritual fitness: Everyday exercises for body and soul*. San Francisco: HarperCollins.

Eliade, M. (1957). *The sacred and the profane: The nature of religion*. New York: Harcourt, Brace, Jovanovich.

Eliade, M. (1958). *Patterns in comparative religion*. Cleveland: World Publishing Company.

Erickson, M., & Rossi, E. (1976). *Hypnotic realities*. New York: Irvington.

Fox, M. (1979). *A spirituality named compassion and the healing of the global village, Humpty Dumpty, and us*. Minneapolis, MN: Winston Press.

Fox, M. (1980). *Breakthrough: Meister Eckhart's creation spirituality in new translation*. New York: Doubleday.

Fox, M. (1981). *Whee, we, wee all the way home: A guide to sensual, prophetic spirituality*. Santa Fe: Bear & Co.

Fox, M. (1996). *Confessions: The makings of a post-denominational priest*. New York: HarperCollins.

Frankl, V. (1946). *Man's search for meaning*. New York: Beacon Press.

Frankl, V. (1955). *The doctor and the soul: An introduction to logotherapy*. New York: Alfred A. Knopf.

Frankl, V. (1958). The will to meaning. *Journal of Pastoral Care, 12,* 82–88.

Gyatso, T., the Dalai Lama. (1989). *Ocean of wisdom: Guidelines for living*. Santa Fe, NM: Clear Light Publishers.

Ingersoll, R. E. (1994). Spirituality, religion, and counseling: Dimensions and relationships. *Counseling and Values, 38*(2), 98–112.

Jung, C. G. (1923). *Psychological types: The psychology of individuation*. London: Routledge & Kegan Paul.

Jung, C. G. (1958). The practice of psychotherapy. In *Collected works (Vol. 16)*. Princeton, NJ: Bollingen.

Jung, C. G. (1959). *The archetypes and the collective unconscious*. Princeton, NJ: Princeton University Press.

Jung, C. G. (1961). *Memories, dreams, reflections*. New York: Vintage Books.

Kivly, L. R. (1988). Elements of healthy religious beliefs. *Counseling and Values, 32*, 236–239.

May, G. G. (1982). *Will and spirit: A contemplative psychology*. New York: Harper & Row.

Merriman, M. (1992). *Living the sacramental life*. Unpublished lecture given in the Episcopal Diocese of Northern Ohio, March 8.

Nussbaum, P. D. (1998). *Aging and the brain*. Unpublished lecture, Akron, OH.

Peck, M. S. (1978). *The road less traveled: A new psychology of love, traditional values, and spiritual growth*. New York: Simon & Schuster.

Peck, M. S. (1993). *A world waiting to be born: Civility rediscovered*. New York: Bantam.

Perls, F., Hefferline, R. F., & Goodman, P. (1951). *Gestalt therapy: Excitement and growth in the human personality*. New York: Dell.

Polster, E., & Polster, M. (1973). *Gestalt therapy integrated*. New York: Vintage Books.

Sasonkin, M. (1995). Unpublished interview with R. Elliott Ingersoll, Akron, OH.

Schoen, S. (1991). Psychotherapy as sacred ground. *Journal of Humanistic Psychology, 31*, 51–55.

Smith, H. (1996). *The wisdom of faith with Bill Moyers*. Video series, New York: Newbridge Communications.

Smith, H. (1976). *Forgotten truth: The common vision of the world's religions*. San Francisco: Harper.

Smith, M. L. (1991). *A season for the spirit*. Cambridge, MA: Cowley.

Spong, J. S. (1998). *Why Christianity must change or die: A bishop speaks to believers in exile*. New York: HarperCollins.

Stotland, E. (1969). *The psychology of hope*. San Francisco: Jossey-Bass.

Watts, A. W. (1950). *The supreme identity: An essay on oriental metaphysic and the Christian religion*. New York: Random House.

Watts, A. W. (1963). *The two hands of God: The myths of polarity*. New York: George Braziller.

Westgate, C. E. (1996). Spiritual wellness and depression. *Journal of Counseling and Development, 75*, 26–35.

Wilber, K. (1995). *Sex, ecology, spirituality: The spirit of evolution*. Boston: Shambhala.

Wilber, K. (1997). *The eye of spirit: An integral vision for a world gone slightly mad*. Boston: Shambhala.

Woldt, A. L., & Ingersoll, R. E. (1990). Where in the yang has the yin gone in Gestalt therapy? *British Gestalt Journal, 1*, 94–102.

# EVIL AND COUNSELING

*When I praise things god-like, I find evil in the Gods.*

—Philoctetes

Great human suffering exists in the world. Some of this suffering is endemic to the existential givens of the human condition (aging, disease, and death). Some is the result of complex human dynamics that lead to conflict on various levels—in our homes, in our schools, on our streets, and between our nation states. As many spiritual leaders have taught, suffering seems to be woven into the fabric of life. Many of us become counselors to ease human suffering, accepting that we will never erase suffering from the human condition. Some suffering, far from being caused by existential givens, is clearly unnecessary and deeply malevolent. Consider the following comments of those who witnessed fellow students gun down students and faculty at Columbine High School in 1999:

> "A gunman looked under a desk in the library and said 'Peek-a-boo,' then fired. . . . Anyone who cried or moaned was shot again. One girl begged for her life, but a gunshot ended her cries." One student saw one of the gunmen pull a sawed-off shotgun from under his coat. "They were laughing after they shot. It was like they were having the time of their life." Another student commented, "Every time they'd shoot someone, they'd holler, like it was, like, exciting." (Associated Press, 1999)

To signify intentions and actions that cause this degree of suffering, we use the word *evil*. In this chapter we address evil within the context of suffering and counseling.

*Evil* is a word with a lot of emotional baggage. Traditionally, we have assigned evil to the natural world, to human nature, and to the gods themselves. As Sanford and Comstock (1971) have noted, evil does not require acts or behaviors that are "sins" in and of themselves, or crimes according to the law. Evil is reserved for actions and intentions that inflict needless pain and suffering on others. One reason we have written this chapter is because our clients use the

**41**

word *evil* to describe situations that they have survived. We sometimes wonder at their choice of words and as many times as not we let their words pass unnoticed. One theme we refer to throughout this chapter may seem apparent but still bears stating and repeating: Clients don't come to counseling when everything is going well; they come when they are suffering. Often, this suffering has components that—for lack of a better word—can be described as bearing evil to some extent.

## THE PROBLEM OF TRYING TO ERADICATE EVIL

Clients on the hero's journey of counseling undergo trials and adversity. Again, this is the stuff of life. As counselors, some of our trials seem to involve easing the suffering of others and, at times, cutting off the very source of this suffering at its roots. Reality is complex. Can we ever be certain that our actions will decrease suffering and not inadvertently cause more suffering? In trying to identify and eliminate evil we often perpetuate it. In the fourth century, Christian monks hacked to death the female scholar Hypatia. St. Cyril noted that this had occurred because Hypatia, a woman, presumed to teach men, which was against God's commandments (Ellerbe, 1995). The founder of Islam was also the originator of the notion of the jihad—the holy war. The idea of using ovens to murder people was not originated by the Nazis, but by the Christian Inquisition in Eastern Europe (Walker, 1988).

If, as Huston Smith (Wagner, 1996) has noted, humans trying to contemplate God are like dogs trying to contemplate algebra, are we really up to the task of even trying to eradicate evil? Alan Watts (1968) has said that perhaps the best humanity could do is stop crusading for abstract causes (such as good, righteousness, social justice) and devote our energies to farming, cooking, engineering, the arts, education, and making love. In Watts's plan, the more abstract concepts would be taken care of through concrete action.

On the other hand, we recognize that cases have been made for inflicting great suffering in the name of a higher ideal. In the *Bhagavad Gita*, young prince Arjuna is tortured when he realizes that the battle he must fight (the Great War of the Sons of India) involves loved ones, on both his side and on the "enemy" side. The prince is instructed by the god Krishna. He is told that it is indeed his duty to enter this situation and concern himself with the action of his duty and not the fruits of his action. This story is set in an India where the caste system dictated what one's duty was and that one's spiritual salvation involved saying "yes" to this duty.

A more recent example of saying "yes" to one's duty is discussed by philosopher Philip Hallie (1988), who became suicidal after his experience in World War II, shelling German villages. Hallie at first thought his salvation could be achieved by studying the nonviolent practices of the French villagers of Le Chambon. During the war, these villagers tried to save lives and did not violently resist Hitler's troops. Hallie wrote a book on this topic (Hallie, 1979), but then he realized that the peaceful resistance of which he wrote did not stop Hitler. After decades of agonizing, Hallie concluded, "A thousand Le Chambons would not have stopped Hitler. It took decent murderers like me to do it. . . . The cruelty that I perpetrated willingly was the only way to stop the cruel march that I and others like me were facing" (Woodruff & Wilmer, 1988, pp. 127–128). As Hallie's recollection makes clear, reality is truly complex.

## OUR POSITION ON EVIL

We undertake this chapter keeping the above scenarios in mind. We take the position that if evil exists, it is within us, and our best efforts to eradicate it may in fact perpetuate it. However, we also believe there are times when one must "fight the good fight" where evil is concerned. In accepting responsibility for our possible ratification of evil, we believe we can also act responsibly, lovingly, and compassionately, with what Scott Peck (1987) referred to as "maximum awareness." Often, our work with clients involves helping them to "fight the good fight."

Generally, how will we "fight the good fight"? Certainly, one place to begin is with a recognition that evil is a rebellion against truth (that which is real) and that both avoiding and seeking truth are human choices. Ancient religious thinkers (like Zarathustra, founder of Zoroastrianism) as well as contemporary thinkers (like C. S. Lewis) have regarded the difference between truth and lies the essential difference between good and evil. Even in India there are evil spiritual figures like Namuci, whose name means "he who never lets go." Namuci is the god of lies, hatred, evil, death, and darkness.

Regarding the rebellion against truth, fighting the good fight requires a commitment to truth, what Van Der Post (1988) called "the responsibility of consciousness" (p. 13) or Peck (1997) has called living with maximum awareness. Our commitment to truth is best carried out through practices that increase our awareness and our consciousness (Wilber, 1999).

Another progressive way to "fight the good fight" is through what we have referred to as facing oneself. Throughout history, cultures have sought to understand the evil in human action through exploring a personification of that evil in a figure like the devil. We explore psychological perspectives of evil in this chapter. To fight the good fight in this sense is to cultivate self-awareness. As Russell (1977) has noted, we often deal with our own potential for evil by projecting it onto others. The Delphic motto, "know thyself," is important in this respect. In Russell's words, "The devil is understood, and ultimately confronted and defeated, as he is integrated into our experience as individuals" (p. 37). Finally, we can fight the good fight against evil through education. Educator Nel Noddings (1989) recommended that "a primary purpose of education should be to reduce pain, separation, and helplessness by encouraging people to explore the nature of evil and commit themselves to continue the search for understanding" (p. 230). In this chapter, we act on Noddings's advice—exploring the nature of evil while encouraging the use of reason and relation in describing, examining, and responding to it. This chapter is an attempt to empower the reader with strategies both to face evil and to engage in healing responses to it.

## BACKGROUND: THE NATURE OF EVIL

The literature describing evil encompasses theological, philosophical, and psychological sources. The reader need not have scholarly expertise in these areas to appreciate a little background. By and large, the sources are derived from Western, patriarchal traditions, as Eastern traditions are typically more focused on seeking the source that transcends polarities of good and evil.

First, "Evil is never abstract. It must always be understood in terms of the suffering of an individual" (Russell, 1977, p. 17). Russell describes evil as senseless and meaningless destruction that strives to turn all things to nothing. Evil is generally described as that which is destructive and opposed to the good that preserves. For Baumeister (1997), finding an adequate definition of evil was difficult; he described human evil as involving actions that intentionally harm others. Similarly, Goldberg (1996) defined evil as malevolence (when one's actions cause another unnecessary suffering). Haase (1992) and Noddings (1989) focused on evil as pain, helplessness, separation, and an inability to experience joy. These general definitions are expanded below.

## THREE CATEGORIES OF EVIL

Russell (1988) described three categories of evil. The first was metaphysical evil, which he defined as a lack of the perfection that existed in the created order. Further, metaphysical evil is absolute and there is nothing an individual can do to eradicate it. If metaphysical evil in fact exists, we can combat it only by striving for the good and trying deliberately not to aid or fuel it (Wilmer, 1988). Russell's second category was natural evil; here, suffering results from the processes of nature (tornadoes, backaches, disease, etc.). Russell's final category was moral evil, which is demonstrated when an intelligent human being knowingly and deliberately inflicts suffering on other sentient beings. This final category involves conscious knowledge as well as full awareness that others dread pain and suffering.

Noddings (1987, 1989) addressed moral evil by focusing on the emotions felt by people (particularly women) who have experienced evil. Noddings presented pain, helplessness, and separation as the trinity of evil. A person commits evil by inflicting any of these without rigorously determined just cause (as in surgery, when pain is inflicted for a greater good). Also, anyone failing to alleviate these conditions when it is clearly in their power to do so also commits evil. Although moral evil concerns us most, as we explore counseling and various spiritual responses to it we will briefly explore Russell's three categories of evil, including some client examples. These examples illustrate that even ancient thinking on the topic of evil lives on in our clients' perceptions and experiences.

There is clearly overlap in these three categories, as metaphysical evil implies a metaphysical good—a god. If this god is assumed to be the creator of the universe, he or she must be in some way responsible for evil, be it metaphysical, natural, or moral. The study of the relationship of a god to the existence of evil is called *theodicy*.

## *Metaphysical Evil*

In summarizing the dynamics of a metaphysical view of evil, the philosopher Radoslav Tsanoff (1931) noted that evil and the problem of evil arise from a clash between what we experience with our ideals. Tsanoff paraphrases Reginald Ray's thoughts in Chapter 1, in describing how we suffer when things aren't as we would like them to be but we try to force them anyway. We recall many clients, thwarted unfairly on the road to their goals, who summoned the gods and the heavens themselves to strike down obstacles.

*In a nursing home where I was providing psychological services, I was asked to see a client whom staff felt was oppositional and becoming "a behavior problem." The 86-year-old man (Jack) had been wheelchair-bound since breaking a hip two years earlier. Jack had lived on his own until age 83, when a stroke left him unable to care for himself. He had been doing physical therapy in the nursing home and making some progress until an unfortunate fall that resulted in a hip fracture. On my way to his room, I could hear him yelling "Goddamn it!" across the wing. Upon arriving in his room, I realized that Jack was trying to maneuver his wheelchair around a guest chair left in the center of the room by his roommate. As I moved the chair out of Jack's way, he asked, "And who the hell are you?" When I explained that I was one of the staff counselors, he quickly responded that I had already provided the only service he needed (moving the chair) and suggested that I kindly get the hell out of his room. A bit unnerved by his intensity, I honored his request and noted that I'd try to meet with him after lunch. Jack was a bit more approachable after lunch and we had several sessions on the "neutral ground" of the cafeteria. Clearly, Jack's most-used angry word was "Goddamn." In our third session I was reflecting this when Jack started laughing and said, "Well, if there is a God I figure if I ask enough he just might strike down all the damned things that get in my way."*

## Eastern Monism

The clash between our ideals (the way we'd like things to be) and reality (the way things are) varies from person to person and culture to culture. This clash accounts for the great diversity in attempts to explain metaphysical evil. The earliest Eastern religions postulated a single divine principle underlying existence and the cosmos. This is a form of monism. Monism posits that there is one god or one ultimate principle in the universe. It may be polytheist in the sense that the numerous gods in a polytheistic religion are simply manifestations of the one god or ultimate principle. For early Eastern philosophers, God was the ultimate One who created the illusion of the world by becoming the many things that make it up. A more colloquial understanding of this view is Watts's (1966) statement that in the Eastern view, God plays hide-and-seek with herself. Since the phenomenal world was considered an illusion, the Eastern religions reasoned that evil is only experienced in the phenomenal realm.

The notion of the world as "illusion" should not be taken too concretely. This notion does not imply that what we see and what we experience aren't real; it simply means that our understanding of what we see and experience is incomplete. This is important, as we have heard colleagues echoing popular "new age" ideas saying, "Oh, suffering is all in your mind." Well, yes and no. Because the world we experience with our mind is incomplete, we suffer. Still, this suffering is certainly not "all in our mind."

## The Introduction of Dualism

According to Russell (1988), the Iranian prophet Zarathustra in 1200 B.C.E initiated the first totally dualistic religion. Zarathustra believed that evil was not an aspect of the divine and that evil existed exclusive of the divine. By denying any connection between the evil and divine, the divine could then be conceptualized as perfect goodness. With Zarathustra's unique proposition, the first real "devil" of the world religions (variously labeled "Angra," "Mainyu," and "Ahriman") was conceptualized. The dualistic influence of Zoroastrianism resulted in exclusive categories of good and evil that were later used by Manichaeans and Gnostics. In the literature of Judaism and Islam, this devil is again transformed and portrayed as an angel administering the wrath of God (Watts, 1963). Judaism, Islam, and Christian writers all drew from the dualistic notions developed in Zoroastrianism and added to them. In Judaism, Islam, and later Christianity, the relationship of the devil to God becomes increasingly complex, reinforcing the notion that we really can't understand metaphysical matters.

*One client I had, an elderly Jewish woman named Margaret, enjoyed reading the psalms. Her roommate complained that the psalms were by-and-large depressing passages and she wondered why Margaret would want to go over "all that wailing" in her reading. Margaret said that the psalms reminded her that life was full of trials and that she was not the first person to suffer trials. She also said that it was important to remember that we can't understand how God works.*

## Classical Conceptions of Evil

Although human beings may be inadequate at understanding metaphysical matters, we do keep trying. We struggle with our clients to make sense of belief, faith, and life. This struggle incorporates the problem of evil. Greeks of the Classical period encountered similar challenges. Their own conceptions of metaphysical evil began with Greek Orphism, which originated around the sixth century B.C.E. The central myth in Orphism was the struggle between Dionysus and the Titans. The Titans were referred to as the elder gods and were supreme rulers of the universe until they were dethroned by one of their own sons, Zeus. Reminiscent of the legend of Lucifer's rebellion in heaven, the Titans plotted to take control of the cosmos and Zeus fought to stop them. After the Titans were defeated, they devoured Zeus's son Dionysus. Athena (goddess of wisdom) saved Dionysus's heart and Zeus was able to resurrect him. After Dionysus's resurrection, Zeus blasted the Titans to ashes and from these ashes came the human race. According to this myth, the dual nature of humanity begins here, with our physical nature stemming from the Titans and our spiritual being from aspects of Dionysus that the Titans ingested.

*One of our clients said he could feel good and evil wrestling within him. Tim had suffered from polysubstance abuse and depression. His drug use began as an attempt at self-medication and degenerated into dependence on alcohol and benzodiazapines. Tim had attended 12-step meetings, but they didn't work for him. One day he was walking in the woods near his house when he felt a sudden connection with the natural environment—a connection that he hadn't felt since childhood. This experience "stuck" with him, coming to represent an awakening of spirit that he could subsequently summon when the stresses of daily life and his recurring depression pulled him toward the liquor store. Tim described these moments as seeming like a devil and an angel locked in a struggle for his soul. At last, by meeting the angel, he (Tim) gained the upper hand.*

## Early Christian Conceptions of Metaphysical Evil

The later Manichaeans combined Zoroastrian philosophy with both Gnostic Christianity and the Greek dualism of God and matter. Although attracted to the Manichaean philosophy in his youth, St. Augustine was a strict monist and could not accept the ultimate duality of good and evil. He settled instead on a doctrine that established God as the supreme good and evil as the privation or absence of good. This privation or departure from the good (the *privatio boni*) is initiated in the human will (St. Augustine, 1963, 1972). For Augustine, the central problem is that human beings do not see the bigger picture that God sees and therefore do not understand how their own will leads them into evil. Thomas Aquinas continued the *privatio boni* argument by maintaining that evil must be the result of creation that has acquired some type of defect. Aquinas argued that there is no one cause of evil and also assumed that evil accidentally showed up in a minority of creatures, first generated and then corrupted.

*In a 1999 course on psychopathology, we were discussing the school shootings in Littleton, Colorado. We had students meet in small discussion groups and charged them to identify (based on what we knew from our studies and from news accounts of the two young gunmen) variables that might have been partially implicated in the tragedy. Among other common variables, students discussed at length the lack of supervision many youths suffer today, the possibility of sociopathic personality structures, prolonged exposure to and desensitization to violent imagery in the media, lack of parent involvement, and a social structure that almost forces both parents to work in many families. Toward the end of this discussion, one student raised her hand and said, "What if these two boys just developed into evil characters or were somehow defective to begin with?" We had to admit that, given an operational definition of evil, this question was indeed a good one.*

## Conclusions on Metaphysical Evil

It may not be possible for us to say that metaphysical evil is a reality. We will have clients who believe that it is and those who do not. Either way we can learn more about human psychology by examining the evolving images of metaphysical evil since, at the very least, they are projections of the human psyche and represent the struggle of all individuals beset with urges to do both good and evil. The history of the concept of metaphysical evil thus brings us one step closer to understanding, if not the cosmos, at least ourselves.

## *Natural Evil*

*For years I worked with clients who suffered from various forms of schizophrenia. Several of these clients had documented symptoms associated with a physiologically based schizophrenia (early onset, enlarged brain ventricles, decreased electrical activity in the frontal lobes). Many of these clients also had family members who suffered from the disease, raising suspicion of a genetic component. One of the more difficult things to see was one particular client's awareness that he was "different." Paul, though a young and attractive man, knew that his prospects regarding work, love, and leisure were limited. He suffered from aural hallucinations that, early in his illness, he believed to be God yelling at him. After several years, he said he didn't believe in God, because God wouldn't make people who were so sick. Paul said, "Only nature makes these types of mistakes."*

Simply put, natural evil consists of those elements in our natural world that threaten our survival and/or cause us pain and suffering. Natural evil includes a broad number of things, like the back problems resulting from bipedalism, like tornadoes and earthquakes, cancer, meningitis, and perhaps destructive aspects of humankind. Various metaphysical conceptions of evil are often used to account for natural evil. As Peterson (1992) pointed out, explanations of this type have been challenged by some philosophers, who remain resistant to the idea of an omnipotent, omniscient, and all-loving deity who apparently allows evil to run unchecked amid the created order. Similarly rational efforts to explain evil have often focused on evil as it is perceived in the natural world by organisms of that world.

## The Evolution of Evil

Writer Timothy Anders (1994) posited a rational explanation of how evolution accounts for much physical pain as well as the dynamics underlying social or moral evils. Anders concluded that both types of evil are the price paid for our biological capacity for suffering, which developed as a result of evolutionary adaptations within the species. Anders suggested bipedalism as a notable example of this type of adaptation and a cause of many problems that still plague humanity. Challenging notions that evolution is always "good" or "advantageous," Anders described how bipedalism resulted in back trouble, foot ailments, circulatory problems, and painful childbirth. For Anders, understanding evil is synonymous with understanding human evolution.

Perhaps one of the more lucid accounts of natural evil is offered by Bloom (1995), who describes the "Lucifer Principle" as the element of evil that is inherent in nature. Bloom's examples range from the biological to the sociological and historical. In one of Bloom's examples, although more than 200 billion red blood cells die each day in the interest of keeping a person alive, this person does not mourn the death of these cells. Bloom posed the chilling hypothesis that each of us may actually be cells in a social superorganism, whose maintenance and growth at times may require our pain or elimination, the suppression of our individuality, and the restriction of our freedom. For Bloom, these conditions may be a necessary part of life as a superorganism. Quoting the philosopher Georg Hegel, Bloom pondered the nature of tragedy as a battle between two forces, both of which are good, but only one of which can win. Such battles develop around hierarchies ("pecking orders") and ideologies. Bloom concluded that "nature has woven that struggle into the superorganism," stating also that while superorganisms, ideologies, and pecking orders are primary forces behind much of human creativity and earthly good, they are also "the holy trinity of the Lucifer Principle" (p. 326).

If Bloom's Lucifer Principle is woven into the fabric of nature, humanity may have to accept that "nature creates by destroying" (Bloom, 1995, p. 328). In this scenario, our hope lies in an ability to bind together for right action. As the Fourteenth Dalai Lama once noted, our best hope for an ethical society is "to turn toward the wider community of beings with whom we are connected (through) conduct that recognizes others' interests alongside our own" (Gyatso, 1999, pp. 23–24). For Bloom and the Dalai Lama, such right action can grow from reason. Reason is the evolutionary development that allows us to mediate between impulse and action. Such mediation has a greater chance of producing "right action." Certainly, there is far more to "right action" than reason, but reason is where most of us must begin. Even for people who do not have a belief in any particular god, this experience of "right action" may help them to transcend and rechannel destructive impulses. This notion of right action may have additional implications for human wellness. Toward this end, Bloom cited the work of McClelland, Ross, and Patel (1985). These researchers studied the boosting of immune system functions in subjects who viewed a documentary depicting Mother Teresa in her work with the poor. Drawing from this study, Bloom hypothesized that to deal effectively with evil in the natural world (including the evil within ourselves), we must first develop ways in which superorganisms (nations and subcultures) can "compete without carnage" (p. 328).

Bloom implied that competing without carnage favors certain state systems over others. In the same vein, Russett (1993) noted that democratic states are only one-eighth as likely as other states to resort to threats of force against each other and only one-tenth as likely to use force at all. Bloom also alluded to the fact that certain approaches to diversity and pluralism could essentially be movements toward competition with less carnage. Citing the conclusions of several researchers, Bloom (1995) stated that "pluralism is one of the most potentially effective forces for promoting global development" (p. 329).

### Conclusions on Natural Evil

As far as counseling goes, we need not look far to see the effects of natural evil. We and our clients suffer illness and die, we embody the changes that evolution—for better or worse—has brought to the species, and we are embedded in large superorganisms that may not see our survival and well-being as we see those things. Even conceptualizing evil and suffering through nature, we find that we have access to abilities that may help us transcend that evil and suffering. Far more confounding than metaphysical evil and natural evil is moral evil.

## Moral Evil

Moral evil occurs "when an intelligent being knowingly and deliberately inflicts suffering upon another sentient being" (Russell, 1988, p. 1). Moral evil is regularly addressed in theological, philosophical, and psychological discourse. Moral evil also results in many clients seeking the services of counselors. Whether causing direct or indirect trauma, moral evil is one of the most severe problems for twenty-first-century Americans.

Russell's definition of moral evil is synonymous with Baumeister's (1997) description of human evil and Goldberg's (1996) notion of malevolence. Noddings (1989) suggested that moral evil could also include cultural evil. Noddings cites cultures that prohibit women's autonomy and freedom as examples of cultural evil. Lifton (1986) and Katz (1994) addressed cultural evil in Nazi Germany, describing how physicians took an active role in the systematic destruction of human life. Sometimes moral evil may be as commonplace as apathy toward other people.

*We would like to think that cultural evil has always reared its face in extreme forms, that it is easy to point out but rarely the rule. But cultural evil is subtle. One of my clients, an African-American male who had been court-ordered to counseling for a drug-related assault, made little effort at dialogue for several sessions. Neither of us was very pleased with the arrangement. I was not only fed up with court-ordered clients but also felt underpaid and was in the early stages of burnout. My client had grown up in a poverty-ridden area, where crime was a fact of daily life and where people like me seemed to represent a large part of the problem. One day I asked my client what he really wanted out of his life, to which he responded, "What the hell do you care anyway?" His question hit me like a brick—at that point, in that moment, I realized that I in fact didn't care and that he knew this. I had slid down the slippery slope of those old tapes, imprinted with racism, classism, and indifference. I had seen this man as one of society's problems, just another client who was going to waste my time because the jails were overcrowded. From our very first meeting, I had ruled out any potential for growth. That day I clearly saw the part that I was playing in the perpetuation of cultural evil.*

## Moral Evil and Psychological Thinking

Some of the great minds of Western psychology have been captivated by the notion of moral evil, and counselors may learn from reflecting on their perspectives. In his groundbreaking work on the psychology of religious experience, William James (1929) spoke of moral evil as a disease and the soul wrestling with moral evil as "sick." James even went so far as to claim that worry over the disease was actually a form of the disease. James felt it was far healthier for people to "act for righteousness" than to dwell on their errors or lament their wrongdoing. Clinically, James called the mind burdened by evil "morbid" and noted that a person could experience different levels of morbidity. A lesser level of morbidity is simply maladjustment within one's environment, alleviated by changing the environment or one's relationship to it. More difficult to address is a "high-grade" morbidity, manifesting itself as a flaw in a person's essential nature, which no change of the environment or rearrangement of the inner self will cure. James went on to imply that in these instances one could either become deeply disturbed—a healing response in itself—or simply accommodate oneself to what was happening—a capitulation to evil.

Freud (1920) addressed the notion of moral evil in his theory of *thanatos*— the "death instinct." According to Freud, the death instinct manifests as a destructive force that can discharge either toward the self or toward others. After witnessing the carnage of the First World War and the death of his daughter Sophie, Freud postulated that the final aim of this instinct was to reduce living things to an inorganic state. In positing that destruction is built into the human organism, Freud's notion holds certain parallels to Bloom's Lucifer Principle.

In describing thanatos as that which is opposed to life, Freud was echoing various cultures' definitions of evil.

Carl Jung addressed evil extensively. Jung (1968) began his argument by claiming that good and evil are abstract principles as well as experienced realities. As principles, good and evil are simply aspects of God that "exist long before us and extend far beyond us" (p. 456). As realities, good and evil exist in things and situations that happen to us, that are too big for us, where we "are always as if facing death" (p. 462). Jung (1958) vehemently disavowed the doctrine of *privatio boni* and instead discussed the shadow side of the creator and creation. For the creator, Jung emphatically believed that evil derives from the dark side of God. Jung contended that this dark side is implied in a line from the Lord's prayer, which asks that God "lead us not into temptation." Jung saw evidence of this dark side in the wrathful lamb of the Book of Revelation and in the poem of Job (which we address in Chapter 4).

Jung believed that each individual, as a creature of God, has a dark side (shadow) in his psyche that could manifest as evil. One aim of Jungian counseling and psychotherapy is to increase awareness of this shadow, allowing it to be integrated with more conscious aspects of personality. For Jung, the process of denying one's own darkness results in one projecting it onto others. These "others" then become targets of destruction for disowned aspects of the self. Needless to say, the projective process is never satisfied in these cases, since the true source of evil is never addressed.

*As a client, Robert was—as the popular saying goes—no box of chocolates. For a 39-year-old man, he had developed a level of cynicism that some people don't approach after even 80 years of negative thinking. Robert suffered from recurrent bouts of depression and alcohol abuse. Little wonder, as his worldview was so bleak that I was amazed he hadn't attempted suicide. Robert was keen at picking out faults in other people (myself included). This quality seemed to help him in business ventures that sometimes led to material success, but it also precluded any meaningful relationships. Robert would frequently state his belief that I continued to meet with him only because I needed an image of myself as someone who could help people. He commented constantly on the ulterior motives of others. Finally, we reached a point when it became appropriate for me to note that he was good at seeing ulterior motives in others primarily because he harbored so many himself.*

Psychoanalyst Carl Goldberg (1996) noted that Jung (1958) interpreted Job's encounter with the devil as a metaphor for the individual meeting his or her own dark side. Goldberg interpreted Jung's idea to mean that a person's past forever remains a part of the person. If the shadow of these past events is too frightening for a person to face, it will be repressed into the unconscious. These repressed aspects are then projected outward onto others by the individual and are eventually encountered in the form of conflict with these others. For Jung, overcoming the fear and taboo of self-awareness was the antidote for the projective process.

Goldberg echoes Erich Fromm's (1973) view that the genesis of evil is a developmental process. Goldberg depicts those who commit moral evil as evolving malevolent personalities that are resistant to self-examination. The longer these individuals choose to make wrong decisions, the more hardened they become. Conversely, the more often they choose to make the right decisions, the more alive they become. Fromm (1973) noted how increasingly difficult it would be for such an individual to admit a wrong course, knowing that to turn back and accept a right path would require inordinate amounts of time and energy and the admission that he was wrong in the first place. As Goldberg notes, repression of these issues becomes inevitable, resulting in the harmful consequences of projection.

*Robert could only slowly acknowledge some of his ulterior motives. He had learned early not to trust people and he knew how to discern what people really wanted. He used this knowledge to his advantage. Robert's unfulfilled needs as a human being became his primary problem, but to change was incredibly threatening. Robert would make occasional progress in his self-examination, only to backslide into days of old habits, seeing his problems only in others.*

Psychiatrist Robert Jay Lifton (1986) researched the behavior of physicians who participated in murder in the concentration camps of Nazi Germany. Presenting a variation of Jung's notion of the shadow, Lifton coined two psychological terms—*psychic numbing* and *doubling*—to describe the processes that led many physicians to maintain "normal" social and family lives, while simultaneously participating in acts of enormous horror and cruelty. Psychic numbing is a lessened capacity to feel empathy for victims, fully supported by the projective process. It is an interruption in the process of seeing the victim as an essentially human other. Doubling involves the splitting of one's self into separate functioning wholes, with each part capable of acting independently. This splitting would finally result in what Jung (1933) referred to as "complexes." These complexes would then become repressed and function autonomously, encouraging the projective defense process. Simply put, the degree of repression correlates directly with the degree of projection in the repressor. Lifton noted high levels of concentration camp personnel alcoholism as one of the side effects of this repression. Hannah Arendt (1964) spoke of a related self-centeredness and self-delusion on the part of the Nazis, noting their ability to conveniently view the Final Solution—total extermination of Jews and other targeted ethnic groups—as their own heavy burden, rather than the atrocity against humanity that they themselves had created and perpetuated.

Karl Menninger (1973) discussed the concept of *sin*, stating that modern psychotherapy was doing more harm than good in assigning clinical labels to certain people who may be better labeled evil. Menninger believed that psychiatry was fostering hopelessness by doing away with the concept of sin, thereby leaving the criminal justice system and the medical community as gatekeepers of misbehavior. This, he postulated, resulted in large numbers of people denying responsibility for much of the moral evil that surrounds us.

Framing moral evil as criminal behavior or mental illness also diverts responsibility away from those of us living in the society where the moral evil is perpetrated. By encouraging us to shift responsibility for dealing with moral evil to the criminal justice or mental health systems, we may ignore our own role in perpetuating it. Menninger believed the concept of sin was still useful in describing the evil of which humans are capable.

Menninger's line of thinking was amplified by M. Scott Peck (1983) who, unlike Menninger, postulated that there are cases that psychiatry could appropriately diagnose as evil. Peck affirmed that by naming something we gain power over it. He strongly believed that we ought to name evil as an illness. Peck explained that the central defect of evil people is not their sins (or inappropriate, destructive behaviors) but their refusal to recognize these sins. Repression and psychic numbing are used in service of both this blocking awareness and the projective process discussed above. Peck contends that it is not their sins per se that characterize evil people, but the subtlety, persistence, and consistency of their sins. Individuals who commit moral evil refuse to recognize their own sin, demonstrating a trait that Peck suggests lies at the core of the *malignant narcissistic personality*—a term first used by Fromm (1973).

Peck suggests that moral evil exhibits an extreme, aggressive willfulness and a focus on power. To face their own sense of inadequacy is, for those committing moral evil, a form of death. Unlike Menninger, Peck asserted that the evil character as a singular personality disorder can be conceptualized as a subcategory of the narcissistic personality disorder found in the *Diagnostic and Statistical Manual of Mental Disorders* (American Psychiatric Association, 1994).

According to Peck, other primary characteristics of evil people are consistent and destructive scapegoating behavior, excessive intolerance to criticism, obsessive concern with public image, and intellectual deviousness. When Peck (1983) said that in order to treat evil we must be more "aligned with truth" than against evil, he implied that we "treat" evil with a methodology of love and a commitment to truth. This means that in a therapeutic setting, evil may be smothered with or absorbed in a force of love and truth.

*I have a colleague who works with adolescent sex offenders who themselves also suffered abusive childhoods. One client was frequently beaten as a child, burned with cigarettes, sexually abused, and frequently left alone for days at a time while his mother was off on drug binges. This client had been in the custody of the state since sexually molesting several children in his neighborhood at the age of 13. I asked my colleague how one would even begin treatment of such a client. My colleague described various cognitive, behavioral, and empathy-enhancing treatments sanctioned by the state in such cases, describing the theory and application of each treatment at great length. After a long and informative description, my colleague sighed and said, "None of that really helps much if you can't baste them in love while you treat them."*

# RESPONSES TO EVIL

What can we do when faced with evil? This question is central to most religious traditions and spiritual movements and is frequently a focus of counseling and psychotherapy. Does our response to this question differ depending on whether the evil is metaphysical, natural, or moral? Readers may have already ascertained that it is difficult to separate these three categories. They are useful to begin a dialogue but soon start to blur at the edges. Where metaphysical evil is concerned, each person must come to her own conclusions regarding its existence and what the best response to it might be. Natural evil is less ethereal and may be effectively combated through mutual cooperation. Natural evil frequently assists in this process by providing a common enemy, such as a virus or natural disaster. When considering psychological dynamics, we cannot help seeing that self-examination and education go a long way toward precluding our participation in moral evil. Yet, what will we do when we meet moral evil in the consulting room or in our personal lives? This is not so easily answered, but there are some guidelines we can start with as well as using some of the archethemes explored in Chapter 2. In considering potential responses to evil, we discuss childhood sexual abuse as an example of moral evil and detail one counselor's approach to the treatment of clients who commit this evil.

## *Taking the First Step*

First, we have to risk the first step, which will often be frightening. The first step involves acknowledging the moral evil in question and confirming our commitment to truth, both in our thoughts and in our actions. A colleague of ours works with sex offenders who suffer from pedophilia. Originally, he believed that he was called to help these people, but he also felt revulsion at their behaviors. To overcome his initial anger, he reflected on the Dalai Lama's (Gyatso, 1999) advice: Try to view all people as wanting happiness as well as wanting to avoid suffering. For our colleague, this practice of compassion helped to prepare the sacred ground on which the counseling process could successfully take place. Our colleague also noted that taking this first step helped him with his own pain. As Yalom (1995) wrote in his discussion of healing factors in group therapy, altruism may in and of itself be a healing factor. Being able to reach out to others, to take the first step, requires a sense of self that is not threatened by reaching out. Facing oneself, as described in Chapter 2, fosters this process. Additionally, a person must also be able to accept support from others in order to affirm the common ground of the human condition. This is a spiritual action in that it is another variation of saying "yes" to life.

## Fostering and Using Support Networks

Responding to evil is never a solo effort. As the adage goes, "There is strength in numbers." One of the great losses of postmodern life is the loss of support-ive communities. Communities where people once easily connected with and depended on each other have dissolved as the pace of our society and the geo-graphic spaces covered by the average person in an average day have increased. When we can foster them, supportive networks and communities are a conta-gious resource. By "contagious," we mean that they encourage love and breed strength. Evil, by its very nature, encourages isolation and breeds weakness.

Our colleague referred to above noted how much he needed support from his family and his colleagues in order to work with sex offenders. The suffering he encountered sometimes "wore down" his optimism and his belief that life was a beautiful thing. At these times, he allowed himself to be refueled by colleagues and family. This did not come easily, as he viewed himself as a "cowboy" of sorts—independent and able to act without any need for others. He observantly noted that if he had acted out the cowboy motif in his current work, he would have been burned out within one year.

## THE ARCHETHEMES REVISITED

How may we utilize the archethemes described in Chapter 2 in our responses to evil?

### Hope

In considering responses to evil, we return to the importance of hope. Examples of cultivating hope may range from a global optimism to an understanding that pain is often time-limited. Even for the nonreligious, optimism about life is essential when responding to evil. It is once again a variation of saying "yes" to life. The counselor doing work with sex offenders could not continue effectively without hope that some clients would eventually be helped by this work. He may be the first to note that pedophilia is often resistant to treatment, but he would also have seen enough success and had enough faith in his work to con-tinue. As Frankl (1946) noted, our last freedom is the attitude that we will take toward life. In a confrontation with evil, letting go of hope is the quickest path to defeat. You may ponder how you maintain a hopeful outlook and how you cultivate such an outlook with clients as one step to how you address evil.

### Virtue

Virtue is about being in touch with one's power. Nowhere is this more important than in a confrontation with evil. How do you use the power you have to allevi-ate the suffering caused by evil in the world? How does that power translate into your work as a counselor? We have noticed that counselors often fall into a caricature of themselves as people who do not show anger. In responding to evil, our anger may in fact be our greatest virtue. Reaching out in compassion or love does not mean that we avoid anger, or that we cannot make judgments, or that we are unable to set and abide by limits. Anger and compassion may effectively join forces. Our colleague who counsels sex offenders uses his anger to reinforce boundaries that the client must learn, particularly regarding what constitutes appropriate sexual attraction and behavior. This counselor must be judgmental regarding appropriate boundaries, recognizing the important role of his anger.

An attempt to deny this anger would constitute what Wilber (1999) called "idiot compassion" (p. 99). Real compassion makes judgments and honors those things that are informed by wisdom and care. Idiot compassion feigns the spirit of kindness but may actually perpetuate evil. Wilber provides the hypothetical example of an alcoholic friend who may die from one more drink but then begs you to get him one anyway. Idiot compassion leads us to get the drink for the man, assuming, "Who am I to impose my views on my friend who is making an adult choice?" Real compassion assesses the situation within the context of a commitment to truth and does not get the drink. Compassion requires making judgments. In Wilber's words, when you hear someone say that he is being nonjudgmental, "run!" (p. 101).

Making judgments requires taking authority. Part of our virtue, our power, lies in taking authority rather than giving it away. We all know that there are times when it would be easier to "follow orders" than to do what seems like the proper alternative. Much evil has been committed in the name of "following orders." Arendt (1964) explored this side of evil in her account of Nazi war criminal Adolph Eichmann, a bland bureaucrat who was "just following orders." Again, owning one's authority implies thinking for one's self, making use of both head and heart. As Arendt makes clear, the banality—the *ordinariness*—of individuals like Eichmann is precisely what becomes so frightening. Eichmann's behavior illustrates the way that evil seems to fester wherever responsibility and accountability have become fragmented.

## Sacred Ground

Counseling and spirituality both share a use of sacred ground or sacred space to bring about transformation. Just as religions across cultures set aside particular places to engage in ritual and to render themselves vulnerable to the divine, the space of the counseling session is one in which client and counselor enact the rituals of counseling and render themselves vulnerable to the forces of personal transformation.

## Polarities

Earlier, we defined a polarity as a pair of opposites that work in complementary fashion. Could it be that good and evil constitute such a polarity? Bear in mind that this question forms the basis of theodicy, which, as described earlier in this chapter, is the unanswered question of how, if a god exists, that god could allow evil to run unchecked in the world. The most compelling theodicies seem to leave us with three conclusions. First, the existence of evil is inexplicable and seems woven into creation. Second, if there is a divine being, that being is ultimately responsible for evil in ways we simply cannot fathom. Third, despite this we have the option of saying "yes" to a life that includes evil and "fighting the good fight" against it.

## Facing Oneself

If we are to decrease the probability that fighting the good fight will perpetuate evil and suffering, we must begin that fight by facing ourselves. As the psychological views on moral evil described in this chapter advise, we must be willing to assess our parts in the evil and suffering we see and experience in the world. As noted, it is much easier to identify an external enemy who needs to be destroyed than to admit our own culpability in evil and suffering. How willing are you to consciously examine your shortcomings? How do those shortcomings relate to what you view as evil in the world? These are questions that can initiate some self-reflection.

There are tools that can aid the self-reflective process. For example, see Chapter 9 of this book on counselor self-assessment, as well as the discussion in Chapter 8 of the "personal inventory" suggested in the 12-step program. Entering counseling certainly helps us keep aware of our virtues, our shortcomings, and the ambiguity of the human condition that may result in any one of us engaging in good or evil. The myths of figures like the devil, if read as myth, describe not just an ambiguous creation but the ambiguity of human nature as part of creation. Such myths can serve as tools for self-reflection that serve to heighten our awareness of our own potential to cause evil and suffering.

## Compassion and Love

The place of compassion and love is clear in relation to the problem of evil. As the Dalai Lama (Gyatso, 1999) has noted, compassion and love are small words but difficult tasks. You may begin by thinking of those closest to you with whom you practice love and compassion. When you experience an image of someone with whom this is difficult, you have met a challenge to the practices. Most of us don't need to think too long to come across such a person. This is a good place to begin a more intentional practice of love and compassion. For the interested reader, psychiatrist Roger Walsh (1999) has compiled numerous exercises designed to facilitate the practice of love and compassion.

In terms of using these archethemes to address evil and suffering, it is hard to say exactly where that will lead. Clearly much of Western psychology has viewed the human condition as essentially sublimating negative energy into socially acceptable forms. The degree to which this is true is the degree to which we will never be free of evil but only be able to control it. Eastern psychology takes a different position, viewing compassion and love as antidotes to those things considered evil. Which approach is most accurate? The best way to address the question is to practice compassion and love and find out for yourself.

## *Meaning and Transcendence*

We discussed the archethemes of meaning and transcendence as treasures gained from the hero's journey. With regard to evil, we view these archethemes as diluting the apparent claims that evil has over us in life. Even the most horrific evil is weakened and made shallow when just one person uses its occurrence as an occasion to make meaning and to transcend related suffering. In this sense we might say that our ability to choose meaning making and transcendence are among our greatest resources for responding to evil both in our personal lives and in our capacity as counselors.

## CONCLUSION

The construct of evil illustrates a potent reality that more operationalized psychological constructs may fail to capture. If we are truly following our clients' leads, we will want to listen when they speak of evil. Most evil—be it metaphysical, natural, or moral—results in human suffering and may be effectively responded to. We hope that we have offered the reader some clues for such responses. In the next chapter, we shift to the theme of suffering. As we have noted throughout this book, suffering is often woven into the existential givens of life. Whether suffering is existential in origin or not, how we endure it is at the heart of counseling and spirituality. With this in mind, the next chapter turns to a very old story of human suffering and the lessons it holds for us today.

## QUESTIONS FOR REFLECTION

1. Why, in your estimation, do evil and suffering exist? What purpose, if any, do they serve? What are their opposites? How are they used to alleviate clients' suffering?
2. Do you feel people are born good or grow to goodness? Do you see any evidence to support your view?
3. Do you feel evil is a useful construct? Why or why not?
4. Consider some of the psychological theories related to evil (James, Freud, Jung, Menninger, Peck, Lifton) that we reviewed in this chapter. Is there one that you feel is more accurate or useful than the others? If so, why? If not, what do you think should be done with the construct of evil?

5. How do you differentiate "bad" from "evil"?
6. Can you think of a time when you perpetrated evil either directly or indirectly? What was it you did? How did you make sense of your actions at the time? What are your views of the incident presently?

# REFERENCES

American Psychiatric Association. (1994). *The diagnostic and statistical manual of mental disorders* (4th ed.). Washington, DC: American Psychiatric Press.

Anders, T. (1994). *The evolution of evil: An inquiry into the ultimate origins of human suffering*. Chicago: Open Court.

Arendt, H. (1964). *Eichmann in Jerusalem: A report on the banality of evil* (rev. ed). New York: Viking Penguin.

Associated Press. (1999). Student contradicts story of Columbine martyr. Chicago Tribune: Internet Edition, http://cnews.tribune.com/news/tribune/story/0,1235,tribune-nation-35287,00.html.

Baumeister, R. F. (1997). *Evil: Inside human violence and cruelty*. New York: W. W. Freeman.

Bloom, H. (1995). *The Lucifer principle: A scientific expedition into the forces of history*. New York: Macmillian.

Ellerbe, H. (1995). *The dark side of Christian history*. San Rafael, CA: Morningstar Books.

Frankl, V. (1946). *Man's search for meaning*. New York: Beacon Press.

Freud, S. (1920). Beyond the pleasure principle. In *Standard edition of the complete psychological works* (Vol. 18). London: Hogarth.

Fromm, E. (1973). *The anatomy of human destructiveness*. New York: Holt, Rinehart, Winston.

Goldberg, C. (1996). *Speaking with the devil: A dialogue with evil*. New York: Viking.

Gyatso, T., the Fourteenth Dalai Lama (1999). *Ethics for the new millenium*. New York: Riverhead Books.

Haase, H. (1992). *Confronting evil: A discourse for the education community*. Unpublished doctoral dissertation, University of Vermont.

Hallie, P. P. (1979). *Lest innocent blood be shed*. New York: Harper.

Hallie, P. P. (1988). Cruelty: The empirical evil. In P. Woodruff & H. A. Wilmer (Eds.), *Facing evil: Light at the core of darkness* (pp. 119–129). LaSalle, IL: Open Court.

James, W. (1929). *The varieties of religious experience: A study in human nature*. New York: Modern Library.

Jung, C. G. (1933). *Modern man in search of a soul*. London: Harvest.

Jung, C. G. (1958). *Answer to Job*. Princeton, NJ: Princeton University Press.

Jung, C. G. (1968). Civilization in transition. In William McGuire (Ed.), *Collected works* (Vol. 10). Princeton, NJ: Princeton University Press.

Katz, S. T. (1994). *The holocaust in historical context: Volume I. The holocaust and mass death before the modern age*. New York: Oxford University Press.

Lifton, R. J. (1986). *The Nazi doctors: Medical killing and the psychology of genocide*. San Francisco: Basic Books.

McClelland, D. C., Ross, G., & Patel, V. (1985). The effect of an academic examination on salivary norepinephrine and immunoglobulin levels. *Journal of Human Stress, 11*, 52–59.

Menninger, K. (1973). *Whatever became of sin?* New York: Hawthorne Press.

Noddings, N. (1987). Do we really want to produce good people? *Journal of Moral Education, 16*(3), 177–188.

Noddings, N. (1989). *Women and evil.* Berkeley: University of California Press.

Peck, M. S. (1983). *People of the lie: The hope for healing human evil.* New York: Simon & Schuster.

Peck, M. S. (1987). *The different drum: Community making and peace.* New York: Simon & Schuster.

Peck, M. S. (1997). *The road less traveled and beyond: Spiritual growth in an age of anxiety.* New York: Simon & Schuster.

Peterson, M. L. (1992). *The problem of evil: Selected readings.* Notre Dame, IN: Notre Dame Press.

Russell, J. B. (1977). *The devil: Perceptions of evil from antiquity to primitive Christianity.* Ithaca, NY: Cornell University Press.

Russell, J. B. (1988). *The prince of darkness: Radical evil and the power of good in history.* Ithaca, NY: Cornell University Press.

Russett, B. (1993, November). Peace among democracies. *Scientific American,* p. 120.

St. Augustine. (1963). *Confessions.* Trans. Rex Warner. New York: Mentor.

St. Augustine. (1972). *City of God.* New York: Penguin.

Sanford, N. & Comstock, C. (1971). *Sanctions for evil: Sources of social destructiveness.* San Francisco: Jossey-Bass.

Tsanoff, R. (1931). *The nature of evil.* New York: Macmillan.

Van der Post, L. (1988). The dark eye in the world. In P. Woodruff & H. A. Wilmer (Eds.), *Facing evil: Light at the core of darkness.* LaSalle, IL: Open Court.

Walker, B. G. (1988). *The woman's dictionary of symbols and sacred objects.* San Francisco: Harper & Row.

Walsh, R. (1999). *Essential spirituality: Exercises from the world's religions to cultivate kindness, love, joy, peace, vision, wisdom, and generosity.* New York: Wiley.

Watts, A. W. (1963). *The two hands of God: The myths of polarity.* New York: George Braziller.

Watts, A. W. (1966). *The book: On the taboo against knowing who you are.* New York: Vintage.

Watts, A. W. (1968). *Could be hidden, whereabouts unknown: A mountain journal.* New York: Vintage.

Wilber, K. (1995). *Sex, ecology, spirituality: The spirit of evolution.* Boston: Shambhala.

Wilber, K. (1999). *One taste: The journals of Ken Wilber.* Boston: Shambhala.

Wilmer, H. A. (1988). Introduction. In P. Woodruff & H. A. Wilmer (Eds.), *Facing evil: Light at the core of darkness.* LaSalle, IL: Open Court.

Woodruff, P., & Wilmer, H. A. (Eds.). (1988). *Facing evil: Light at the core of darkness.* LaSalle, IL: Open Court.

Yalom, I. D. (1995). *The theory and practice of group psychotherapy.* New York: Basic Books.

# The Story of Job and Human Suffering

Human suffering is the vortex of spirituality and counseling. As we have noted, few clients come to us for counseling when everything is going well, and many people turn to spirituality when everything is going bad. Our clients suffer, we suffer, all human beings suffer. The first of four noble truths taught by the Buddha is that life is characterized by suffering (*duhkha* in Pali). Although this truth is simply worded, it is nevertheless complex.

The word *suffer* comes from a Latin root meaning "to endure." An ironic twist to human suffering is that when we are suffering, we are also enduring. To *endure* comes also from the Latin, meaning "to harden" or "to make lasting." Perhaps this is the source of the annoying saying many of us heard as children, about suffering breeding character. Many clients go to counselors thinking that they want their pain to go away altogether. If there is anything to the first noble truth of the Buddha, this desire is impossible. In some cases, we can assist clients in diminishing their pain, but we cannot erase the source of pain (which may be existential in origin). Ideally, we can help clients become more aware of their style of enduring (suffering) and more artful in applying that style to the ongoing challenges of living.

## SUFFERING AND PROSPERING "AMERICAN STYLE"

One unfortunate characteristic of the dominant American culture is that we are trained to think that we can and should avoid pain (and hence, suffering). Anglican priest Michael Merriman (1992) suggested that our culture functions from an oversimplified Deuteronomic theology that maintains the righteous are rewarded and the wicked are punished; therefore, if we are suffering it is our own fault and we are to blame. The origin of this theology is the Hebrew text called *Devarim*, known more commonly as Deuteronomy, found in the Old Testament of the Bible. In the 28th chapter of Deuteronomy the author summarizes the earthly blessings that will be bestowed on the righteous and the evils that will be suffered by the wicked. Bear in mind that such theologies have been the source of heated debate for millennia since there have always been those quick to point out that the wicked often prosper while the righteous suffer greatly. The oversimplification of this theology is assuming that those who suffer do so because of their own faults, and those who prosper do so because they have adhered to the true path.

If this simplified notion that the righteous are rewarded and the wicked punished were true, then to accept our suffering would be to accept that we are somehow wicked. As Ingersoll (2000) has discussed, it is amazing how many people find it easier to assume their wickedness than to wrestle with the painful realization that they live in an unjust world. Additionally, if this theology were true, there would not be much motivation for those prospering to help those suffering. It would make sense to allow them to suffer the consequences of their wickedness. This theology makes the privileged and the destitute equally responsible for their situations, allowing an artificial barrier to separate them. One spiritual challenge facing counselors is their commitment to questioning such a theology that basically "blames the victim." At least in the counseling session, such a philosophy could result in countertransference.

We have known novice counselors who appear to believe that the righteous are rewarded and the wicked are punished. This belief provides counselors with an illusory sense of control regarding what may or may not occur. They are frightened by a client's pain when it seems that they, the counselors, may be vulnerable to the very same suffering. To question this illusory control is threatening, as it leaves us vulnerable to existential givens that we all must face. It is not just the breaching of a folkway that is threatening, but that in doing so, we come face to face with our own pain, suffering, and vulnerability. This is a considerable challenge, but it is also a common human response. Upon hearing that an acquaintance has cancer, how many of us ask or wonder "Oh, did she smoke?"

## POLARITY AND SUFFERING

Lyn Bechtel (1993) of Moravian Theological Seminary has addressed prospering and suffering—what we described in Chapter 2 as the archetheme of polarity. She summarized the problem of suffering by noting that living is the interplay of life and death, of oppositional forces (like the yin/yang metaphor from Taoism). Life feeds on death. Life is poetry and pain: "pain deepens and verifies the poetry" (p. 3). This polarized nature of life becomes problematic in a culture like ours, where we seek an unrealistic, sometimes impossible amount of control. If life is the interplay of control and a loss of control, the society that seeks total control will only breed denial of an essential truth—that there are many things that are simply beyond our power to affect. As the

Buddha noted, in denying the truth, we suffer. In rebelling against the truth, we perpetrate evil.

Our clients may come to us hoping to find a way to stop suffering. Such a state is not possible as long as one is alive. What we help clients to accomplish is receptivity to what life brings us, placing us in a better position to exert control where it is most needed. As Viktor Frankl (1946) reminds us, this may be solely in the attitude that we take to what life has brought. Such a simple equation nevertheless may require a great deal of counseling if it is to be put into action.

Our "free-market spirituality" is not much help when we attempt to recognize a darker side to existence. This spirituality capitalizes on a Western aversion to pain and suffering, explaining why spiritual vendors often sell a variety of "feel-good trips." Many new-age spiritualities simply give people new ways to think about themselves, but do not open them up to any transformation that might result in a radical change in the experience of the self (Wilbur, 1999). Whenever we conduct workshops on spirituality and counseling, we ask people to co-create descriptions of spirituality. Often workshop participants generate a list of adjectives and positive descriptors like "lovely" and "peaceful." Occasionally, one or two people with a knowing glint in their eye will say "spirituality is terrifying." These people seem to have crossed the boundary between a safe theology based on illusions and the sometimes-frightening nature of a true spiritual journey. They have crossed the boundary of illusory control, to meet life as it truly is—to say "yes" to life. In spiritual literature, the book of Job stands out as a wonderful guide to crossing these boundaries—to saying "yes" to a life that necessarily involves suffering.

## THE BOOK OF JOB: BACKGROUND

Most scholars agree that the text of Job was written late in Hebrew history (500 BCE), but the first Hebrew manuscript did not surface until some time after this (Mitchell, 1979; Reichert, 1946; Spong, 1991). The book, actually a poem, is based on a tale from a much earlier era (circa 2000 BCE), about the sufferings of a righteous man. This earlier poem may actually have origins in Sumerian and later Babylonian tales about the suffering of righteous men. In the Sumerian version the gods intervene and end the author's suffering, thus restoring order to the universe (Russell, 1977). In the Babylonian version, the righteous man who is suffering receives no satisfactory reply from the gods (Lambert, 1958).

The book of Job (along with the other Old Testament books of Ruth and Jonah) can be categorized as "biblical protest literature" (Spong, 1991), continuing Ezekiel's theology of the individual (as opposed to the group or the tribe). Job's story challenges the notion from Deuteronomy (and Proverbs) that suffering is reserved for the wicked, that the righteous do not suffer. Job is probably one of the oldest, most exquisite poems addressing the nature of suffering and related spiritual transformation. The book contributes much to our understanding of suffering, helping us also to understand a counselor's urge to deny personal vulnerability and to want solely to rescue clients from suffering.

The story of Job also affirms the reality of suffering. There has been an abuse within the new-age movement to attempt to pass off suffering as a psychological "trick-of-the-light" or an "illusion." Eastern traditions typically depict evil as one aspect of a polarity that emanates from a divine source. The divine source underlies the entire polarity (good and evil), but people tend to see only the polarity and not its divine origin. In this sense, an appearance of the polarity in the world has been called "illusory." Not in the sense that it is not real, but in the sense that it is not "all there is." Many people misinterpret Eastern texts, assuming that an "illusory" nature of the world means that it is simply not real and that if they meditate "hard enough" it will finally vanish. This interpretation is not supported in the esoteric traditions. In enlightenment one sees both the polarities *and* the divine source underlying them. Far from a "feel-good trip," Job's story provides human suffering with the dignity that is its due. The book points out the insight that suffering can lead to—insight into the ground of all polarities, the source of life itself. Our own view of Job is that of myth. A myth is not something untrue, but a metaphor weaving perennial truths with history. Joseph Campbell (1988) stated that myths are clues to the spiritual potential of human life. These clues help us to resonate with the experience of being alive.

## THE STORY: AN EARLY CASE STUDY IN SUFFERING

*Once upon a time, in the land of Uz, there was a man named Job. He was a man of perfect integrity, who feared God and avoided evil* (Mitchell, 1979, p. 5).

Thus begins Job's tale. As the story unfolds we learn that Job has done quite well for himself. He is "the richest man in the East," with "seven sons and three daughters; seven thousand sheep, three thousand camels, five hundred donkeys and many slaves" (the ancient equivalent of a $300,000 home, two SUVs in the garage, and a trust fund for college educations at private universities). Job is so righteous that he even offers sacrifices in the temple for his children, on the outside chance that they have sinned. Job is the type of person who files his taxes on time, coaches Little League baseball in the summer, and walks the dog at night. Job is undeniably righteous. However, Job is righteous because he is a good businessman. His theology tells him that it is profitable to be "good" because the "good" are rewarded. This is not to say that Job is trying to "con" the Almighty. Job truly believes his theology because his life experience has given him no evidence to disbelieve it. All seems well in this ancient Hebrew version of the "American Dream."

From here, the scene shifts to a dialogue in heaven between God and a pre-Christian form of Satan, playing a type of "prosecuting attorney." Satan has just returned from a trip to earth. God, almost as if offering a dare, praises Job to Satan: "How about that Job—is there any more righteous man in the land?" The stage is set for Satan to introduce some doubt into God's mind. He replies, "Sure, he's devoted to you now—but turn me loose on his family and fortune and he'd curse you to your face." So, with doubt properly introduced, God agrees to let Satan test Job, on the condition that Satan not harm him. At this point, Job loses everything. Despite this, he does not curse God, but instead looks to his theology and concludes "The Lord gives and the Lord takes away; may the name of the Lord be blessed."

From here, we return to heaven: Again, God and Satan are passing the time of day and the Lord cannot resist the temptation to boast a bit more on account of Job's stalwart response to trial. To this Satan responds, "A man will give up everything to save his own skin. Just reach out and strike his flesh and bones, and I'll bet he curses you to your face." To this dare the Lord gives the chilling reply: "All right, he is in your power. Just don't kill him." Now, in addition to the loss of his fortune and offspring, Job is afflicted with all manner of physical illness. Even his wife has had enough, and advises Job to quit clinging to his innocence, to curse God and to die. Job is well aware of his theology, which states he must have been truly wicked to have such suffering visited upon him. For the first time, he rejects his theology and maintains that he has not sinned. Job experiences firsthand that not all who suffer are wicked.

Now enter three of Job's friends: Eliphaz, Bildad, and Zophar. They have heard of Job's suffering and have come a great distance to be with him. Upon their arrival, they see how great Job's suffering is and—rather than offering him the shallow comfort of words—they sit with him for three full days. Finally, they begin one of the most brilliant dialogues known to literature. Job curses his life (but not God) and maintains his innocence. The friends, although trying to be comforting, become increasingly disturbed. If Job is innocent, their theology is wrong. And if their theology is wrong, they could suffer just as Job suffers, with no just cause. At this realization, they begin to argue. If Job is suffering and Job is righteous, they too are vulnerable to such suffering. Like the beginning counselors that we mentioned earlier, Job's friends seek to avoid confrontation with their vulnerability by finding a way to "blame the victim."

At the climax of Job's story, he challenges God to show him where he has sinned. God answers him out of a whirlwind. The image of God has transformed greatly within the story. Far from the well-meaning bungler of the story's beginning, the voice from the whirlwind is a frightening articulation of the unrestrained, natural life force itself. Through a stunning array of naturalistic imagery, God definitively demonstrates that Job and his theology were asking the wrong questions all along. God illustrates the awesome, infinite nature of life, along with the feebleness of the theology that Job was using in his attempt to capture it. After this confrontation, a spiritually awakened Job says, "I have spoken of the unspeakable, and tried to grasp the infinite. I have heard of you with my ears, but now my eyes have seen you" (Mitchell, 1979, p. 88).

In the end, Job's fortune is returned tenfold. The Lord reprimands his friends and their theology and Job gets new offspring, giving his daughters equal share with his sons. "After this, Job lived for a hundred and forty years. He lived to see his grandchildren and his great-grandchildren. And he died at a very great age" (Mitchell, 1979, p. 91).

## SOME ANALYSIS

The story of Job is ripe with polarities. The polarities of good and evil and the ways in which we try to make sense of them are the main themes of the story. Lurking below this theme is the polarity of activity and receptivity. In the beginning of Job's story we come across a very active, controlling man who follows every ritual, leaving nothing to chance. This Job does all the right things, but without much passion. This Job lives in a type of "behavior modification" cosmology, where reinforcement and punishment emanate directly from God. Job's problem becomes his diminished capacity for receptivity and vulnerability. His recipe for theology has cultivated an illusion that the universe is a predictable place, controllable by activity. What Job learns is that his activity must be complemented with an appropriate amount of receptivity.

Stephen Mitchell (1979) has noted that the greatness of this poem lies in part with the strength of its characters. Job's friends are at once noble and disappointing—quite like most of us. Just as good counselors would, they arrive and sit in silence with Job. They do not try to mask their discomfort with idle chatter, but sit receptively with him. They know Job is suffering and they nobly resist the temptation to offer platitudes to ease their own discomfort. In their silence, they enter the sacred space of Job's suffering. In relation to counseling, Job's friends are modeling the receptivity that is necessary, if counselors are to have an experience of the client. Recall Erich Fromm's (1950) statement that a therapy may either help clients adjust to the sickness of their culture or address the pain in their soul. The receptivity of silence directs the client toward the soul, where the distractions of the culture have no jurisdiction.

Job is wrestling with a common counseling theme. What must a person do when his usual way of understanding the world ceases to make sense? Whether it is a theological stance, a career, or a particular role that we are playing, we can quite easily be shaken to our very foundation when our approach to life no longer provides meaning. As counselors pressured to work in a competitive culture largely shaped by the medical/mechanistic paradigm, it is sometimes tempting to provide a "new-and-improved" meaning, a cognitive reframe, from the lofty perch of supposed expertise. Providing such interventions under the guise of "reality testing" may be more an effort to cloak our own discomfort than to offer relief to the client. Imagine Job walking into an HMO and hearing the counselor say, "Well, Job, you are dealing with issues of loss and I can lead you through that grieving in six to eight sessions."

We saw in Chapter 1 that powerful idols in American culture are the scientific method and the control that it offers us. Certainly, science is an impressive tool. It has cured disease, added comforts to our lives, and freed us from the tyranny of oversimplified theologies like that of Job's friends. Negative by-products of the scientific method include developing more power over nature than we may have the wisdom for as well as a typically Western habit of denying the inherent polarities of life (for example, the natural polarity of control and lack of control). Because technology is truly marvelous, it feeds our craving for absolute control. If we transcend our egos, we may recognize that control must be balanced with ambiguity or uncertainty. As the Chinese proverb suggests, "To be uncertain is uncomfortable, to be totally certain is ridiculous." Total certainty is "not in the cards," but as counselors and psychotherapists continue to ape the scientific paradigm, a temptation to control increases, while we defer directly to treatment manuals for our interventions.

Perhaps the most striking aspect of Job's story is his spiritual transformation in the face of the whirlwind. Mythically, Job becomes a whole (holy) person. Job's suffering has been transformed through his arrival at wholeness. This has been accomplished through a realization that life does not respect recipes for existence—stemming from theology, a business ethic, or anything else—that feign total control. In terms of the polarity of activity/receptivity, we might say that Job was primarily "active" in his close observance of the law. He lived in an ordered universe with predictable outcomes. He had lost touch with his receptive elements. It is the receptive that allows us to experience awe, mystery, and ambiguity. Through his confrontation with the whirlwind, Job reclaimed his capacity for awe and strengthened his tolerance for ambiguity.

And what of the story's ending? Certainly, it is hard to imagine losing all your loved ones and then having them replaced with new ones, much like a parent replacing a child's broken toy. Such literal understanding does little to enhance our ability to endure suffering. Job's story is a myth, and his story's ending demands a deeper reading. As the poem concludes, the author makes a special point of saying that Job gave his sons *and* daughters equal shares of his fortune. This was not a common practice in the patriarchal Hebrew culture of Job's day. Mitchell (1979) stresses that this gesture is symbolic of Job's transformation, wherein he has integrated his masculine and feminine characteristics, as well as his active and receptive sides. This symbolism is further appreciated through our close examination of the Hebrew names given to Job's daughters: Dove (peace), Cinnamon (plenty), and Eye Shadow (feminine grace) (Mitchell, 1979).

## THEMES FOR COUNSELORS

### Affirming Suffering

Several themes arise through a careful reading of Job. Here, we elaborate on and expand themes first suggested by Anglican priest Matthew Fox (1991). First, the story of Job may be viewed as a framework for affirming the reality of suffering—for not blaming the sufferer for his or her situation. As noted previously, many in our culture struggle to deny the reality of suffering. Realities like HIV/AIDS, cancer, hopelessness, poverty, violence, war, and child abuse all point to the unmistakable fact that suffering is a large part of life. A Jewish mother once told her daughter, "I will not wish for you the absence of suffering in life for that wish will not come true. I will wish for you the strength to endure suffering and the wisdom to derive meaning from it" (Adams, 1995). As we train counselors, we must help them to work through their struggles as they seek to affirm the reality of their clients' suffering. We must remain in touch with our own struggles to affirm the client's suffering—to affirm it without necessarily attempting to fix it. The difficulties that we face in our attempts to affirm suffering are at least partially connected to our own fears of suffering.

Rabbi Harold Kushner (1981) wrote that the German word *schadenfreude* refers to the uncomfortable feeling of relief that we experience when something bad happens to someone else, rather than to us. This may partially explain what Job's friends are dealing with as they condemn Job's insistence of innocence. It relates to the current trend toward a model of counseling that includes social advocacy. Counselor responsibilities can extend to education of the public, particularly when the public's *schadenfreude* reveals itself in areas such as the condemnation of gays, lesbians, or the homeless. To blame the sufferers is easy—we fear, "There, but for the grace of God, go I," and we project our fears. The writer of Job protested blaming those who suffered, knowing finally that good people suffer as well. As counselors, we must certainly come to grips with this existential given, if we are to be of assistance to clients.

### Balancing Activity and Receptivity

A second theme in Job emphasizes our need to balance activity with receptivity. The story of Job illustrates the crisis that arises when one aims to control all aspects of life, ignoring the necessary counterpart of surrender. Our culture overemphasizes activity and control, much to the neglect of receptivity and surrender. Counselors need to be aware that time spent with clients in the therapeutic setting may actually be the only opportunity for the client to experience real receptivity. The Anglican monk Martin Smith (1991) once said, "Few people give us much encouragement to ask 'who am I?' We are expected to carry on; we have no business indulging in such introspection" (p. 31). Smith held that the spiritual life would thrive only by defying these prohibitions. In a secular sense, meaning or existential well-being can develop only with a proper balance of activity and receptivity. An hour in the therapist's office may be one of the few receptivity-cultivating opportunities that people allow themselves.

## Honoring Ambiguity

A third theme in Job—closely related to the balancing of activity and receptivity—is honoring ambiguity. In other words, it is not a sin to say, "I don't know" (recall that *sin* in Greek means "to miss the mark"). As we live in a culture that values "experts" and "expertise," it has become anathema in many circles to say, "I don't know." This dynamic is particularly malignant in academic, political, and business circles. The "expert" is meant to have an informed opinion, usually at the drop of a hat. This is indicative of Western culture's typical overvaluing of activity, its undervaluing of receptivity, and its dread of ambiguity. The cultural pressure to "have an answer" is almost overwhelming. Living by the letter of the law appears to work no better in academia, politics, or business than in religious pursuits. We give birth to far more fruitful ideas by recovering our capacity for awe and wonder, thereby enhancing the eventual processes of data gathering and literature citation. In this type of complementary relationship, we may find that recovering our capacity for awe and wonder leads to far more useful data.

Counseling's research paradigm of prevention capitalizes on the reality of ambiguity, since it is harder to show that a problem was prevented than to show that a problem that existed was solved. In recognizing ambiguity's value, someone has also suggested that one of the best things a counselor can say when faced with a client's suffering is, "I don't know how you feel" (Adams, 1995). Perhaps counselors should thank God that they *don't* know! Just as Job's friends are primarily frightened by the potential breakdown of their theology, people's discomfort with suffering or their feeling that they should always "have an answer" will lead them to empty chatter. A time of deep spiritual, emotional, or physical pain is a time to listen, not a time to talk.

## Hope for the Spiritually Abused

A fourth theme in Job is hope for the spiritually abused who experience spiritual hunger. These are individuals who have had abusive experiences, primarily at the hands of others whose original job was to nurture spiritual growth. The abusers, damaged in their own way, have abused their position and hurt those who seek spirituality or who have surrendered themselves for the purpose of spiritual growth. Though they may not yet be able to pull away from various harmful ideologies or groups, persons who have been spiritually abused may gain much from Job's experience of living legalistically (under the oversimplified, Deuteronomic theology), of suffering, and of seeking meaning through his suffering. Yao (1985) and Brewer (1991) found that distrust of religious groups is a common experience for the spiritually abused individual. Counselors with an understanding of Job may have a valuable resource to offer such individuals. Here, freedom from dogmatic attachment to tradition may actually provide a great boon to the counselor.

## Job and Addiction

A fifth theme of Job's story is an allegory for understanding addiction (unhealthy attachment). The second noble truth of Buddhism emphasizes that craving and attachments cause suffering. Gerald May (1988) described addiction as a process of attachment that can enslave one's will and desire. Schaef (1987) saw American culture as riddled with such addictions. If we define addiction broadly to include worldviews, we may perceive Job as experiencing a type of withdrawal from the worldview that had served him for so long. Just as Job experiences the pain that accompanies a rearrangement of his view of life, our clients consistently face some transformation in their own worldview that will inevitably cause them pain; still, this is not a pain without meaning! Indeed, it is Job's courage to endure such transformation that makes him an inspiring character. The very nature of addiction supports the authenticity of Job's manifested God of the whirlwind, as well as his resulting transformation. Addiction often implies an attachment to the illusion of security. We can see that if God were truly the God of Job's friends he would be concrete and graspable—an easy target for addictive attachment. We will deal more specifically with addiction (and the 12 steps) in Chapter 8.

## Job as a Patron Saint

Finally, Fox (1991) has suggested that Job is a good patron saint for first-world people. Fox felt that Job experienced what the so-called first-world nations must now experience. Job lived by the letter of law until he lost everything and rediscovered his capacity for awe and surrender. Job "shut up" not out of submission but out of awe. Job reveled in the awe of mystical wonder, experiencing true *metanoia* (change of heart). Job had succeeded in his culture by "following the rules" unswervingly. Many people holding power in our current culture adhere to a national myth that says we live in a land of plenty ("one nation under God") with a humanistic political ideology. This has led many to assume, in some way, that we are God's chosen people. Fox believed that our democratic structure and our efforts to deter nuclear war might have contributed to the idea that we are successful, because we are "walking with God." Merriman (1992) notes that this national myth does not take into account those suffering from the ills of a technocratic society—ill health, poverty, lethal addictions, and meaninglessness (among many). As Anglican bishop John Spong (1991) pointed out, the danger in believing yourself to be chosen is that it becomes easy to view those who are not in your group as unchosen. This is the same projective process that was discussed at length in Chapter 3 on evil. Spong concluded that the emotional distance between God's unchosen and God's rejected is very small, as we are not actively encouraged to look at our own shadow but instead are emotionally reinforced to avoid it.

## CONCLUSION

The book of Job is one of many windows that counselors may look through to learn more about counseling, spirituality, and suffering. We recognize that our view of Job as myth rather than a sacred scripture belonging to a particular religious tradition may not resonate with all readers. As with the other material in this book, we remind readers to ponder those points that arouse interest and leave those that do not.

## QUESTIONS FOR REFLECTION

1. Where did you first hear of the story of Job? Does our presentation of it differ from your understanding of it?
2. Can you think of a situation in which another person's suffering frightened you because you thought the same thing might happen to you? How did you react to your fear? How did you react to the person whose suffering inspired your fear?
3. Which of the themes for counselors presented in this chapter resonated most with you? How might you apply that theme in your counseling practice?
4. Can you think of other stories or myths that help us make sense of human suffering? Which ones stand out for you as useful metaphors in counseling and why?

## REFERENCES

Adams, S. (1995). Unpublished interview on spiritual wellness. In R. E. Ingersoll, *Construction and initial validation of the spiritual wellness inventory*. Unpublished dissertation, Kent State University.

Bechtel, L. (1993). *Exploring the book of Job*. Unpublished manuscript. Bethlehem, PA: Moravian Theological Seminary.

Brewer, C. (1991). *Escaping the shadows, seeking the light: Christians in recovery from childhood sexual abuse*. San Francisco: Harper.

Campbell, J. (1988). *The power of myth*. New York: Doubleday.

Fox, M. (1991). *Creation spirituality: Liberating gifts for the peoples of the earth*. San Francisco: Harper.

Frankl, V. (1946). *Man's search for meaning*. New York: Beacon Press.

Fromm, E. (1950). *Psychoanalysis and religion.* New York: Bantam.

Ingersoll, R. E. (2000). Gentle like the dawn: A dying woman's healing. *Counseling and Values, 44,* 129–134.

Kushner, H. (1981). *When bad things happen to good people.* New York: Avon Books.

Lambert, W. G. (1958). The Babylonian theodicy. In D. W. Thomas (Ed.), *Documents from Old Testament times* (pp. 97–110). New York: Knopf.

May, G. (1988). *Addiction and grace: Love and spirituality in the healing of addictions.* San Francisco: Harper.

Merriman, M. (1992, March 8). *Living the sacramental life.* Unpublished lecture given in the Diocese of Ohio, Cleveland.

Mitchell, S. (1979). *The book of Job.* San Francisco: North Point Press.

Reichert, V. E. (Ed.).(1946). The book of Job. In *Sancino books of the Bible,* Vol. 11. Jerusalem: Sancino Press.

Russell, J. B. (1977). *The devil: Perceptions of evil from antiquity to primitive Christianity.* Ithaca, NY: Cornell University Press.

Schaef, A. W. (1987). *When society becomes an addict.* San Francisco: Harper & Row.

Smith, M. L. (1991). *A season for the spirit.* Cambridge, MA: Cowley Publications.

Spong, J. S. (1991). *Rescuing the Bible from fundamentalism: A bishop rethinks the meaning of scripture.* San Francisco: Harper.

Wilber, K. (1999). *One taste: The journals of Ken Wilber.* Boston: Shambhala.

Yao, R. (1985). *Fundamentalists anonymous: There is a way out.* New York: Luce Publications.

# CHAPTER
# 5

# GUILT AND MENTAL HEALTH

In Chapter 3, we discussed various types and aspects of evil, including moral evil. We now consider one potential consequence of evil—guilt. It is important that we distinguish between appropriate and inappropriate guilt, examining connections between guilt and religious faith while also describing the real influence of guilt on mental health. Guilt can carry both positive and negative consequences, with implications in both directions having a significant impact on the client/counselor relationship and the entire counseling process.

In Chapter 1 we spoke of the "psychological fact of interest" and spirituality. Even though they are aware that religion and spirituality are central in many Americans' lives (Gallup, 1995; Gallup & Castelli, 1989; Kosmin & Lachman, 1993), many mental health professionals continue to neglect an active consideration of these issues within their counseling practices (Barnhouse, 1979; Hoge, 1996; Ingersoll, 1994; Kelly, 1995; Lovinger, 1990; Miller, in press). As we have seen in previous chapters, religious belief and the construct of spirituality continue to gain an increasing amount of attention within our field, despite this overriding neglect by practitioners. A growing number of mental health professionals have begun to acknowledge openly that active religious belief and/or spirituality can contribute to sound mental health. Literature concerning the importance of spiritual and transpersonal issues continues to emerge, with counselors becoming increasingly comfortable confronting clients with related issues. Still, many practitioners persist in a misunderstanding of clients with overtly religious or spiritual issues (Judy, 1996).

A perpetuated misunderstanding of religious and spiritual dimensions of client experience has generally been attributed to a simple lack of alertness on the part of practitioners. Environmental constraints have been viewed as significantly less influential (Kelly, 1995). As Worthington (1989) makes clear, even practitioners who share a particular religious background with a client may—in some cases—believe that strictly religious issues belong outside the traditionally secular counseling session. Lack of alertness by the practitioner and a related view of the counseling process as strictly secular have their roots in

74

peculiarly Western cultural distinctions discussed in Chapter 1. Again, we might ask: Are religion and spirituality not as much a part of the human experience as everyday thoughts and feelings?

This book is about counseling and spirituality. In this chapter we focus more on specifically religious aspects of spirituality and their relationship to guilt and mental health. From a mental health perspective, religion functions as either a source of strength or a source of negative and debilitating emotions, depending on a client's level of relative health or dysfunction regarding his or her religious belief (Allport, 1950; Arterburn & Felton, 1991; Faiver & O'Brien, 1993). Wulff (1996) considers the psychology of religion to be either descriptive or explanatory. A descriptive psychology of religion seeks to document the many varieties and types of religious experience, while an explanatory approach seeks to locate the origins of religious experience in psychological, biological, or environmental events. The explanatory approach, exemplified by practitioners such as Sigmund Freud, James Leuba, and B. F. Skinner, has typically been hostile to religion, presenting religion as a potential and specific cause of pathology. Humanistic values have occasionally been the target of a related form of enmity, though they have typically been thought to underlie various therapeutic systems and the work of many practitioners (Bergin, 1980; McMinn, 1984). Ellis (1980) highlights a similar perspective, implying that religion is a clear source of pathology. Yet, he views humanism as capable of conveniently providing the values of religion with none of the resulting neuroses. A central aspect of this debate is the construct of guilt and its relation to religion, spirituality, and mental health. A review of the relevant literature makes relationships between these constructs evident, shedding light on many potential implications for practitioners.

## RELIGION AND GUILT

In our discussion of religion and its relationship to guilt and mental health, we have chosen to emphasize primarily Judeo-Christian examples of what Smith (1976) refers to as exoteric forms of religion. As mentioned in Chapter 1, exoteric religion focuses on public, concrete, outer forms and doctrines, just as esoteric religion focuses more significantly on a personal experience of some Divine Reality. Exoteric religion is a social phenomenon, involving a gathering of people within a specific faith perspective (Roberts, 1990). Faith is a transcultural dynamic, through which trust in some object, principle, or event is recognized as central to worth and meaning in a person's life (Fowler, 1981). Our use of the term *religion* includes notions of institutional affiliation (predominantly Christian in the United States, according to Gallup Poll Monthly, 1993), church involvement, and corresponding personal behavior. This same religion has been described as "a system of symbols, which acts to establish powerful, persuasive, and long-lasting moods and motivations by formulating conceptions of a general order of existence and clothing these conceptions with such an aura of factuality that the moods and motivations seem uniquely realistic" (Geertz, 1966). The word *religion* itself derives from the Latin root *religio*, indicating a "rebinding" or a belonging to some larger whole. Religion may result in an individual's religiosity, a quality of *being* religious that Allport and Ross (1967) describe as either extrinsic (utilitarian, used primarily for socialization and self-justification) or intrinsic (sincerely committed, central to the individual's life). Whether extrinsically or intrinsically motivated, religiosity results inevitably in some sense of a moral code. When we speak of guilt, we may describe a type of self-reproach and remorse for one's behavior. These feelings result from perceived violations of important moral principles included in a person's moral code (Klass, 1987). For many Americans, this moral code stems directly from formalized religion.

It is useful to think of guilt as the state in which religion and psychology meet (Belgun, 1960; Collins, 1980; Narramore, 1974a). Existentially oriented practitioners refer to an "existential guilt" that stems from living an incomplete or inauthentic life (Yalom, 1980). We see guilt conceptualized quite differently within the various primary therapeutic approaches and Yalom's description provides just one example. Though we view this theoretically diverse treatment of guilt as important, our primary concern relates to a client's personal experience with guilt and the role that guilt plays in a client's life. Guilt may be experienced as a client's sense of having done wrong, which implies indeterminism—if a person *feels* that he or she should have acted differently in a certain situation, an implication may be made that he or she *could* have acted differently (Smith, 1988). In this way, guilt involves a self-awareness and a self-consciousness and relies on developmental mechanisms to directly facilitate this self-awareness and self-consciousness. By the same token, we believe that it is necessary to differentiate the concept of guilt from shame. While guilt suggests condemnation of a single, specific act or behavior, shame indicates a more global condemnation of the entire self (Lewis, 1971; Lewis, 1992; Meehan et al., 1996; Tangey, 1990; Tangey & Fischer, 1995). Shame has traditionally been associated with a larger range of psychopathology while guilt has been associated with more nonpathological tendencies, such as empathy and social adjustment (Tangey, 1990). In a study that we have found useful, Jones and Kugler (1993) identify three types of guilt—pervasive trait guilt, a more immediate state of guilt, and guilt related to moral standards. In the estimation of Jones and Kugler, pervasive trait guilt becomes most problematic and is related most closely to a larger range of psychopathology, typified by the inclusion of shame.

In the field of counseling and psychotherapy, any discussion of the etiology of guilt must begin with Freud. Freud (1974) theorized that a sense of guilt was the source of all religion and morality, with guilt primarily related to unconscious hostility toward some other distinguishable entity. Freud asserted that humankind most likely acquired a characteristic guilt at the outset of human existence, resulting from a complex negotiation of incestuous desires. Eventually, Freud and other prominent psychoanalysts moved beyond this oversimplification. A modified understanding of guilt relied finally on an important assertion: What significant authorities (religious, familial, political, etc.) teach children about sexuality, anger, and other emotional issues does have a significant impact on the adult consciousness (Meissner, 1984). In psychoanalytic theory, this modified understanding is embodied in the construct of the superego, the body's purveyor of an idealized self-image as well as various internalized messages of "significant authorities." Freud asserts that a sense of guilt that is endemic to human nature (and exercised through the superego) stems most significantly from violations of internalized social injunctions and, to a lesser degree, from violations of religious doctrine or directives. In either case, guilt evolves from the presence of a moral code that has been breached.

Recent interpersonal conceptualizations of guilt (Meehan et al., 1996; O'Conner, 1995) negate Freud's psychodynamic perspective and view guilt instead as painful affect stemming from a person's belief that he or she has harmed someone else. Violation of a moral code is indicated once again, with this moral code instructing us to avoid harming others. The guilt that is present in these cases helps us to appropriately facilitate and maintain attachments, but this same guilt can become problematic and maladaptive when exaggerated. A psychodynamic schema of guilt that is possibly more palatable than Freud's has been outlined by Narramore (1974a), who interprets guilt as emanating primarily from the superego. He divides the superego into three implicated mechanisms—the ideal self, the corrective self, and the punitive self. The ideal self functions as the nucleus of conscience, containing our values, standards, and aspirations. The ideal self acts as a measuring stick against which we gauge our behavior and our self-image. Narramore defines the corrective self as the source of "healthy guilt," internalizing caregiver reprimands and eventually utilizing these same reprimands in a self-reflective way. The punitive self is described as an opposing source of "unhealthy guilt," originating in caregiver threats of punishment, rejection, or shaming. These caregiver threats are also internalized and utilized in a self-reflective manner, with what Narramore perceives to be negative (unhealthy) consequences. Though Narramore approaches the etiology of guilt from a psychodynamic perspective, the guilt that he associates with the ideal and/or punitive selves may be conceptualized as "maladaptive schemas." These schemas are "stable and enduring themes that develop during childhood and are elaborated upon throughout the individual's lifetime" (Young, 1990). It is important to note that these schemas have their origin in both individual temperament and dysfunctional development, which may actually integrate religious themes or experience.

# THE EFFECT OF GUILT ON MENTAL HEALTH

When an individual actively pursues a state of mental health, the process can be envisioned as one of balance, with individuals allowed to grow while also maintaining contact with consensual reality (Wilber, 1997). The guilt that an individual experiences may serve to either maintain or diminish this contact with consensual reality, depending on the type and intensity of the guilt feeling. Historically, there has been widespread agreement regarding the merits of appropriate forms of guilt and the harmful nature of inappropriate guilt (Horney, 1937; Hyder, 1971; Narramore, 1974a; Peck, 1993, 1997). Skilled practitioners often encourage clients to discriminate between more appropriate forms (where awareness of one's shortcomings might ultimately enhance personal growth) and increasingly neurotic or excessive forms (where growth may be impeded by emotional baggage). Narramore and Counts (1974) discriminate in their own amplification of this view, referring to "real guilt" as a message from the Holy Spirit in response to breaking God's law and to "false guilt" as a more elemental message from the potentially oversocialized superego.

It has become possible to assess guilt as appropriate or inappropriate based on client self-reports. These self-reports indicate that, in moderate amounts, guilt serves positive functions (Ferguson & Crowley, 1997; Steketee, Quay, & White, 1991; Tangey & Fischer, 1995). In its fourth edition of the *Diagnostic and Statistical Manual of Mental Disorders*, the American Psychiatric Association (1994) makes clear that a more immoderate amount of guilt (survivor guilt, exaggerated guilt over uncontrollable factors, excessive guilt) acts as a direct symptom in a number of prevalent pathologies, including Major Depressive Disorder (Single Episode—296.2, Recurrent—296.3) and Posttraumatic Stress Disorder (309.81). Malatesta and Wilson (1988) note that long-term exposure to messages inducing a particular emotion may lead to "surfeit pathology," indicating an overload of the emotion in question. When this type of pathology occurs, personal experience can be interpreted through maladaptive schemas that are caused by this emotional overload. A particularly debilitating example of this pathology occurs when guilt becomes the emotion in question. We share the view of Malatesta and Wilson, and we encourage practitioners to assist clients by cognitively challenging these maladaptive schemas or patterns.

For both practitioner and client, orientation to guilt may have a significant impact on the counseling relationship. McMinn (1984) calls this orientation to guilt the "G orientation," attributing either guilt-accepting (G+) or guilt-suppressing (G−) traits to specific individuals. Individuals who demonstrate a guilt-accepting orientation view guilt as a by-product of inappropriate behavior. The practitioner with a G+ orientation may utilize this orientation to assist clients in identifying inappropriate behaviors that guilt responses might signify. Practitioners with a G+ orientation are more likely to view guilt as a natural and potentially helpful response, capable of influencing clients toward future avoidance of inappropriate or negative behaviors. Practitioners demonstrating a G– orientation view guilt as a purposeless entity that directly produces psychopathology. For the G– practitioner, guilt is to be either entirely avoided or, at the very least, eliminated in order for client improvement to occur. Elimination of inappropriate behaviors (which may easily preclude the client's experience of guilt) is less important to the G– practitioner. Rather than debating a more global stance on the relevance of religion in counseling and psychotherapy, McMinn focuses on potential client-therapist matching with regard to religious values. McMinn feels confident that practitioners with a prominent G+ orientation will lean toward theism, while those with a more prominent G– orientation will identify with more secular values. McMinn notes the potential value inherent in matching therapist-client orientations, since clients also carry their own guilt-accepting or guilt-suppressing orientation.

Belief that guilt is consistently pathological in nature has found support in the writings of Albert Ellis (1980). Though this is an extreme view, evidence does exist to positively correlate guilt, or specific types of guilt, with psychopathology. Comparatively, Tangey (1990) has asserted that guilt is anchored primarily on the nonpathological end of the behavior continuum. This more common view is supported by Narramore (1974a), who qualifies guilt as a prevalent factor in all psychological problems, but in a generally inappropriate (exaggerated, excessive) form. Narramore sees inappropriate guilt emanating largely from the punitive self and its three major themes—fear of punishment, loss of self-esteem, and fear of rejection. With Narramore's view in mind, practitioners might utilize the presence of inappropriate guilt to dictate treatment methodology.

Primary problems of excessive guilt have been closely associated with emotional distress or with problems of addiction. In this regard, Weiss (1986) and O'Conner and Weiss (1993) have connected excessive guilt with disturbing childhood experiences and an eventual avoidance of growth. This psychodynamic view has similarities with the interpersonal theory of "altruistic guilt." An individual suffering from altruistic guilt fears harming another person, thereby often neglecting the pursuit or attainment of developmentally appropriate goals for himself or herself. The challenge of correlating levels of religious devotion with levels of guilt has been taken up by a number of recent researchers, with varying results. Steketee, Quay, and White (1991) have demonstrated that greater religious devotion may be positively correlated with greater levels of inappropriate guilt in clients suffering from Obsessive-Compulsive Disorder, but that clients suffering from other anxiety disorders are not susceptible at similar levels. These researchers also conclude that religiously devoted clients who do not suffer from Obsessive-Compulsive Disorder do locate relief within the Sacrament of Reconciliation (confession), while those still suffering from Obsessive-Compulsive Disorder do not.

# GUILT IN THE JUDEO-CHRISTIAN TRADITION

The religiously devoted tend to seek guidance and solace actively in the primary texts of their respective faiths. Examination of the sacred writings of the Judeo-Christian tradition reveals a number of direct references to guilt. Traditional, Old Testament Jewish writings typically portray guilt as collective, relating tales of idolatrous worship practices and inappropriate interfaith marriages. In these traditional writings, public confession of guilt is seen as a proper response to the prevailing conditions. We see here that the corrective self (Narramore, 1974a) is implicated, rather than the more destructive punitive self. In New Testament Christian writings, a more individual sense of guilt develops. The individual's personal awareness of sin (frequently revealed as the missing of some ideal mark) becomes a prominent theme, with those who experience a resulting guilt reflecting varying degrees of remorse. Frequent allusions to a Jewish image of the heavenly record of each person's sins and a similar sense of "counted sin" relate directly to awareness of a moral law and a self-awareness that is dictated by moral law. Standards or laws against which to measure behavior are emphasized significantly in New Testament writings, comprising a moral code that, if breached, may easily result in an individual's experiencing a sense of guilt. This relates directly to Narramore's notion of the ideal self and the specific values, standards, and aspirations for which the ideal self strives. Narramore (1974b) notes a significant New Testament absence of any emphasis on guilt as a strictly emotional entity. Three Greek words found in biblical translations—*hupodikos*, *opheilo*, and *enochos*—describe guilt as a specifically social condition, where one is either liable to judgment, guilty of an offense, or indebted to someone, respectively.

If an individual commits an act that goes against traditional religious belief or religious training, it is normal for this individual to experience feelings of guilt. New Testament writers allude to the potentially positive ramifications of this experience, speaking directly to the wonder of redemption. Both Narramore (1974b) and Collins (1980) describe this sense of godly grief or godly sorrow in relation to constructive, corrective guilt, with more worldly grief or worldly sorrow presumably linked to inappropriate forms of guilt. Excessive or inappropriate guilt may follow when individuals assume unrealistic demands or react in exaggerated ways to real or fancied transgressions rather than simply accepting appropriate levels of responsibility. In a majority of instances, guilty feelings lead to a loss of self-esteem, a need to make amends, and a desire to seek forgiveness and atonement. If these tasks remain incomplete, the guilty individual may either consciously or unconsciously react in a self-defeating manner, usually in the form of self-punishment (Osborne, 1967). This punishment will be expressed somatically, emotionally, behaviorally, or even in the language of dreams (Drakeford, 1967).

Whatever the case, our focus here is on inappropriate guilt, stemming from what Narramore considers the punitive self. If one's level of individual guilt becomes more appropriate, we may witness a more reasonable acceptance of what has been done, a making of necessary amends, and some movement forward. The process described here can be ultimately healing, freeing, and interpersonally healthy (Donnelly, 1993). Even when only appropriate levels of guilt are present, self-defeating response patterns may occur. These patterns may be positively worked through with the assistance of a counselor, and guilt-experiencing individuals may eventually become capable of making necessary amends. These amends are extremely difficult to accomplish in the presence of excessive, inappropriate guilt, due simply to this guilt's inordinate quality and the likely unresolved nature of related issues.

*Ed, age 47, felt a heavy burden of guilt. Due to his abusive drinking, he had neglected his children during most of their early childhood. He had now been sober for several years and was participating in Alcoholics Anonymous. His A.A. program suggested that he make amends for the harm that he had done in the past. However, Ed became depressed as he considered that there was no realistic way to go back in time to be present at his children's school or sports events or their early home life. His sadness was made even more immediate by the current attitudes of his children, who were now in their teens and twenties. These attitudes ranged from coldness to real hostility. Ed's therapist made arrangements for the entire family to participate in a number of Ed's counseling sessions. During these sessions, some long-standing resentments were aired, with Ed finally apologizing for his past actions. With further amends in mind, Ed's therapist suggested that he now make an extra effort to be present to his wife and children. As he found ways to do this, Ed exhibited behavioral changes that diminished his feelings of depression and helped to relieve him of the guilt he had carried for so long.*

Processes implicated in the presence of excessive guilt are ultimately "diseasing," confining, and interpersonally unhealthy in their effect. Consider how many mental health professionals have worked with clients suffering from depression or experiencing some form of inappropriate guilt!

Narramore (1974b) has clearly articulated the discrepancy that occurs when guilt is deliberately utilized in religious settings as a motivational tool. This practice is not supported in the sacred texts of the Judeo-Christian tradition, yet Narramore shows that many religious leaders use the primary themes of the punitive self (fear of punishment, loss of self-esteem, fear of rejection) to their advantage, unfairly impacting the consciousness of believers as a result. This is a clear exacerbation of inappropriate guilt. On a related topic, Narramore (1974c) concludes that—with regard to the punitive self and "unhealthy guilt"—the Sacrament of Reconciliation (confession) may be effective in alleviating a fear of punishment or rejection, but not a loss of self-esteem. Narramore credits this discrepancy to a client's potential feeling of unworthiness.

Those suffering from unhealthy guilt and a subsequent loss of self-esteem may believe themselves undeserving of the relief that confession affords.

Bynum (1994) joins Narramore in signifying the desire for forgiveness or atonement in response to guilt as a universal dynamic. Early in this century, Weber (1922) described pastoral care (including the practice of confession) as an evolved product of prophetically revealed religion, with its source in an oracle or diviner. The diviner was normally consulted when suffering was believed to have resulted from a transgression against one of the gods. This consultation was meant to lead to the confession of either a single individual or an entire community so as to pacify the aggrieved spirits and restore peace to the group. Weber claimed this practice as the original source of the confessional, claiming that the current affiliation between the practice of confession and individual ethics is a more modern phenomenon.

More recently, Smith (1985) traces the Sacrament of Reconciliation to the "Second Epistle to the Corinthians," authored by Clement of Rome, and an additional work entitled "The Shepherd of Hermas." These works are products of the second century and—when combined with the third-century works of Tertullian—they reveal an early form of confession, conceived as a second method of repentance for those who sin following the initial sacrament of baptism. Bishops and clergy eventually took full control of this ritual, which evolved into present-day private confession. In tracing the history of this sacrament, we see the notable retention of the rite in the revised Anglican prayer book of the 1970s (Smith, 1988). It would seem that alongside the rise of psychiatry and the practice of counseling during the twentieth century, a consensus formed regarding the therapeutic value of individual confession. In relation to this, we have described the archethemes of confession and forgiveness in Chapter 2. In Chapter 8, we will describe the use of one form of confession as a component of the suggested 12 steps of Alcoholics Anonymous.

Raised within the Lutheran faith as the son of a Lutheran pastor, Carl Jung was particularly critical of the loss of regularly practiced confession in the majority of Protestant religions. Jung (1958) suggested that just as the psyche develops to the point of self-awareness, the psyche also develops an ability to harbor secrets about its various functions and actions. Jung believed that this resulted in guilt and the imperative need for an earthly confessor. "The Protestant is left to God alone," Jung writes. "He has to digest his sins by himself" since the absence of confession has put grace beyond his reach (p. 48). Jung believed that the psychotherapist, within a healing process that included self-disclosure, had essentially replaced the traditional priest as confessor. In this confessor role, the therapist listens in a nonjudgmental fashion with unconditional positive regard (Jung, 1958; Rogers, 1957), just as the client experiences unhindered acceptance. As Jung (1933) states, "We cannot change anything unless we accept it. Condemnation does not liberate, it oppresses. I am the oppressor of the person I condemn, not his friend or fellow sufferer" (pp. 234–235). When guilt is experienced at an appropriate level, the therapist's thorough acceptance of the client can potentially lead to client self-acceptance. In learning self-acceptance, the client may accept forgiveness and make atonement for his or her perceived transgressions. When guilt is inappropriate, transgressions can be neither forgiven nor atoned for, since they essentially exist solely in the heart and mind of the supposed transgressor.

*Father Everett, a priest in his early fifties, had been suffering with a degenerative neuromuscular disease for several years. He was also suffering from the depression that so often accompanies this type of illness. His depression had gone untreated for far too long. He believed that he had "a right to be depressed," due to his experience of chronic pain and loss of function. By the time he was brought to a therapist, Father Everett's symptoms had become severe. Prominent among them was an obsessive thought that he was sinful, that he had sinned early in his priestly career, that he had not properly confessed or been absolved, and that all of his subsequent priestly work was therefore worthless. He had been assured by colleagues in the ministry that he had now done his best to confess properly and that God had indeed forgiven him. He even possessed a letter from his bishop—who he believed to be a kind and thoughtful man—which assured him that he had appropriately confessed and had been absolved. However, none of these assurances had taken away his obsessive thoughts. Father Everett's excessive and inappropriate guilt moderated only after several months of treatment for clinical depression.*

## IMPLICATIONS FOR PRACTITIONERS

Because of the historical division between most prominent psychological theorists and organized religion, it is important for practitioners to acknowledge openly a willingness to discuss religious issues with clients. Many clients, especially those middle aged or older, are reluctant to address guilt or related concerns with religious overtones. Central to this reluctance is the stereotypically tenuous relationship between religion and the therapeutic professions. As practitioners, we should be willing to ask clients whether religion is important in their lives, listening also for some indication of any positive or negative impact that religion has had on them. If a client reports that religion holds little or no interest, practitioners need not pursue the issue further. If a problem does exist, however, and is closely tied to issues of religion, practitioners may address the problem directly, if so qualified. If practitioners feel that a problem is beyond their own realm of competence, they should refer the client to a qualified, empathic member of the clergy (Faiver & O'Brien, 1993; Faiver, O'Brien, & McNally, 1998).

*Tanya, a chronically depressed mother of four adult children, was making a slow recovery from a depressive episode. She was a deeply religious person*

*who had always been active in her church. Tanya's obsessive thoughts con-*
*cerned what she believed to be her own responsibility for a tragic sexual assault*
*on her youngest daughter, which had occurred at the school Tanya had insisted*
*her daughter attend. In Tanya's recovery, it proved helpful for her therapist to*
*arrange a meeting with her pastor, who discussed with Tanya the fact that she*
*was apparently making herself "more responsible than God," since not even*
*the deity had intervened to stop the attack on her daughter. The phrase "I'm*
*not more responsible than God" became a sort of mantra for Tanya, helping to*
*relieve her of inappropriate guilt.*

Figure 5.1 outlines a number of practical steps that qualified practitioners might take when assisting clients with guilt-oriented issues. In this figure, the assumption is that the counselor is willing to adopt unconditionally either a guilt-accepting (G+) or guilt-suppressing (G–) client orientation. We assume also that no client sociopathy is present. If a client is genuinely guilt suppressing (G–), the practitioner might successfully approach treatment from a cognitive-behavioral perspective, attentive to the possibility of maladaptive schemas. Once these schemas are identified, client guilt might subsequently be confronted through active disputing of the schemas themselves. If a client's values and the identified schemas are widely divergent, they may be explored along with whatever client behaviors remain incongruent with the client's established value system. If the client presents as guilt accepting (G+), client guilt might be explored so as to determine its relative appropriateness or inappropriateness.

Practitioners might effectively proceed by listening attentively to the client's story—acting, in effect, as confessor. If client guilt emerges as an appropriate presence, practitioners might then work with the client to discern any potentially religious themes. If religious themes surface, a client's moral code can be identified and implications of client past and future behavior can be examined from this perspective. In the absence of obvious religious themes, knowledgeable practitioners might assist clients in identifying values held for the ideal self, or possibly assist clients in adjusting their behavior to match these values. If client guilt emerges as an inappropriate presence, we assume that the client will gain a lesser degree of relief from sharing her individual story, due largely to the excessive or otherwise inappropriate nature of the guilt itself.

As we work with clients who harbor inappropriate guilt with attached religious themes, we might benefit from an examination of these themes in light of Narramore's (1974a) established metaphors for the ideal and punitive selves. These metaphors can be framed as maladaptive schemas, most likely deviating a great deal from the actual teachings of the client's chosen religion. This type of therapeutic practice demands practitioner familiarity with the primary tenets and teachings of the major religions, enabling successful disputation of maladaptive schemas.

We are strong advocates of assessing the client's belief system within the context of the intake interview (Faiver & O'Brien, 1993). In this process, we

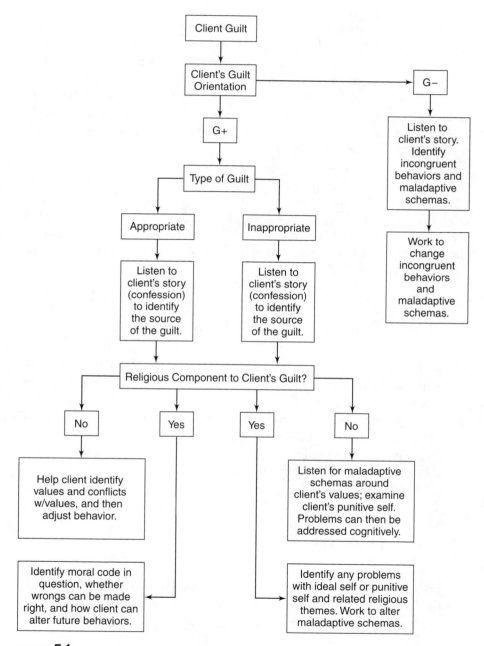

**FIGURE 5.1**

Flow chart for conceptualizing client guilt

Reprinted from Faiver, C., O'Brien, E., & Ingersoll, R. (2000). "Religion, guilt, and mental health," *Journal of Counseling and Development*, 78(2), 155–161. (2000 ACA.) Reprinted with permission. No further reproduction authorized without written permission of the American Counseling Association.

may witness guilt with religious overtones negatively impacting client affect, behavior, or cognition. Client depression or anxiety may be related directly to dysfunctional belief systems. Client obsessions or compulsions may be directly associated with excessive religiosity. A client's description of a personal problem may focus unrealistically on guilt-oriented thoughts. If a client demonstrates a healthy expression of religion, practitioners may still assess levels of appropriate guilt, possibly eliciting details regarding a client's breaching of his own moral code and the status of any personal amends in relation to this breach. In considering these items, practitioners need to acknowledge that—in some cases—a demonstrated increase in religious practice may serve as an appropriate method of handling guilt. The client's particular commitment to religious practice should be understood and included within the process of conceptualizing each individual case. When long-standing religious commitment is indicated, practitioners will benefit through utilization of specific steps to address potential guilt-oriented issues (delineated in Figure 5.1).

## CONCLUSION

Client guilt reveals itself in a variety of ways. Religious underpinnings may prove influential in both appropriate and inappropriate forms of client guilt, manifested through client affect, behavior, or cognition. What remains imperative is the practitioner's ability to understand and conceptualize guilt-oriented dynamics within clinical practice settings. By achieving a thorough comprehension of guilt dynamics in relation to religion and mental health, practitioners will more effectively meet the needs of clients for whom these constructs are highly relevant.

## QUESTIONS FOR REFLECTION

1. Is there any functional purpose to guilt? If so, what? When does guilt cross the line into the dysfunctional? How can you discern the difference? How might this discernment be applied to therapy?
2. Referring to Figure 5.1, what sort of guilt orientation do you have? How would you use this in working with clients?
3. How do you see guilt and forgiveness working together in a healthy manner?
4. What are some of the common themes of your "punitive self"?
5. How might you work with clients whose guilt overwhelms them? Give case examples.

# REFERENCES

Allport, G. (1950). *The individual and his religion*. New York: Macmillan.

Allport, G., & Ross, J. M. (1967). Personal religious orientation and prejudice. *Journal of Personality and Social Psychology*, 5, 432–443.

American Psychiatric Association. (1994). *Diagnostic and statistical manual of mental disorders* (4th ed.). Washington, DC: Author.

Arterburn, S., & Felton, J. (1991). *Toxic faith: Understanding and overcoming religious addiction*. Nashville, TN: Oliver Nelson.

Barnhouse, R. T. (1979). Spiritual direction and psychotherapy. *Journal of Pastoral Care*, 33(3), 149–160.

Belgun, D. (1960). *Guilt: Where psychology and religion meet*. Chicago, IL: Scott, Foresman.

Bergin, A. E. (1980). Psychotherapy and religious values. *Journal of Consulting and Clinical Psychology*, 48, 95–105.

Bynum, E. B. (1994). *Transcending psychoneurotic disturbances: New approaches in psychospirituality and personality development*. New York: Haworth Press.

Collins, G. (1980). *Christian counseling: A comprehensive guide*. Waco, TX: Word Books.

Donnelly, D. (1993). *Spiritual fitness: Everyday exercises for body and soul*. New York: HarperCollins.

Drakeford, J. W. (1967). *Integrity therapy*. Nashville, TN: Broadman Press.

Ellis, A. (1980). Psychotherapy and atheistic values: A response to A. E. Bergin's "Psychotherapy and Religious Values." *Journal of Consulting and Clinical Psychology*, 48, 635–639.

Faiver, C. M., & O'Brien, E. M. (1993). Assessment of religious beliefs form. *Counseling and Values*, 37, 176–178.

Faiver, C. M., O'Brien, E. M., & Ingersoll, R. E. (2000). Religion, guilt, and mental health. *Journal of Counseling and Development*, 78(2), 155–161.

Faiver, C. M., O' Brien, E. M., & McNally, C. J. (1998). "The friendly clergy": Characteristics and referral. *Counseling and Values*, 42(3), 217–221.

Ferguson, T. J., & Crowley, S. L. (1997). Measure for measure: A multitrait-multimethod analysis of guilt and shame. *Journal of Personality Assessment*, 69, 425–441.

Fowler, J. W. (1981). *Stages of faith: The psychology of human development and the quest for meaning*. New York: HarperCollins.

Freud, S. (1974). Totem and taboo. In J. Strachey (Ed. and Trans.,), *The standard edition of the collected works of Sigmund Freud* (Vol. 13, pp. 1–161). London: Hogarth Press. (Original work published in 1912)

Gallup Poll Monthly. (1993). *Report on Trends*, 331(4), 36–38.

Gallup, G. (1995). *The Gallup poll: Public opinion 1993*. Wilmington, DE: Scholarly Resources.

Gallup, G., & Castelli, J. (1989). *The people's religion: American faith in the '90's*. New York: Macmillan.

Hoge, D. (1996). Religion in America: The demographics of belief and affiliation. In E. P. Shafranske (Ed.), *Religion and the clinical practice of psychology* (pp. 21–42). Washington, DC: American Psychological Association.

Horney, K. (1937). *The neurotic personality of our time*. New York: W. W. Norton.

Hyder, Q. (1971). *The Christian's handbook of psychiatry*. Old Tappan, NJ: Fleming H. Revell Co.

Ingersoll, R. E. (1994). Spirituality, religion, and counseling: Dimensions and relationships. *Counseling and Values*, 38, 98–112.

Jones, W. H., & Kugler, K. (1993). Interpersonal correlates of the Guilt Inventory. *Journal of Personality Assessment, 61,* 246–258.

Judy, D. (1996). Transpersonal psychotherapy with religious persons. In B. W. Scotton, A. B. Chinen, & J. R. Battista (Eds.), *Textbook of transpersonal psychiatry and psychology* (pp. 293–301). New York: Basic Books.

Jung, C. G. (1933). *Modern man in search of a soul.* (W. S. Dell & C. F. Baynes, Trans.). New York: Harcourt Brace.

Jung, C. G. (1958). Psychology and religion. In H. Read, M. Fordham, & G. Adler (Eds.), *The collected works of C. G. Jung* (Vol. 11, pp. 3–106). Princeton, NJ: Princeton University Press.

Kelly, E. W. (1995). *Spirituality and religion in counseling and psychotherapy: Diversity in theory and practice.* Alexandria, VA: American Counseling Association.

Klass, E. T. (1987). Situational approach to the assessment of guilt: Development and evaluation of a self-report measure. *Journal of Psychopathology and Behavioral Assessment, 9,* 35–48.

Kosmin, B., & Lachman, S. (1993). *One nation under God: Religion in contemporary American society.* New York: Crown.

Lovinger, R. J. (1990). *Religion and counseling.* New York: Continuum.

Malatesta, C. Z., & Wilson, A. (1988). Emotion cognition interaction in personality development: A discrete emotions, functionalist analysis. *British Journal of Social Psychology, 27,* 91–112.

McMinn, M. R. (1984). Religious values and client-therapist matching in psychotherapy. *Journal of Psychology and Theology, 12,* 24–33.

Meehan, W., O'Connor, L. E., Berry J. W., Weiss, J., Morrison, A., & Acampora, A. (1996). Guilt, shame, and depression in clients in recovery from addiction. *Journal of Psychoactive Drugs, 28,* 125–134.

Meissner, W. W. (1984). *Psychoanalysis and religious experience.* New Haven, CT: Yale University Press.

Miller, G. (in press). The development of the spiritual focus in counseling and counselor education. *Journal of Counseling and Development.*

Narramore, S. B. (1974a). Guilt: Where theology and psychology meet. *Journal of Psychology and Theology, 2,* 18–25.

Narramore, S. B. (1974b). Guilt: Christian motivation or neurotic masochism? *Journal of Psychology and Theology, 2,* 182–189.

Narramore, S. B. (1974c). Guilt: Three models of therapy. *Journal of Psychology and Theology, 2,* 260–265.

Narramore, B., & Counts, B. (1974). *Guilt and freedom.* Santa Ana, CA: Vision House.

O'Connor, L. E. (1995, August). *Survivor guilt and depression: Empirical studies.* Paper presented at the meeting of Division 39 of the American Psychological Association, Los Angeles, CA.

O'Connor, L. E., & Weiss, J. (1993). Individual psychotherapy for addicted clients: An application of Control Mastery Theory. *Journal of Psychoactive Drugs, 25,* 283–291.

Osborne, C. (1967). *The art of understanding yourself.* Grand Rapids, MI: Zondervan.

Peck, M. S. (1993). *Further along the road less traveled: The unending journey toward spiritual growth.* New York: Simon & Schuster.

Peck, M. S. (1997). *The road less traveled and beyond: Spiritual growth in an age of anxiety.* New York: Simon & Schuster.

Roberts, K. A. (1990). *Religion in sociological perspective* (2nd ed.). Belmont, CA: Wadsworth.

Rogers, C. R. (1957). The necessary and sufficient conditions of therapeutic personality change. *Journal of Consulting Psychology, 21,* 93–103.

Smith, H. (1976). *Forgotten truth: The common vision of the world's religions*. New York: HarperCollins.

Smith, M. L. (1985). *Reconciliation: Preparing for confession in the Episcopal church*. Cambridge, MA: Cowley Publications.

Smith, S. G. (1988). *The concept of the spiritual: An essay in first philosophy*. Philadelphia: Temple University Press.

Steketee, G., Quay, S., & White, K. (1991). Religion and guilt in OCD patients. *Journal of Anxiety Disorders, 5*, 359–367.

Tangey, J. P. (1990). Assessing individual differences in proneness to shame and guilt: Development of the self-conscious affect and attribution inventory. *Journal of Personality and Social Psychology, 59*, 102–111.

Tangey, J. P., & Fischer, K. W. (Eds.). (1995). *Self-conscious emotions: The psychology of shame, guilt, embarrassment and pride*. New York: Guilford.

Weber, M. (1922). *The sociology of religion*. Boston: Beacon Press.

Weiss, J. (1986). Unconscious guilt. In J. Weiss & H. Sampson (Eds.), *The psychoanalytic process: Theory, clinical observation and empirical research* (pp. 43–67). New York: Guilford.

Wilber, K. (1997). *The eye of spirit: An integral vision for a world gone slightly mad*. Boston: Shambhala.

Worthington, E. L. (1989). Religious faith across the lifespan: Implications for counseling and research. *The Counseling Psychologist, 17*, 555–612.

Wulff, D. M. (1996). The psychology of religion: An overview. In E. P. Shafranske (Ed.), *Religion and the clinical practice of psychology* (pp. 44–70). Washington DC: American Psychological Association.

Yalom, I. D. (1980). *Existential psychotherapy*. New York: Basic Books.

Young, J. E. (1990). *Cognitive therapy for personality disorders: A schema-focused approach*. Sarasota, FL: Professional Resource Exchange.

# DISCERNMENT TO EPIPHANY

## Inclusion of Religion and Spirituality in the Assessment Process

*I do not know how to teach values . . . without reference to theories about the* meaning *of human existence. I do not know how to teach about meaning without reference to theories of the soul. And I do not know how to teach about the soul without reference to theories of God. A secularist is entitled not to believe in either God or the soul, but is he entitled not even to be exposed to these concepts?*

—M. Scott Peck (1997)

## APPROACH TO RELIGIOUS/SPIRITUAL ISSUES IN ASSESSMENT

Within the counseling relationship, clients deserve the very best care that practitioners can provide. For counselors to fulfill this obligation, client information of the greatest relevance must be gathered in the most expeditious way possible. In gathering this information, we advocate a macroview of the client's environment and worldview. Author James Michener often begins his novels with a depiction of the formation of the universe, with his narratives then evolving in a telescopic fashion, straight into the present day and into the real grist of the story. In the assessment of clients, we advocate a similar format and rationale—progressing from the gathering of general client information to a more specific ascertainment of a client's belief system (which may or may not include the religious/spiritual domain). In this chapter we present a basic model for gathering client data. This model incorporates an examination of client religious/spiritual beliefs and includes guidelines for appropriate referral for religious/spiritual issues.

# THE ASSESSMENT PROCESS—
# RELIGION/SPIRITUALITY INCLUDED

As a unique opportunity for both client and counselor to question each other, to share goals and expectations for therapy, the assessment interview allows the topic of religion/spirituality to be addressed in an integrated way. Conducting a comprehensive clinical interview as the foundation for successful therapeutic intervention may necessitate several interview sessions. Any sound assessment interview should eventually provide an opportunity for diagnostic impressions and treatment recommendations for the client (Faiver, 1988). We believe that the counselor who actually performs this assessment should provide direct treatment to the client as well. Yet, this may be neither possible nor advisable, depending on agency policy and organizational structure, as well as the various competencies and interests of the assessing counselor.

## Aspects of Assessment

Types and methods of assessment depend largely on agency policy, funding, and organizational and individual style. Some assessments may be relatively informal, calling for only a minimal amount of information; others may be highly formalized procedures that gather large amounts of client information and data. Time required for client assessment procedures may vary widely, as a result of different levels of client functioning and variations in client willingness to participate in the assessment process itself. Ideally, all methods of assessment are directed toward the facilitation of client empowerment, permitting the client to appropriately address presenting problems. As a systematic process of information gathering, the formal assessment process normally includes a client description, a client problem description, a client psychosocial history, a client mental status examination (addressing cognition, affect, and behavior), the counselor's diagnostic impression of the client, and treatment recommendations for the client (Faiver, Eisengart, & Colonna, 2000). During the assessment process, the client should be encouraged to ask questions and share expectations regarding treatment.

Each piece of the assessment process demands a full concentration of counselor energy on the client and the client's unique personhood (Benjamin, 1987). Through the client's description, a counselor works to establish a general framework through which a relationship with the client may be initiated. This relationship then enables the client and counselor to define specific problems and concerns. Of enormous relevance here is a delineation of the scope of these problems and concerns, as well as a measurement of their impact on the client and significant others within the client's life. Throughout this second phase of the assessment process, counselors must be aware that presenting problems may mask more significant underlying issues. These issues may not surface until a further trust is established between the client and counselor. In an effort to determine the etiology of client problems and concerns, a psychosocial history becomes imperative within the assessment process. This history may be obtained as a rough social sketch (Sullivan, 1970) or an extensive, detailed life history, addressing significant developmental milestones (MacKinnon & Michels, 1971). Whatever the case, a psychosocial history should effectively convey client strengths and weaknesses, in relation to interpersonal and environmental factors within the life span.

The mental status examination includes a detailed assessment of client cognition, affect, and behavior. This information is often most successfully obtained by interspersing relevant questions throughout the assessment interview rather than posing a litany of related questions to the client all at once. Siassi (1984) effectively conveys the critical nature of the mental status examination, comparing it legitimately to the physical examination common in general medicine. As a result of this examination, a client's current thought processes, overall pervasive mood, and present appearance and functioning create a final "palette" from which the counselor may develop a diagnostic impression. We encourage counselors to be cautious here, recognizing the importance of this diagnosis and the essentially fluid nature of the impression that is conveyed by the client. Each client holds various degrees of potential for future development and changes in functioning level. The counselor's diagnosis, which will lead to various treatment recommendations, should be tentative in this regard and conscious of the essentially human, malleable qualities of the client. We believe that the process of counseling is a collaborative process. This collaboration may be incorporated into the final phase of assessment. Clients willing to assist counselors in the development of treatment recommendations may recognize a newly defined responsibility to themselves, resulting in an increased commitment to treatment.

We have found a number of particular questions, when posed to the client, to be of great benefit within the assessment process. Alfred Adler's "The Question" (Adler, 1964) is particularly useful for determining the origin of client conflict. It asks, "What would be different in your life if you didn't have this problem?" By the same token, Ellis (1989) describes worrying types who tend to catastrophize, making their troubles seem more dire than they actually are. To put client problems into proper perspective, Ellis asks, "What is the worst thing that can happen?" Along the same lines, the question "Is there anything that I haven't asked that you think I should know?" may be utilized as an effective summarization question. This often elicits additional information relevant to client concerns. All of these questions may facilitate client centering, permitting a flow of information that leads to accurate focus on relevant issues. Quite commonly, we have witnessed issues of spirituality unfolding within these lines of questioning. It is our belief that if a professional resistance persists regarding the incorporation of spiritual awareness within the clinical setting, many client issues may be misinterpreted or missed.

## Discovering the Client's Spirituality

As counselors evaluate relevant areas of psychosocial and mental status functioning within the context of a thorough client assessment, we suggest that they maintain a concurrent awareness of religious/spiritual factors that may be contributing to client problems and their potential resolution (Faiver & O'Brien, 1993). They may address the topic of religious/spiritual issues directly as they gather general descriptive information regarding the client's presenting problems. The counselor may note the client's current religious/spiritual belief system, or lack thereof, as well as the denomination or faith (if any) under which the client was raised. Significant differences in current and past belief or practice may indicate areas of potential exploration, regarding specific sources of conflict. The counselor may also explore, in a general fashion, the role that religion or spirituality currently plays in the client's life. Clients may consider themselves spiritual or religious, advocating a certain ethic or maintaining certain rituals, but this may not be an accurate indication of the actual role that religion or spirituality actually plays in their lives. How much does the client have invested in this area? In essence, the counselor might ask Adler's question in a slightly different way: "What would be different in your life if you didn't have this religion or spirituality?"

Examination of cognition, affect, and behavior that is integral to the mental status examination (and, therefore, integral to client assessment) may be applied directly to a holistic assessment of client spiritual values and/or religious beliefs. Regarding cognition, religious/spiritual assessment should ideally include an exploration of the client belief system itself—its concepts, values, precepts, and guidelines. Cognitive dissonance is a distinct, directly related possibility here. We have found it valuable to assess this cognitive dissonance, as well as the complex issue of guilt (see Chapter 4 for a detailed discussion of guilt). If guilt is present, what is its source? How long has it been present and how pervasive is it? Does this guilt serve some functional purpose? Any appropriate developmental process demands this type of examination (Watson, Morris, & Hood, 1988). Regarding affect, religious/spiritual assessment should ideally include an exploration of potentially related sources of depression, anxiety, or labile mood. Emotions present within or elicited by the belief system itself might be investigated in terms of their positive or negative impact on the client. Counselors may find it useful to then utilize exercises that incorporate these emotions within the therapeutic process itself. Regarding behaviors, religious/spiritual assessment should ideally include an exploration of habits and/or rituals present in the client's regular routine. Counselors should note any excessive religiosity, bizarre related gestures, or prevailing habituation on the part of the client. Interest in a religiousness and spirituality composed of developmentally appropriate behavior—not impeding but, rather, fostering growth and positive interaction—is at issue here (Worthington, 1989).

## RELIGIOUS OR SPIRITUAL PROBLEM: A NEW DIAGNOSTIC CATEGORY

It is important that we include a section in this chapter on the new category for religious/spiritual problems now found in the DSM-IV (V62.89) (American Psychiatric Association, 1994). The intent of this diagnostic category was to address problems that were topically spiritual or religious, presenting them as areas of concern that may or may not be related to mental or emotional disorders (Turner, Lukoff, Barnhouse, & Lu, 1995). The intention of this category is particularly important, given the fact that many theories of psychological change have viewed religious or spiritual experiences as strictly pathological symptoms, ignoring them as potentially positive supports (Wulff, 1996).

The need for this diagnostic category was first raised in both psychiatric and transpersonal psychology circles. Psychiatrist Robert Turner and psychologist David Lu led the effort to have the category included in the DSM-IV. The logic of this category is that it can be placed on Axis I, much like an adjustment disorder that is a phase of life problem and not a mental/emotional disorder. This diagnostic category assumes that a person's spiritual life is an organismic variable that may or may not be related to an organized religion. Recently, this same view has appeared in numerous papers and books by both psychologists and counselors (Ingersoll, 1994; Miller, 1990; Vaughan, 1995). For many people, becoming increasingly autonomous with regard to a spiritual life may be a normal developmental process. Disillusionment with the organized church has played a large role for some. Yet, while confidence in religious institutions and leaders decreases, there is an increase in the number of people who say that they believe in God, that they engage in a spiritual practice, or that they have had a mystical experience (Gallup Poll Monthly, 1993).

When dealing with client religious or spiritual issues in the counseling session, there are some general guidelines that we believe to be helpful.

- Affirm the importance of the client's spiritual/religious path even before you discern whether this path is helpful or harmful to the person. In order to strengthen the therapeutic alliance, we must experience and communicate empathic understanding of the importance that clients' religious/ spiritual paths may have for them.

- Attempt to enter the client's worldview through use of congruent vocabulary and imagery. In conceptualizing problems and treatment, this will strengthen the counselor's empathic encounter as well as the therapeutic alliance.
- Be willing to consult with other "healers" or religious authorities (friendly clergy) in the person's life. This can give the counselor deeper insight into a client's religious/spiritual path while also strengthening the therapeutic alliance.
- Attempt to discern the client's cognitive, moral, and faith-oriented developmental levels. There are numerous models that counselors may use here, including Fowler's (1981) stages of faith development.
- Be willing to distinguish healthy from unhealthy practices and consider whether there are pathological elements to the client's belief system. This willingness demands great experience, sincerity, and caution.

(The final guideline is as dangerous as it is important. Religious mystics like John of the Cross or Sri Aurobindo—if interviewed during difficult developmental periods in their spiritual journeys—could easily have been diagnosed as depressed or even delusional by current clinical standards [Lukoff, 1996]. These diagnoses never occurred, for obvious reasons. Modern clients, with equally elusive difficulties impacting their sense of spirituality or religion, are regularly diagnosed with medically defined mental and emotional disorders. These diagnoses must be made with great care, also for obvious reasons.)

*A 25-year-old client named Ricky had been diagnosed with a form of schizophrenia after several episodes of hearing voices. He had decompensated to the point that he would not bathe or eat, for fear of being poisoned by the devil. Ricky's symptoms began at age 19, although he had experienced numerous difficulties in school since the age of 16. Ricky frequently stated that God was ordering him to do certain things. He would stand cruciform in the front yard for hours at a time, howl at the bankers going to work downtown, and collect rocks to build an altar in his mother's living room. These orders came upon him suddenly and in a loud, thundering voice that Ricky was too terrified to disobey. While in these frightened states, Ricky apparently heard demons snickering at him, trying to distract him from what he viewed as his divine destiny. When Ricky began taking intramuscular injections of an antipsychotic medication, the voices stopped.*

Ricky's case illustrates many extreme characteristics of pathological religious/spiritual experiences. The experiences in question were illusions and hallucinations, apparently the result of dysfunctional dopaminergic activity in the mesolimbic area of Ricky's brain. When Ricky began to take medications designed to decrease the dopaminergic activity in this brain area, his peculiar experiences stopped. It may certainly be argued that if we administer typical antipsychotic medication to a mentally healthy mystic, this individual too will experience a disruption in his or her religious/spiritual experiences. Although impossible to test because of ethical constraints, the differences between the religious/spiritual impressions of the mystic and the hallucinations of a person afflicted with a brain disease like schizophrenia remain important.

Transpersonal psychiatrist Stanislav Grof (primarily with his wife, Christina) has devoted much time to training professionals to recognize differences between psychopathology and religious/spiritual experience. Grof, who at one time was an aspiring cartoonist, drew a cartoon of a Hindu mystic hanging from a tree by one leg. A person suffering a psychotic break was also restrained at the trunk of the tree. The person at the trunk of the tree asked the mystic, "Why do they call me crazy and you a mystic?" The mystic answered, "Because I know who not to talk to." Grof's cartoon highlights a very important principle regarding ego strength. Developmentally speaking, many transpersonal theorists (Grof, 1990; Vaughan, 1995; Wilber 1999) emphasize that a person must have a stable, healthy ego structure to transcend this same structure through religious/spiritual experiences. Certainly, such experiences come at all stages of development. Still, as a separate and distinct line of development, they require the basis that a healthy ego provides.

Wilber (1980, 1990, 1999), who described three general stages of human ego development, has elucidated this point. In the prepersonal stage, the infant/small child is prerational and just beginning development of a sense of self. In the personal stage of ego development, the adolescent/adult functions from a rational sense of self that corresponds with Piaget's concrete and/or formal operational stages. In the transpersonal stage, the person has transcended (and included) the previous two stages, now using them as a basis for moving on to the next stage. If a person is not functioning adequately in the prepersonal and personal stages, he or she will be unable to cultivate transpersonal or transrational levels of development. Because the prepersonal and transpersonal are both nonrational, people often confuse them. This confusion results in "elevationism" and "reductionism." Wilber (1999) noted that Freud was a classic reductionist, since he tended to see all transpersonal experiences as prepersonal and thus pathological. Freud stated that Jung was an elevationist, in that he tended to elevate prepersonal myths to transpersonal greatness.

Gabbard, Twemlow, and Jones (1982) have cautioned that clinicians need to be able to discern differences between unusual experiences that are integrating in nature and experiences that are disorganizing or dis-integrating. Barnhouse (1986) observed that clinicians cannot necessarily discern the health or pathology of religious/spiritual experience through content alone. The clinician needs to understand the context (primarily the cultural context) within which the content arises. Grof and Grof (1989) and Greenberg and Witzum (1991) have developed the following useful guidelines for distinguishing religious/spiritual experiences from—most notably—psychoses:

- Psychotic experiences are typically more intense than spiritual experiences.
- Psychotic experiences are typically ego-dystonic and are consistently terrifying to the individual, whereas religious/spiritual experiences—though uncomfortable at times—have ego-syntonic elements and frequently offer some degree of comfort to the individual.
- Psychotic experiences are often associated with a progressive deterioration in self-care.
- Psychotic experiences often involve special messages from religious figures unverified by communities of esoteric practitioners within the given tradition.
- Spiritual experiences are usually associated with good pre-episode functioning, whereas pathology is less often associated with good pre-episode functioning.
- In psychopathology there is usually a slower onset of symptoms when there are more stressful precipitants.
- In spiritual issues, there is usually a positive explanatory attitude toward the experience.

With these guidelines as background, review the case of Ricky, noting how many of them apply to his case.

## TYPES OF RELIGIOUS PROBLEMS

A number of religious problems, described by Turner et al. (1995), often lead clients to seek help in counseling.

### Change in Denomination or Conversion to a New Faith

Sometimes a client may have difficulty because of a recent change in religious orientation. This event may be on a continuum from forced conversion to voluntary conversion. The extent to which this life event becomes problematic for various clients may differ greatly. A degree of loss must be established with the client, with an increasing amount of loss indicating an increasing amount of grief work to be done. This problem frequently arises when a couple marries.

*In one such case, both the man and woman had strong ties to their faith communities. The woman was Presbyterian and the man Roman Catholic. The man's parents insisted that they would not support the marriage unless their son's fiancée converted to Roman Catholicism. This caused quite a rift between both the marrying couple and their two families. Finally, the woman decided to convert, since she did not want any tension to exist between the two families. Although she was being treated for a different disorder at this same time, working through the anger and grief associated with the conversion became this woman's clinical focus for several counseling sessions.*

## Intensification of Practices or Adherence to Beliefs

A change toward more fervent religious practices or beliefs may be an intensification of the exoteric resulting from an esoteric experience. Frequently, when
people have an experience that they interpret as religious, they may turn to the
practices of whatever tradition they know as a result. In some cases, people may
seek out the more esoteric practices of their tradition—for example, fasting.
At times, a person may not feel supported in these efforts and even clerics in
the person's religion may not know how to respond. Intensification can also be
due to guilt or trauma. As counselors, we need to look for the meaning that lies
behind this intensification.

*One woman came to me following some problems between herself and her
teenage son. They had been fighting rather fiercely about her decision to attend
a church after six years of not going to church at all. The woman's husband had
died seven years earlier from cancer. At that time, the family had been members
of a small, charismatic, Christian church. The pastor of this church had told the
woman and her son that prayer could save the husband, healing his cancer.
When the husband died, this same pastor told them they had not exhibited
enough faith.*

## Loss of or Questioning of Faith

The earlier one's stage of spiritual development occurs, the more typically exoteric one's focus becomes. A loss of faith or questioning of faith can be difficult, especially in the earlier stages of faith development. This is particularly
true if ostracism from a faith community occurs as a result. At later stages, loss
or questioning may be accompanied by deep sadness, as one moves out of a
faith that has been secure and comfortable and into the ambiguity of unknown
spiritual waters. We support clients in this seeking process, believing that a
faith system that does not tolerate questioning will not have the allegiance of
a sincere spiritual seeker for long.

## "Toxic Faith" as a Religious Problem

Arterburn and Felton (1991) have approached unhealthy dynamics in religious
groups through what they call "toxic beliefs" or "toxic faith." Although these
authors address a Christian audience, we feel that their constructs have cross-
traditional applications. Listed below are various "toxic beliefs" that contribute
to an unhealthy religious/spiritual path.

### Conditional Love
God may become or be presented as the "critical parent" whom many people
experienced or feared in childhood, an authority figure who gives love only con-
ditionally. People who adhere to a notion of God as a critical parent typically

emphasize performance over God's love. In most religions, God's love is not earned but is freely given. In unhealthy groups, one way that leaders promote member dependence is through their presentation of God as a critical parent. In actuality, it is the leader who is critical, hiding behind a facade of divine inspiration.

### Instant Peace
Another toxic belief centers around the notion that when tragedy strikes, the believer should have instant peace. This is a delusional understanding of spiritual health. Even believers need time to deal with their emotions. People promoting a quick, "feel-good trip" of instant peace are usually the same people who are uncomfortable with the distress of others (remember Job's friends). This doesn't mean that God or life can't sometimes intervene in ways that may result in instant peace. It simply means that this is more the exception than the rule.

### Guaranteed Healing
Some people develop or are taught the notion that if you have real faith, God will heal you or someone for whom you are praying. Faith helps us adapt to life but may not necessarily change the existential givens. It is important to remember that even if you possess the most mature, passionate faith in the world, this does not mean that healing is in your destiny. It is important here to differentiate "healing" from "cure." While a physical cure may not occur for a terminal illness, often the person suffering from this illness may report feeling "healed" of tangential problems like bitterness, anger, and frustration. From the perspective of each individual life, it is impossible to say which result is more important.

### Irreproachable Clergy
Not all people claiming to be (or ordained to be) people of God can necessarily be trusted. As in all professions, the clergy includes a wide variety of personalities. Trust may be earned through interpersonal or community interaction. We need to be cautious of leaders who claim to speak directly for God, without a process of discernment. Many times, clients feel conflicted over what they perceive to be God's law when they are in actuality conflicted over the law of their religious leader, who tells them that he or she is interpreting God's law. This is a very important distinction. Wilber (1999) makes the related point that when a religious or spiritual group makes the shift from experience to law, there is always a chance that such a group will spawn leaders who have experienced no real spiritual inspiration. Wilber noted that over several hundred years, the Christian church moved from an emphasis on spiritual experience to an emphasis on a specific set of beliefs. When this happened, "a priest was no longer holy (*sanctus*) if he was personally awakened or enlightened or sanctified, but if he held the office. Likewise, you could become 'saved' not by waking yourself up, but merely by taking the legal sacraments" (p. 359).

## Emphasis on Monetary Rewards

Material blessings are not necessarily a sign of spiritual blessing. If they were, we would probably all be like Job's friends, attempting to secure divine favor through correct behavior. No, riches are not necessarily a sign of blessing and poverty is not a sign of wickedness. This misconception is more a reflection of our consumer society than any divine will. We have all known people who believe that a spiritual commitment might remedy their fiscal problems. While a healthy spiritual life can certainly provide motivation toward goals and impart meaning to one's struggle, they by no means guarantee economic prosperity. Investment tithing is a variation on the notion that spiritual health equals fiscal health. This practice is based on the toxic belief that as one gives more money to the church, more will be given back in return. Essentially, this reduces the divine place in the cosmos to a mere certificate of deposit.

## Salvation by Works

Salvation by works is a toxic belief that you can work your way to enlightenment or heaven. There is a variation here on cult dynamics, in which a leader receives cheap labor from his followers by claiming that this labor (and the leader's supervisory position) are somehow the will of God and the workers will be repaid through spiritual salvation. A variation of this toxic belief is a syndrome called "slavery of the faithful." In this state, the faithful believe that they must not stop meeting others' needs, even when doing so interferes with meeting their own needs. Typically, the faithful, through their extreme catering to others, eventually begin to deny their own humanity and resent those whom they serve. The ultimate evolution can become a type of personal martyr complex.

## Irrational Submission

Another toxic belief is that *"I must always submit to authority."* "Authority" refers here to the leader or leaders of a group. This belief can reach absurd proportions, as in cases where women have allowed children to be abused because they did not believe that they should question the head of the household. In some cases, this head of the household—the supposed authority to be obeyed in the home—is defined as such only by the leader of a group.

## Passivity

Related to many of the previous beliefs, passivity is the belief that having true faith means waiting for God to do whatever you (or the leader of your group) wants or needs done.

*We remember a client named Gladys. She suffered from recurrent major depressive episodes as well as diabetes. She would frequently violate the low-sugar diet that her physician had prescribed, putting herself at serious risk for diabetic shock. When confronted about this and other unproductive actions, she would sigh and say, "It's all in God's hands." She was frequently asked how she believed "God's hands" worked. She would say that if God really had a plan for her he would inevitably make it happen. Although she often stayed home in bed for days at a time, Gladys usually attended the Baptist church each Sunday, where her sisters and mother worshipped. After obtaining a release from Gladys, we contacted her pastor, who was more than happy to set up a few co-counseling sessions for Gladys's benefit. In these sessions, the pastor proved to be a member of what we have called the "friendly clergy"—a non-judgmental and caring person, not unfriendly toward Gladys's efforts in counseling. He was very clear with Gladys, describing that their tradition required members to serve God through taking care of themselves and preparing themselves as useful vessels through which God's hands could work. In one session, he held Gladys's hands lightly, saying, "These hands are God's hands too, you know." Following these sessions, Gladys put more effort into maintaining her diet and combating many irrational thoughts. She now realized that such thoughts only fed her depressive cycle.*

## Textual Exclusivity

Another damaging belief is that if something is not explicitly spelled out in the sacred texts of a particular religion, it is not relevant. We need to understand that most religious texts were formulated in largely illiterate societies and that much has changed since their formulation. The ancient Hebrews did not have to worry about computer viruses or the dramatic impact of the violence shown in today's movies. Although the sacred texts may inspire us with direction regarding how to live a human life, our modern society dictates much that we must improvise on or figure out as we go.

## The Belief in the Perfect Mate

There have always been people who believed that God will provide them with a perfect mate. Although many people feel a divine hand in their significant relationships, others take such a belief too literally, pairing it with their own definition (often irrational) of "perfect." Certain leaders of spiritual/religious groups may fuel such beliefs, leading to frustration in the believer and, in some cases, premature termination of a relationship. In some respects, the idea that one's partner should be handpicked by God is not rational, if paired with a belief in free will. If the mate is chosen by God, this could very well require the person to relinquish her or his free will. God can certainly be a central fulcrum in one's relationship, but such centrality does not guarantee the perfection of either the mate or the relationship. We have found that very often it is the imperfections in relationships that people come to love, since they are markers signifying the work that a couple has done in and on their relationship.

## The Pollyanna Perspective

"Everything that happens to me is good"—this view can be damaging. Many movements related to new-age marketing and consumer culture emphasize this perspective. As we noted in our chapter concerning archethemes, life comes to us in polarities. There is always the good and the bad. Many times, people seek to avoid the difficult emotional work that comes with labeling something as "bad." By saying a difficult illness or loss is "good," such people may in fact be avoiding the experience of sadness, anger, and helplessness that frequently accompanies such life events. The Pollyanna perspective can also be adopted when one wishes to avoid looking realistically at the bad elements of some aspect of his or her life.

*We recall one client who was in a relationship with a man who regularly abused numerous drugs and who would become emotionally abusive to her while intoxicated. This woman had met the man after being left by another man that she had dated for four years. She was afraid of being alone and even more fearful of examining how difficult she found being alone. She could not bear to be alone, even if only temporarily, while between relationships. She would frequently say, "Oh, Stan has a problem with drugs, but he's really not that mean to me and it does teach me patience." It took escalation to physical violence for this woman to realize both that this relationship was not healthy for her and that she needed to examine her issues of dependency.*

**Bullet-Proof Faith**
Being convinced that a sufficiently strong faith will protect you from pain and suffering is another toxic belief. It is similar to one of the main themes of the book of Job. A spiritual faith or practice may help as we deal with pain, but it is no guarantee against pain's occurrence. As the Buddha taught, suffering is inherent in life. Our greatest control is contained in the way that we meet and deal with suffering.

**Divinely Ordained Happiness**
There is more to life than merely being happy. Happiness is paired with sadness in the polarities that make up our experience.

## TYPES OF SPIRITUAL PROBLEMS

When diagnosing a religious or spiritual problem through use of the DSM-IV V-Code for that purpose, we may encounter numerous client problems that include religious elements but are more commonly described by clients as spiritual, rather than religious.

### *Mystical Experiences*

The words *myth*, *mysticism*, and *mystery* are all derived from the same Greek verb *musteion*, which means to close the eyes or mouth (Armstrong, 1993). Armstrong concludes that all three words are rooted in an "experience of darkness and silence," adding, "They are not popular words in the West today"

(p. 210). She notes that myths are associated with lies, that mysteries are things that need to be cleared up, and that mysticism is often in the company of cranks and charlatans. In counseling and psychotherapeutic circles, genuine mystical experiences and direct apprehensions of the divine may be viewed as pathological by the untrained, inexperienced eye. Counselors should remember that clients may come to them seeking assurances of their mental state, following mystical experiences.

## Near-Death Experiences (NDEs)

Near-death experiences have become a topic of both medical (Greyson, 1996) and psychological (Ring, 1985) study. Once regarded as a type of hallucination or illusion, the NDE is being explored as a nonordinary experience. Research supports the hypothesis that NDEs are not attributable to a mental or emotional disorder (Basford, 1990). Gallup (1982) estimated that about 5% of Americans have had an NDE. These experiences have been documented as drastically altering the experiencer's attitudes, values, beliefs, and spiritual growth. Along with the positive sequelae of NDEs, some researchers have commented that the NDE may also be followed by depression, anger, isolation, and interpersonal problems, as the experiencer seeks to integrate the experience into her or his life (Greyson & Harris, 1987).

## Spiritual Emergence or Emergency

Grof and Grof (1989) have pioneered study in this area, which refers to problems that may arise spontaneously for individuals in the midst of some spiritual practice. Spiritual emergence is a more gradual and less disruptive unfolding of spiritual development, while spiritual emergency is an acute unfolding that may cause severe distress and impairment. This type of spiritual development may include physical symptoms, psychological distress, and even paranormal experiences. It has been explained as the "life force" manifesting within the individual. The Grofs liken this to periods of development associated with the practice of Kundalini yoga and the shamanistic initiation that occurs in certain indigenous cultures. More severe forms of this problem may exacerbate preexisting mental/emotional disorders or precipitate a disorder to which the individual is vulnerable. In these cases, an Axis I diagnosis should be made and treated, as well as the spiritual or religious problem. Italian psychiatrist Roberto Assagioli (1989) also addresses the overlap between spiritual practices and psychological problems. Both the Grofs and Assagioli espouse views similar to Wilber's (1999), asserting that ego issues must be dealt with adequately for the person to be able to integrate the spiritual aspects that are surfacing. Ultimately, the spiritual emergence and spiritual emergency are calls to wholeness.

## Meditation-Related Issues

In many meditation practices, a person voluntarily induces depersonalization and, in some cases, dissociation. For some people, this sense of depersonalization or dissociation may be uncomfortable. It may pass as the practice continues or, if the practice is stopped, the condition may abate in a short period of time. Walsh and Roche (1979) have observed that altered perceptions occur as one develops in meditative practice and that these perceptions are not pathological. Rather, they seem to be part of the developmental meditative path for some people. Buddhist forms of meditation may also draw people suffering from Borderline Personality Disorder and Narcissistic Personality Disorder, since these forms may help people to legitimate and rationalize their lack of integration and self-structure (Lukoff, Lu, and Turner, 1996). The possible correlations noted here need to be monitored by counselors when clients are engaged in some meditative discipline.

There is no clear consensus regarding the domains of counseling and meditation. The two may certainly function in a complementary fashion, and there are times when one or both are appropriate. When counseling and psychotherapy are directed toward strengthening and expanding the ego, meditation practices are concerned with looking into this ego, to understand how it is structured (Welwood, 1983). Welwood noted that in focusing meditation, one concentrates on the breath and usually becomes more aware of churning confusion of thoughts and emotions that may be a driving force (usually unconscious) in one's life. In counseling and psychotherapy, the client attempts to sort out these thoughts and feelings. In focusing meditation, the confusion is allowed to arise and exist with no attempt to analyze it. Counseling and psychotherapy are more goal-oriented than meditation of this type. The way we structure thoughts and emotions feeds into the stories that we tell ourselves about who we are. The product of these stories is what emerges as significant in counseling and psychotherapy. We cling to these stories in defense against the uncertainty that is an existential given of life. When we cling too much, we develop unhealthy tendencies such as hatred, greed, envy, pride, and ignorance—all regularly addressed in counseling and psychotherapy.

Welwood wrote that in meditation "we learn how to 'keep our seat,' how not to get thrown or carried away by the wild horse of the mind, but rather to stay alert and keep riding no matter where the mind may go" (p. 46). The reader may wonder, "Might meditation be therapeutic in some cases?" To this we answer "yes," although this conclusion is best reached by a person with experience in both realms. In counseling and psychotherapy, we build meaning structures, while in meditative practices we allow those structures to dissolve (Welwood, 1983).

Wilber (1999) has taken the position that both disciplines are useful. We need counseling and psychotherapy to build up meaning structures to contribute to a strong ego. We need a strong ego from which to begin engaging in a dissolving of meaning structures, so that our awareness may transcend the ego. This is necessary if we are to deal with the existential challenges in life like impermanence, aging, and death. Whereas counseling and psychotherapy certainly deal with one level of well-being, "the process of meditation reveals a deeper core of well-being beyond ego strength in the therapeutic sense of a well-adjusted, functioning personality structure" (Welwood, 1983, p. 47). For Welwood, psychotherapy and meditation overlap in the Buddhist notion of *Maitri*, an unconditional friendliness to ourselves. In Maitri we stop chastising ourselves; we stop feeling that we aren't the way we "should" be and accept how we are in this moment as a part of the human experience. Both counseling and meditation help us to become friendlier to ourselves through disciplined attention, self-acceptance, respect for the unknown, and a holistic understanding of who we are.

## Terminal Illness

A terminal illness can induce profound changes in a person's spiritual belief and practice. The prospect of death, the threat to one's integrity, and the ambiguity of life after death are all stressors for people who suffer from a terminal illness (Lukoff, Lu, & Turner, 1996). People suffering from terminal illnesses may also experience nonordinary states of consciousness and unusual, paranormal experiences. The attending clinician needs to assess such experiences carefully before assuming that they are linked to pathology.

*I was seeing an elderly client, Myra, who was in a nursing home and in the final stages of a struggle with terminal cancer. Although relatively free from severe pain, Myra began having nonordinary experiences that included visits from dead relatives. No one but she could see these visions. As with many people who have had similar deathbed experiences, Myra found them comforting, although staff was unsure what to make of them. One nurse consulted with my supervisor and me regarding whether the client would need antipsychotic medication. We discussed with this nurse the nature of these nonordinary experiences and explained that in our professional experience, they were rarely linked to degeneration in the client's cognitive functioning or any aggressive acting out. Like many aspects of the dying process, these visions were inexplicable manifestations that helped the dying person to let go, easing her transition.*

## Dark Night of the Senses/Soul

Phenomena that have been addressed by mystics in both Eastern and Western traditions, the Dark Night of the Senses/Soul is an acute feeling that the things of this world have lost their appeal. People undergoing this experience find that they don't enjoy the things they used to—nothing turns them on anymore (Peck, 1997). The Dark Night of the Senses/Soul may be the manifestation of a calling to a higher purpose or increased meaning in life. Obviously, this experience may be mistaken for depression. However, an important developmental difference is that the person genuinely feels something is missing but does not know what it might be. In the Dark Night of the Senses/Soul, a person has had a taste of the Divine, with this experience then fading and bringing with it a sense of being abandoned. In these cases people may find that their only recourse is either to continue their regular spiritual practice or to explore the possibility of integrating a spiritual practice into their lives.

## CULTS AND CULT-LIKE DYNAMICS

A special problem related to religion and spirituality, but not specifically religious or spiritual, has to do with cults and cult-like dynamics. In our workshops and talks we frequently find counselors asking questions about cult-related issues. According to Roberts (1990), cults are distinct from religions. Religions envision themselves in close interaction with mainstream society, and sects are religious groups that break off from established religions, while still interacting with society. Cults, on the contrary, do not typically arise within a church and they usually remain separated from society. Although this differentiation is important, psychiatrist Arthur Deikmann (1990) says that it may be equally important to understand that virtually any group of people—cults, sects, religions—may engage in cult-like dynamics. Deikmann cautions against looking for extreme groups that would colloquially be labeled "cults," as this diverts our attention from equally destructive cult dynamics potentially functioning in socially sanctioned groups, such as religions or businesses.

It is essential to be able to distinguish cult dynamics that are truly harmful and unhealthy patterns. Helpful here is the definition of a destructive cult devised by cult exit-counselor Steve Hassan (1990). He says that a destructive cult is "any group that engages in outright deception to pursue its ends, whether religious or secular in its apparent orientation" (p. 5).

Deikmann (1990) offers the following characteristic cult dynamics (or cult-like dynamics) for discerning the health of a group's practices. The degree to which these characteristics operate in each group is the degree to which they are an unhealthy influence on individual members.

### Compliance with the Group

In this dynamic, the desire for group approval is exploited and people who are vulnerable to group disapproval are recruited. For this dynamic to work, the recruit's fear of disapproval must be very strong. This is partially achieved by isolating group members from other sources of esteem, from financial support, and from emotional closeness. Couples and families are often specifically targeted for separation. Parts of the recruitment dynamic are meant to exacerbate the normal fears and insecurities that we all have. One such tactic is asking potential members such questions as "Are you really happy?" This is a common question and much of the time we may answer "no" in response, based on how our day or our week is going. Happiness may not be the absolute point of life, but if these groups inquire at a vulnerable moment, a person may become acutely aware of what he or she is lacking. This is the design of such dialogue. The group claims to have what you need to feel better. All you must do is comply and you may then have the happiness that you supposedly lack. The late philosopher Alan Watts once commented that this technique is akin to first sitting on someone and then getting up, asking "Now, don't you feel better?" Social psychologist Robert Cialdini's (1993) work on techniques of influence describes the learning techniques typically used to promote group compliance.

## Dependence on the Leader

Psychodynamically, we all have dependency fantasies. Groups and leaders can systematically exploit these fantasies. The dependence dynamic is fueled by our societal practice of placing people on certain pedestals, creating unrealistic role models that inevitably contribute to our feelings of inferiority. Where healthy authority seeks to replace fear and awe with appreciation, cult leaders actually prefer fear and awe. To achieve this effect, cult leaders will tend to appear free from doubt—actually an old evolutionary trick, first practiced by our primate cousins. In chimpanzee groups, dominant males exhibit facial expressions and body language indicating indifference to what is going on around them. Less dominant chimps are constantly glancing at their leader and others for social cues, wondering what to do next. Although the dominant, "cool" chimps may slip away after a confrontation and later show signs of distress or fear, they avoid revealing such natural reactions in the presence of lesser chimps, who may (taking note of their vulnerability) then challenge them for the dominant place (Tiger & Fox, 1971). This level of "cool" does not accurately reflect the complex reality in which we live. It can be used to promote dependence rather than interdependence. Healthy leaders welcome doubt and they process doubt without necessarily being able to reach any meaningful conclusions. Unhealthy leaders prefer to rule by fiat and fear. A primary goal in promoting dependence on the leader is to encourage followers to relinquish choice. A spiritual choice is always, at least interpersonally, a free choice. It is an expression of one's self and not just an expression of one's fears or insecurities. Typically unhealthy leaders claim to have some special powers or a special relationship with some powerful entity. This is a significant problem with book-based spirituality that relies on interpretation of the leader. If the book can indeed be interpreted, this is something that any literate person should be able to do with a moderate degree of effort. If the recipe dictates that only certain people will be inspired to interpret correctly, there is likely a cult dynamic brewing. We must also remember that "spiritual giants" are more often media

products than divine products. There is virtually no end to the number of omniscient and omnipotent images that a good media machine can churn out.
Many times, these portrayed leaders fall prey to their own hype, believing
themselves to possess qualities they do not have.

## Devaluing Outsiders

When a group divides itself and the world into categories of "saved" and
"unsaved," "righteous" and "infidel," "chosen" and "unchosen," it is devaluing
outsiders. The "outgroup" is made to appear as the "other" and from there,
they can be made to look less than human. Once this shift has occurred, a
psychological mind-set is in place for what we described in Chapter 3 as
"moral evil." It is a necessary prerequisite for the enacting of violence. Devaluing of outsiders relies heavily on the psychological defense of projection,
whereby we see in others those things we are not willing to own in ourselves.
For the group practicing cult dynamics, devaluing outsiders decreases the
possibility that group members will have contact with outsiders, who may
raise legitimate questions about the worth of the group. However, as Hassan
(1990) explained, "If the group is a legitimate, valid organization, it will stand
up to any scrutiny" (p. xviii). Hassan concluded that people who have been
able to remove themselves from destructive cults (he calls such people "walk-
aways") are those who have been able to maintain contact with others outside
the cult.

## Avoiding and Stifling Dissent

Dissent, in moderate doses, is healthy and corrective. Cult dynamics punish
and stifle dissent, even when it emerges in moderate doses. One method of
avoiding dissent is to decrease contact with nonmembers. The degree to which
outsiders think for themselves is also the degree to which they become a threat.
Anyone who thinks or chooses for herself and also has contact with group
members becomes a potential threat (interestingly, the Greek root of heretic
[heretikos] means "to think for one's self"). Dissent is also avoided and stifled
by promoting dependence on the leader and compliance with the group.
If these goals are achieved, the members' sources of approval and community
are easily manipulated, with dissent punished through isolation. For both humans and primates, isolation is a powerful aversive stimulus (Kaplan, 1983).

Deikmann (1990) makes the important point that cult dynamics can in fact
be functioning in socially sanctioned groups of which clients may be a part. By
maintaining an awareness of these dynamics, counselors are in a better position
to discern whether a client's religious/spiritual group is contributing to a diagnosed religious or spiritual problem.

# RECOMMENDATIONS FOR REFERRAL

## The Importance of "Friendly Clergy"

In all assessments, recommendations such as psychiatric referral, psychological testing, hospitalization, or group counseling may be indicated. When a counselor discovers issues that involve a client's personal spiritual base or religious tradition, referral to specific clergy may be the appropriate action (Faiver, O'Brien, & McNally, 1998). We encourage counselors to acquaint themselves with nonjudgmental and caring clergy of various faiths (we refer to these individuals as the "friendly clergy") for potential referral of clients with religious or spiritual concerns that are beyond the counselor's scope of practice. In suggesting this, we do not assume that a deep understanding of either spirituality or specific religious traditions and beliefs is reserved only for members of the clergy. Still, ordination and the role of the clergy in assuming the most visible and accessible positions of leadership in churches, parishes, and temples does give them a unique teaching authority.

Research indicates that qualified clergy in these positions recognize a need for broad training in the field of counseling and that many view this as a viable offshoot of their training within the faith (Givens, 1976; Lowe, 1986; Stovich, 1985; Virkler, 1979). In certain cases—when a comprehensive investigation of the religious/spiritual realm is indicated—a trained and specifically identified member of the clergy may be more appropriate in the role of adviser or faith system interpreter than a counselor who is less qualified in this area. Remember, however, that our entire premise is founded on the notion that it is impossible to divorce a client from his or her spirituality or religious belief system within the context of the counseling relationship. A sensitive counselor may want to consider the client's beliefs holistically, as part of the context of therapy.

*Mitch, a client whose individual treatment included techniques of clinical hypnosis, received (under hypnosis) the suggestion that it would be useful to experience and identify a dream relevant to his concern. In a subsequent session, Mitch reported that he had experienced a dream in which he had engaged in cannibalism. Examination of his psychosocial history disclosed that Mitch had been raised in the Roman Catholic faith but had married a Protestant woman in a Protestant ceremony. Feelings of guilt regarding a union that had occurred outside the faith he'd been raised in had subsequently distanced Mitch from a sacrament central to that faith. Mitch's identification with his dream was grounded in spiritual issues surrounding the taking of holy communion—the sacramental eating of Christ's body and drinking of Christ's blood. Mitch no longer felt comfortable participating in this sacrament. His conflict could be addressed only by integrating the spiritual domain and his particular religious belief system directly into his therapy, through referral to appropriate clergy.*

Of course, any method utilized by counselor or clergy for therapeutic purposes must be consistent with a client's belief system to begin with. For example, a client from a fundamentalist Christian background may find techniques of clinical hypnosis anathema to his or her faith. A general familiarity with different faith traditions should prevent similar scenarios from occurring.

## Finding Friendly Clergy

How, then, do we identify the friendly clergy? As with any referral, great care must be taken to locate appropriate and qualified help. Clergy possessing an ideal profile for our referrals would be esteemed as seasoned teachers and exponents of their particular spiritual base and religious tradition. These clergy should be accessible, well respected by their congregation, and humane and "friendly" rather than judgmental. The ideal of the nonjudgmental counselor described by Rogers (1952) could be extrapolated to this group of clergy, since they would be expected to have some awareness, understanding, and respect for psychological processes, the effects of stress and depression, and the value of psychotherapeutic techniques. Clergy who have undergone some measure of therapy themselves, gaining personal exposure to various qualities and methods of successful practitioners, are perhaps more qualified in this regard. Providing an equally strong case are the increasing number of clergy who have chosen to undertake formal graduate study of counseling or psychology.

The unique manner in which clergy find themselves involved in the lives of their parishioners and the expectations placed on these clergy due to this position may give them opportunities to use perceptive responding skills and short-term therapeutic counseling methods (Switzer, 1983). Though advanced training is not absolutely necessary for clergy to become adept in these areas, we do feel that the awareness and understanding we have emphasized here are integral to any successful client-clergy dynamic. If a client were referred to a member of the clergy who demeaned all secular counseling efforts, the client would undoubtedly become confused and demoralized. *We are familiar with the experience of an AIDS patient who encountered an unfortunate and extreme example of this preconceived bias when, in the process of seeking solace and guidance regarding his illness, he was admonished by his pastor during a personal consultation and told that he was deserving of God's punishment. It is vital that responses of this uncaring nature be avoided when referral to clergy (or any other professional) is indicated.*

Networking becomes important as we identify clergy from various faiths who are friendly to the cause of counseling and open to client religious concerns that may transcend the predominant pastoral issues of marital and premarital counseling (Givens, 1976; Hong & Wiehe, 1974). Useful sources may include colleagues in the counseling profession, the local council of churches or similar organizational bodies, active lay people of a particular denomination, or various community equivalents of crisis hot lines. The client himself or herself may function as a source, perhaps recalling a particular member of the clergy who was accepting and helpful in the past.

Our treatment of twelve-step methodologies in Chapter 8 indicates our belief in this program as a useful adjunct to counseling. Ideally, networking with the assistance of organizations (like Alcoholics Anonymous) that are similarly attuned to spiritual issues could result in a periodic "listing" of friendly clergy, as described above, under the aegis of well-established organizations within the field. Most twelve-step programs overtly incorporate spiritual qualities in an idiosyncratic way, as addicts and alcoholics are led—with the support of others—through a process of discernment whose goal is to engender a lasting sobriety. This sobriety might consequently be reflected within the course of an assessment that includes consideration of religious and spiritual influences. We refer readers to Appendix B, which reviews the Twelve Steps of Alcoholics Anonymous, and Appendix C, which demonstrates a client assessment format that includes examination of the religious/spiritual domain.

## RELIGIOUS/SPIRITUAL ASPECTS
## OF THE COUNSELING PROCESS

Inclusion of the religious/spiritual domain within the assessment process consequently leads us to consider aspects of the counseling relationship that incorporate religious or spiritual qualities in and of themselves. In the wealth of literature concerning counseling and psychotherapy we see a preponderance of theoretical and clinical material at the notable expense of any related investigation of the essence of the therapeutic encounter itself. If we examine why practitioners become involved in counseling, what they believe is achieved by it, what they observe or witness directly in meeting with clients, and what nonclinical learning is involved in these encounters with clients, we may draw conclusions regarding the place of the counseling process in society (Feltham, 1998). If we are open to this type of process examination, we may continue to make well-supported inferences regarding the current human condition and the role of religious/spiritual qualities in that condition.

Work with a wide range of clients in a wide range of therapeutic contexts suggests that the type of religious/spiritual belief that a person has provides a telling document of an individual's particular psychological development (Randour, 1993). Both Freud and Jung held strong views on the relationship between psychotherapy and religion/spirituality. The influence of these early theorists has played a large role in counselors' increased openness regarding the inclusion of spiritual content within the therapeutic relationship. Acknowledgment of the religious/spiritual dimension as an integral aspect of the counseling experience has led naturally to the development of a number of concrete methods of consciously integrating this dimension into the therapeutic process

(Gendlin, 1996; Hinterkopf, 1997; Ingersoll, 1994). If we are to make inferences regarding the human condition, depth and meaning may certainly be added through exploration of a client's religious/spiritual convictions and an openness (on the part of the practitioner) to the possibly religious/spiritual essence of the therapeutic encounter. Potential differences in process and outcome that result from this openness have emerged as an important area of inquiry within the field (Hinterkopf, 1994; Noam & Wolf, 1993; West, 1998).

This inquiry has furthered Rogers's contention that goodness and self-actualization are likely outcomes when clients are provided the necessary and sufficient therapeutic conditions of unconditional positive regard, empathy, genuineness, and emotional congruence. In Rogers's lifelong adherence to a view of therapy as an essentially spiritual process, these therapeutic qualities can be seen as potentially spiritual in nature. Just as the positive, empathetic, and genuine support of fellow addicts and alcoholics is central to the notably spiritual twelve-step movement, Rogers historically emphasizes the critical importance of these qualities within the therapeutic relationship. Only through appropriate, honest empathy would a counselor be able to perceive the client's internal world and understand his or her subjective experiences (Rogers, 1961).

The type of empathy supported by Rogers may help counselors to be receptive to a wider range of messages from the client. If counselors can suspend the common tendency within the profession to think in predominantly analytic ways, their intuitive functioning may be enhanced. Use of intuition allows the counselor to experience the client in a more holistic, phenomenological manner, with analysis of client behavior as disparate pieces of information subsequently kept to a minimum (Eisengart & Faiver, 1996). The holistic nature of this experience relates directly to standard applications of religion/spirituality. What is religion/spirituality if not an increasingly holistic, enlightened view?

To acknowledge the role of Rogerian/humanistic qualities alongside intuition in the counseling process is to acknowledge less tangible, less measurable aspects of the therapeutic encounter. Just as the typical working environment of the Western counselor emphasizes the active, the measurable, and the quantifiable, therapeutic encounters incorporating aspects of our empathetic, intuitive, counteranalytical selves may exist as spiritually influenced events in and of themselves. A distinct contribution of our more receptive mode (touched upon earlier in our discussion of the major archethemes) comes into play here. Regardless of our ability to apply the receptive mode consciously during our work as counselors, aspects of the counseling process that elicit client dedication to specific religious belief or client attraction to less specific spiritual issues are undeniably present. Forgiveness—a concept with enduring connections to the religious/spiritual realm—has been recently represented in the counseling literature as an effective means of promoting personal and relational development. Forgiveness can help the client accept his or her own humanity and that of others, acknowledge weaknesses and shortcomings of self and others,

| TABLE 6.1 | INVENTORIES RELATED TO SPIRITUALITY | |
| --- | --- |
| **Inventory Title** | **Source** |
| The Spiritual Orientation Inventory | Elkins et al. (1988) |
| The Spiritual Well-Being Scale | Ellison (1983) |
| State-Trait Hope Inventory | Grimm (1984) |
| Mysticism Scale | Hood (1975) |
| The Spiritual Wellness Inventory | Ingersoll (1995) |
| Index of Core Spiritual Experience | Kass et al. (1991) |

and recover from past traumas (Ferch, 1998; McCallister, 1996). Any therapeutic intervention relying even partially on an examination of past experience must touch on elements of forgiveness and, in this way, directly involve concepts and processes with religious/spiritual implications.

We hope that an assessment design that includes an incorporation of the religious/spiritual domain will support additional research and investigation of religious/spiritual experience within the counseling process. Important distinctions have been made regarding the necessary differences between faith-oriented counseling and mental health counseling (Bufford, 1997; McCarty, 1986). These differences should remain prominent in the minds of researchers and practitioners, providing a necessary impetus for continued, increasing recognition and integration of religious/spiritual qualities within the counseling experience.

Readers may wish to explore the inventories related to spirituality listed in Table 6.1. The Ingersoll Spiritual Wellness Inventory may be found in Appendix G of this book.

## QUESTIONS FOR REFLECTION

1. Is a client assessment of beliefs indicated under all therapeutic circumstances? When might beliefs serve a functional purpose? When might they not?
2. In your opinion, what characterizes unhealthy spirituality?
3. Can you think of spiritual or religious organizations that are "mainstream" and yet the participants exhibit what Deikmann has called "cult-like dynamics"?
4. What do you think a client who has been spiritually abused would need most out of counseling? How well equipped would you feel to treat such a client?
5. When is referral necessary? Under what circumstances? Give case examples.

# References

Adler, A. (1964). *Problems of neurosis*. New York: Harper & Row.

American Psychiatric Association. (1994). *Diagnostic and statistical manual of mental disorders* (4th ed.). Washington, DC: Author.

Armstrong, K. (1993). *A history of God: The 4000 year quest of Judaism, Christianity, and Islam*. New York: Alfred A. Knopf.

Arterburn, S., & Felton, J. (1991). *Toxic faith: Understanding and overcoming religious addiction*. Nashville, TN: Oliver Nelson.

Assagioli, R. (1989). Self-realization and psychological disturbances. In S. Grof & C. Grof (Eds.), *Spiritual emergency: When personal transformation becomes a crisis* (pp. 27–48). Los Angeles: Jeremy Tarcher.

Basford, T. K. (1990). *Near-death experience: An annotated bibliography*. New York: Garland.

Barnhouse, R. T. (1986). How to evaluate patients' religious ideation. In L. Robinson (Ed.), *Anglican theology and pastoral care*. Wilton, CT: Morehouse Barlow.

Benjamin, A. (1987). *The helping interview with case illustrations*. Boston: Houghton Mifflin.

Bufford, R. K. (1997). Consecrated counseling: Reflections on the distinctiveness of Christian counseling. *Journal of Psychology & Theology, 25*(1), 111–122.

Cialdini, R. B. (1993). *Influence: The psychology of persuasion*. New York: Wiley.

Deikmann, A. (1990). *The wrong way home: Uncovering the patterns of cult behavior in American society*. Boston: Beacon Press.

Eisengart, S. P., & Faiver, C. M. (1996). Intuition in mental health counseling. *Journal of Mental Health Counseling, 18*(1), 41–52.

Ellis, A. (1989). Rational emotive therapy. In R. Corsini & D. Wedding (Eds.), *Current psychotherapies* (4th ed., pp. 197–240). Itsaca, IL: Peacock.

Ellison, C. W. (1983). Spiritual well-being: Conceptualization and measurement. *Journal of Psychology and Theology, 11*, 330–340.

Faiver, C. M. (1988). An initial client contact form. In P. A. Keller & S. R. Heyman (Eds.), *Innovations in clinical practice: A source book* (Vol. 7, pp. 285–288). Sarasota, FL: Professional Resource Exchange.

Faiver, C. M., & O'Brien, E. M. (1993). Assessment of religious beliefs form. *Counseling and Values, 37*(3), 176–178.

Faiver, C. M., O'Brien, E. M., & McNally, C. J. (1998). "The friendly clergy": Characteristics and referral. *Counseling and Values, 42*(3), 217–221.

Faiver, C. M., Eisengart, S. P., Colonna, R. (2000). *The counselor intern's handbook* (2nd ed.). Pacific Grove, CA: Wadsworth.

Feltham, C. (Ed.). (1998). *Wisdom and vision of the therapists*. Thousand Oaks, CA: Sage.

Ferch, S. R. (1998). Intentional forgiving as a counseling intervention. *Journal of Counseling & Development, 76*(3), 261–270.

Gabbard, G. O., Twemlow, S. W., & Jones, S. W. (1982). *With the eyes of the mind: An empirical analysis of out-of-body states*. New York: Praeger.

Gallup, G., Jr., with Procter, W. (1982). *Adventures in immortality: A look beyond the threshold of death*. New York: McGraw-Hill.

Gallup Poll Monthly. (1993). *Report on Trends, 331*(4), 36–38.

Gendlin, E. T. (1996). *Focusing-oriented psychotherapy: A manual of the experiential method*. New York: Guilford Press.

Givens, R. J. (1976). The counseling ministry of the churches of Christ. *Journal of Psychology and Theology, 4*(4), 300–303.

Greenberg, D., & Witzum, E. (1991). Problems in the treatment of religious patients. *American Journal of Psychotherapy, 45,* 554–565.

Greyson, B. (1996). The near-death experience as a transpersonal crisis. In B. W. Scotton, A. B. Chinen, & J. R. Battista (Eds.), *Textbook of transpersonal psychiatry and psychology* (pp. 303–315). New York: Basic Books.

Greyson, B., & Harris, B. (1987). Clinical approaches to the near-death experience. *Journal of Near-Death Studies, 6,* 41–52.

Grimm, P. M. (1984). *The state-trait hope inventory: The empirical evaluation of an instrument.* Unpublished manuscript, University of Maryland School of Nursing, Baltimore, MD.

Grof, S. (Speaker). (1990). *The cosmic game* (Cassette Recording No. 1-56455-054-0). Boulder, CO: Sounds True Recordings.

Grof, S., & Grof, C. (Eds.). (1989). *Spiritual emergency: When personal transformation becomes a crisis.* Los Angeles: Jeremy Tarcher.

Hassan, S. (1990). *Combating cult mind control.* Rochester, NY: Park Street Press.

Hinterkopf, E. (1994). Integrating spiritual experiences in counseling. *Counseling & Values, 38*(3), 165–175.

Hinterkopf, E. (1997). Defining the spiritual experience. *TCA Journal, 25*(2), 75–82.

Hong, B. A., & Wiehe, V. R. (1974). Referral patterns of clergy. *Journal of Psychology and Theology, 2*(4), 300–303.

Hood, R. W. (1975). The construction and preliminary evaluation of a measure of reported mystical experience. *Journal for the Scientific Study of Religion, 14,* 29–41.

Ingersoll, R. E. (1994). Spirituality, religion, and counseling: Dimensions and relationships. *Counseling & Values, 38*(2), 98–111.

Ingersoll, R. E. (1995). *Construction and initial validation of the spiritual wellness inventory.* Unpublished doctoral dissertation, Kent State University.

Kaplan, J. R. (1983). Social stress and atherosclerosis in normocholesterolemic monkeys. *Science, 220,* 733–735.

Kass, J., Friedman, R., Leserman, J., Zuttermeister, P., & Benson, H. (1991). Health outcomes and a new index of spiritual experience. *Journal for the Scientific Study of Religion, 30,* 203–211.

Lowe, D. W. (1986). Counseling activities and referral practices of ministers. *Journal of Psychology and Christianity, 5*(1), 22–29.

Lukoff, D., Lu, F. G., & Turner, R. P. (1996). Diagnosis: A transpersonal clinical approach to religious and spiritual problems. In B. W. Scotton, A. B. Chinen, & J. R. Battista (Eds.), *Textbook of transpersonal psychiatry and psychology* (pp. 231–249). New York: Basic Books.

MacKinnon, R. A., & Michels, R. (1971). *The psychiatric interview in clinical practice.* Philadelphia, PA: Saunders.

McCallister, R. J. (1996). Forgiveness. In Hatherleigh Press (Eds.), *The Hatherleigh guide to issues in modern therapy* (pp. 243–262). New York: Hatherleigh Press.

McCarty, S. (1986). Spiritual counseling: Realizing third party presence. *Studies in Formative Spirituality, 7*(2), 223–237.

Miller, W. R. (1990). Spirituality: The silent dimension in addiction research. *Drug Alcohol Review, 9,* 259–266.

Noam, G. G., & Wolf, M. (1993). Psychology and spirituality: Forging a new relationship. In M. L. Randour (Ed.), *Exploring sacred landscapes: Religious and spiritual experiences in psychotherapy* (pp. 194–207). New York: Columbia University Press.

Peck, M. S. (1997). *Denial of the soul: Spiritual and medical perspectives on euthanasia and mortality.* New York: Simon & Schuster.

Randour, M. L. (Ed.). (1993). *Exploring sacred landscapes: Religious and spiritual experiences in psychotherapy.* New York: Columbia University Press.

Ring, K. (1985). *Heading toward omega: In search of the meaning of the near-death experience*. New York: William Morrow.

Roberts, K. A. (1990). *Religion in sociological perspective* (2nd ed.). Belmont, CA: Wadsworth.

Rogers, C. R. (1952). *Client-centered therapy*. Cambridge, MA: Riverside Press.

Rogers, C. R. (1961). *On becoming a person*. Boston, MA: Houghton Mifflin.

Siassi, I. (1984). Psychiatric interview and mental status examination. In G. Goldstein & M. Hersen (Eds.), *Handbook of psychological assessment* (pp. 259–275). New York: Pergamon.

Stovich, R. J. (1985). Metaphor and therapy: Theory, technique, and practice of the use of religious imagery in therapy. Special issue: Psychotherapy and the religiously committed patient. *Patient Psychotherapy, 1*(3), 117–127.

Sullivan, H. S. (1970). *The psychiatric interview*. New York: Norton.

Switzer, D. K. (1983). Why pastors should be counselors (of a sort): A response to Richard L. Krebs. *Journal of Pastoral Care, 37*(1), 28–32.

Tiger, L., & Fox, R. (1971). *The imperial animal*. New York: Holt, Rinehart and Winston.

Turner, R. P., Lukoff, D., Barnhouse, R. T., & Lu, F. G. (1995). Religious or spiritual problem: A culturally sensitive diagnostic category in the DSM-IV. *Journal of Nervous and Mental Disease, 183*(7), 435–444.

Vaughan, F. (1995). *Shadows of the sacred: Seeing through spiritual illusions*. Wheaton, IL: Theosophical Publishing House.

Virkler, H. A. (1979). Counseling demands, procedures, and preparation of parish ministers: A descriptive study. *Journal of Psychology and Theology, 7*(4), 271–280.

Walsh, R., & Roche, L. (1979). Precipitation of acute psychotic episodes by intensive meditation in individuals with a history of schizophrenia. *American Journal of Psychiatry, 136*, 1085–1086.

Watson, P. J., Morris, R. J., & Hood, R. W., Jr. (1988). Sin and self-functioning, part 2: Grace, guilt and psychological adjustment. *Journal of Psychology and Theology, 16*, 270–281.

Welwood, J. (1983). On psychotherapy and meditation. In J. Welwood (Ed.), *Awakening the heart: East/West approaches to psychotherapy and the healing relationship* (pp. 43–54). Boston: Shambhala.

West, W. (1998). Therapy as a spiritual process. In C. Feltham (Ed.), *Witness and vision of the therapists*. Thousand Oaks, CA: Sage.

Wilber, K. (1980). *The atman project*. Wheaton, IL: Quest.

Wilber, K. (1990). *Eye to eye: The quest for a new paradigm*. Boston: Shambhala.

Wilber, K. (1999). *One taste: The journals of Ken Wilber*. Boston: Shambhala.

Worthington, E. L., Jr. (1989). Religious faith across the lifespan: Implications for counseling and research. *The Counseling Psychologist, 17*(4), 555–612.

Wulff, D. M. (1996). The psychology of religion: An overview. In E. P Shafranske (Ed.), *Religion and the clinical practice of psychology* (pp. 43–70). Washington, DC: American Psychological Association.

# INTERVENTIONS

At this point we would like to discuss interventions, many of which we have described throughout this book. Counseling is not simply a grab-bag application of techniques, and incorporating spirituality into counseling is no different. All good interventions grow from the therapeutic encounter and are uniquely applied within that context. That said, some generalizations can be made. We posit that all interventions have as their primary goal to ground and center the client, the counselor, or both. Richards and Bergin (1997) said that spiritual and religious interventions aid therapists in interceding therapeutically in their clients' spiritual or religious systems. They emphasized that no mainstream secular psychotherapeutic approach has developed interventions expressly for this purpose. As such, this becomes new ground.

## WHERE TO BEGIN?

Since knowing where to start is extremely important, we recommend three general guidelines developed by Fukuyama and Sevig (1999):

First, it is essential for the counselor to seek clarity about his or her own spiritual/religious beliefs and worldview. We discuss counselor self-assessment in Chapter 9 and offer a self-report instrument in Appendix G. Fukuyama and Sevig also mentioned the importance of understanding how one's cultural background is related to one's spiritual/religious worldview. We refer the reader to their excellent text for exercises related to this area.

Second, it follows that counselors need an in-depth understanding of the client's spiritual/religious beliefs and worldview. No spiritual intervention can be in the best interest of the client without such knowledge. In counseling relationships this information comes to light as the therapeutic alliance develops under the skill and patience of the therapist with the participation of the client.

Third, Fukuyama and Sevig recommend that counselors using (or interested in using) spiritual interventions participate in supervision groups or study groups in which the issues described above can be further explored. Doing so will increase the probability of ethical practice in the use of spiritual interventions.

To these three we add a fourth guideline. Counselors should be actively engaged in their own spiritual journey—one that includes practices congruent with the counselor's chosen spiritual path. In helping a client along his or her spiritual journey there is no substitute for personal experience. Of course, we believe that individuals must choose their own path and that their choices may change as they develop.

## CATEGORIES OF SPIRITUAL INTERVENTIONS

There are perspectives or therapeutic "lenses" through which to examine spiritual interventions. These lenses may be integrated into most settings where counselors treat adult clients. They may also be applied to work with children and adolescents with the consent of the parents or primary caregivers. In reviewing the literature on spiritual interventions, Richards and Bergin (1997) found that most therapists use spiritual interventions as part of an integrated approach to counseling that includes secular theories and techniques. These authors also posited five "either/or" categories through which spiritual interventions can be understood. Table 7.1 summarizes these categories.

First, interventions may take place both within or outside the counseling session. For example, the literature reviewing the use of prayer as an intervention leads us to believe it is far more common for therapists to pray for their clients outside the counseling session than with their clients during the session (Bullis, 1996; Jones, Watson, & Wolfram, 1992; Shafranske & Malony, 1990; Richards & Potts, 1995).

Second, counselors may categorize interventions as "religious" or "spiritual." Although Richards and Bergin acknowledge that separation of the two terms is

**TABLE**

**7.1    FIVE CATEGORIES OF SPIRITUAL INTERVENTIONS**

In-session versus out-of-session

"Religious" versus "spiritual"

Denominational versus ecumenical

Transcendent versus nontranscendent

Affective, behavioral, cognitive, and interpersonal interventions

Richards & Bergin (1997)

not easy, "religious" interventions might be thought of as those that utilize some aspect of the client's exoteric religious path. Exoteric examples include referring to sacred scriptures from the client's religion, encouraging attendance at religious gatherings, or using other resources available in the client's religious community. "Spiritual" interventions draw more from what we described in Chapter 1 as the "esoteric." These interventions focus more on transcendence, subjective meaning, and spontaneous experiences.

Third, interventions designated as "religious" may be either denominational or ecumenical. Denominational interventions refer to interventions drawn from the client's specific religious denomination including its theology. Ecumenical interventions are more universal in nature, devoid of content that would identify them with any particular religious expression.

Fourth, transcendent interventions are those in which the client, the therapist, or both share a worldview that includes a belief in the reality of what Richards and Bergin (1997) call "transcendent spiritual influences" (p. 239) (belief in or a sense of a larger spiritual reality). In this intervention, the client or counselor may petition these transcendent spiritual influences on behalf of the client. Conversely, implicit in "nontranscendent" interventions is the assumption that the clients and therapists do not share this worldview, or that the intervention has nothing to do with the spiritual/religious dimension.

Finally, Richards and Bergin believe that spiritual interventions, like any other type of intervention, may be primarily affective, behavioral, cognitive, or interpersonal. Kelly (1995) also alludes to this in his discussion of spiritual interventions via mainstream counseling theories.

## SPECIFIC INTERVENTIONS

The specific interventions we cover here include assessing, blessing, confessing, disputing, forgiving, giving, guiding, praying, referring, relating, ritualizing, supporting, and teaching.

### Assessing

The intake assessment sets the tone for treatment. Usually, it is the first contact the client has with the therapist. Therefore, we include assessment as an intervention, since it is part of the therapeutic process. Bullis (1996) and Shafranske and Malony (1990) have also described assessment as an intervention. An in-depth treatment of assessment can be found in Kelly (1995) and Hood and Hood (1999). Implicit in assessment is a basic understanding of the structures that support beliefs, such as the person's formal religious upbringing and current belief system. Religion can be a source of conflict and guilt, but also of strength and support. Many therapists have seen a simple question (about the spiritual/religious dimension) suddenly open a passage to a deeper, more personal level. The client may reveal a glimpse of deep faith, of intense anger, of old guilt, or of wistful longing. Powerful forces in the client's life, both positive and negative, can first be glimpsed here.

*Ann, an older client with a Christian background, had been referred because of grief over the death of an adult child. She was reticent and brief in her replies in the initial session, giving the impression that she felt therapy was pointless in her desolation. When asked about the place of faith in her life, however, Ann's voice and her whole demeanor changed. With some emphasis, she replied: "Oh, I'd be lost without my God!" The assessment and initial therapy turned a corner at that point. Ann accepted first that, as she had indicated, she was not lost. She was profoundly grateful that the therapist was willing to talk with her about the support her faith was for her.*

We suggest that the assessment of client beliefs be included as one element in the initial intake assessment (see Appendix C for an example of an intake form incorporating belief system assessment). Further, we recommend that counselors and other therapists avail themselves of a personal assessment of beliefs before applying any clinical assessment to a client population (see Appendix E for the counselor self-assessment form and Appendix G for the Spiritual Wellness Inventory).

## Blessing

Psychologist Stephen Gilligan (1997) encourages us to bless our clients by ratifying their experiences, humanity, and uniqueness. Although the Old English root of *bless* means "to consecrate with blood," a more common understanding of the word is "to bestow good upon." Blessing may be accomplished by our prizing (Carl Rogers's term), honoring, or loving the client. This honoring of the client does not necessarily imply an acceptance of the client's actions, as in the case of acting out or abusive behaviors. It does, however, acknowledge the client as a person in his or her own right through the creation by the therapist of the therapeutic milieu. Blessing the client in the counseling session may also take a more traditional form such as in the practice of "laying on of hands" (Richards & Bergin, 1997). Recall in Chapter 3 the case example of cultural evil. In that example the counselor found himself perpetuating evil by giving in to his exasperation with court-ordered clients and projecting all the failures of past clients onto his present case. Blessing played an important role in the resolution of that conflict.

*After speaking with my supervisor I realized that I had made no effort to understand my client as a person in his own right. He represented to me the problem. I made no progress with that client and he was soon incarcerated for parole violation. Shortly after that I participated in an intensive retreat at a yoga ashram out of state. The theme of the retreat was, as always, self-knowledge, but this time I had some ripe material to work with. My spiritual directors there used imagery exercises to help me access both my anger and fear regarding the dynamics behind many of the ills that led court-ordered clients to my office. The retreat directors reminded me that not only God can bless people, for we all possess the capacity to bestow blessings on others through loving them. "Love" in this sense meant being willing to extend ourselves for the growth of another. Since then, when I have treated court-ordered clients, I try to remember that they are like me. They want to be happy and avoid suffering. They want to live their lives. Remembering this increases the chances that I will extend myself for their growth, that I will love them, that I will bless them. When I am successful I find myself also blessed.*

## Confessing

The counseling process is often one of confession. Step five of the twelve-step program discusses, after a thorough inventory or assessment of ourselves, the importance of admitting the nature of our wrongs "to God, to ourselves, and to another human being" (see Appendix B). In a later case example, we speak of a client who was not fully successful in his recovery (or in his therapy) until he made his fifth, or confessional, step. Every therapist can point to examples of clients' unburdening themselves and in the process, being made whole.

*Della, age 66, had been mugged and was suffering from Post-traumatic Stress. During the course of counseling, some long-buried experiences came to light. She told her therapist of deep shame and anger caused by severe and even sadistic beatings from her father that had occurred over 50 years earlier. She had never shared these feelings, or their source, with any person before.*

The very act of exploring and explicating one's shadow side, as well as discovering or uncovering one's personal treasures, in the accepting presence of the skilled other, has a powerful healing effect. Chapter 2 discussed the "healing pilgrimage" of counselor and client, and the central role of this self-disclosure.

## Disputing

Ellis (1994) in his A-B-C theory includes disputing (D) as an important technique in therapy. While not concerned with the spiritual dimension, Ellis nonetheless espouses the idea of assisting a client in disputing deleterious and dysfunctional beliefs. We agree that a client who unfairly envisions himself or herself as sole judge, jury, and prosecutor may need help in disputing rigid and "soul-slamming" thoughts. We realize how value-laden this task may be, perhaps most vividly in the case of gays, lesbians, and other marginalized individuals. Cultural influences may, in some cases, cause these individuals to view themselves unfairly as less than others in dignity and worth. Certainly, active disputation of these views may prove beneficial for these people.

*Elena, age 39, had been seeing Dr. M. for chronic anxiety and dysphoria. She was hospitalized in an acute depressive crisis. A lover of several years had abruptly broken off their relationship, and the loss had awakened feelings long-buried about the death of her father in an accident when she was 9 years old. She was extremely embarrassed and distressed to find herself in a psychiatric facility, and that therefore she would be seen as "crazy." And, she feared, perhaps she was crazy. Her therapist visited her in the hospital, and reassured her. "You are not crazy," she said. The therapist was amazed what power this simple statement took on for Elena in her recovery. "I'm not crazy. Dr. M. told me I'm not crazy." The relationship of trust and respect that had been established between Elena and Dr. M. allowed the therapist to effectively dispute Elena's fearful and erroneous thought*

Jones, Watson, and Wolfram (1992) describe disputing as simply confronting incongruence between a client's actions and his or her professed beliefs. The stronger the therapeutic alliance, the greater the likelihood of success for this use of disputing. Disputing is also instrumental in what Kelly (1995) refers to as "invalidating." This ethically challenging technique, which requires the utmost discernment on the part of the counselor, endeavors to transform or eradicate a toxic belief or practice adhered to by the client.

## Forgiving and Releasing

Releasing or letting go is a difficult task for many of us, including our clients. "Turning the other cheek" and allowing the psychic energy attached to negative situations to dissolve can be equally challenging. In some form or another, forgiving and releasing are the most widely noted spiritual intervention in the current literature (Jones, Watson, & Wolfram, 1992; Kelly, 1995; Richards & Potts, 1995; Richards & Bergin, 1997). The act of forgiving may include letting go of ancient grudges against persons long gone, or forgiving those who have recently wronged us. Forgiving must include forgiving ourselves as well. Milton Erickson once noted that everyone is entitled to a happy second childhood. Chapter 2 discussed the important archethemes of compassion and forgiveness. Chapter 8 calls to mind the dire warnings in the twelve-step program about hanging on to anger and resentment.

*Dwayne had been disturbed for years by feelings of poor self-worth, depression, and confusion. In an intense session with a Gestalt-oriented therapist, he uncovered feelings of rage against authority figures, including God, Jesus, and Dwayne's father. He was shocked at the depth of rage he tapped. In subsequent sessions, he described his relief and joy at discovering that he was now able to forgive himself for misdeeds and failures over which he had felt guilt for years.*

Regarding forgiveness, Richards and Bergin (1997) make the excellent point that clients must come to forgiveness in their own time. Clients who have been traumatized by others may initially respond with numbness, then move to a healthy period of anger, and finally reach the point at which they are ready to embark on the journey of forgiveness.

# Giving

Giving gifts is a common tradition in many religious systems. Milton Erickson referred to therapy as the "terrible gift," implying its power and potential. Therapists give of themselves and their techniques, while the client ideally gives progress to himself or herself (and to the therapist as well). We like to view each session as a small gift. Perhaps the two primary gifts we offer clients are those of acceptance and challenge. In discussing this intervention, it is impossible not to consider our need, as therapists, for self-care and self-acceptance. If we are overworked, rushing from one commitment to another, one session to another; if we have personal issues left untended, how much of ourselves do we have to give? One of us heard from a theology professor many years ago a simple Latin saying: *Nemo dat quod non habet* ("No one gives what he doesn't have.")

Another important aspect of the gift of therapy is helping clients discover or rediscover their own gifts. One of the archethemes in Chapter 2 addresses one's "virtue" or "power." Often clients who feel disempowered have lost touch with their personal gifts, those things that make them unique and uniquely valuable to the communities in which they live.

Finally, giving may be understood as service to the greater good. Richards and Bergin (1997) observed that service is included in the exoteric forms of all the world's religions. It is also a focus of many religious expressions such as Tibetan Buddhism as described by the fourteenth Dalai Lama (Gyatso, 1999). Service (described as "altruism") has been characterized by Yalom (1995) as one of the therapeutic factors in group psychotherapy. Yalom notes the healing effect that service has on clients, enabling them to focus on helping another rather than on their own pain. We think again of our clients who are recovering in twelve-step programs. Clearly, service and *giving* are part of the very essence of what makes twelve-step recovery work. These clients tend to know what giving is about.

# Guiding

The Judeo-Christian tradition is replete with allusions to the shepherding function of those in leadership, such as David. Christian bishops serve as shepherds of their flocks, their staffs potent symbols of this role. Likewise, we view the therapist as shepherding or guiding the creative process of therapy, providing parameters and protecting the client as clinically indicated. In Eastern traditions, the guru (derived from Sanskrit meaning "one who leads from darkness to light") accomplishes the guiding.

*Joanna was depressed and suffered from poor self-esteem. Her parents had given her very little emotional support during childhood. In therapy, she generously wished only for good things for her young children, not for herself.*

*Her therapist found herself saying, "Trust me in this!"—namely, that Joanna needed to seek good things and good feelings for and about herself; and that this quest would abundantly help her children. Joanna stayed in therapy for herself and her own growth, and for her children's growth.*

## Praying and Meditating

Praying is another intervention widely written about in the professional literature on spiritual interventions. Most studies done on professional therapists' uses of prayer indicate that it is far more common for the therapists to pray silently within the session or outside the session than with the client (Ball & Goodyear, 1991; Bullis, 1996; Jones, Watson, & Wolfram, 1992; Kelly, 1995; Richards & Potts, 1995; Richards & Bergin, 1997). This is not a text on the uses and types of prayer. Nevertheless, we know that prayer is, for many of us—both clients and counselors—an effective, growth-oriented, life-giving intervention. While we may not necessarily pray with our clients, we can certainly pray for them. One of us, in conducting stress management seminars, customarily asks the participants how they manage stress in their lives. Invariably, one of the answers is "prayer." Of course, there are many kinds of prayer. In such considerations, the initial prayer that we typically bring to mind may allow us to address our concerns, our joys, our grief, and our hopes to our God, higher power, or divinity.

If this prayer can be described as a form of expression, then meditation is a kind of listening, or opening ourselves to reality and/or its creator. (See Chapter 2 for a discussion of the "receptive" mode, in which meditation and contemplation take place.) In a long-ago seminary lecture, the following words were attributed to a devout, simple country priest: When asked what he was doing during those long hours he spent in chapel, he replied, "I look at God, and God looks at me." This may be as apt a description of the prayer called contemplation as we have heard.

One colleague sat through many sessions with a young couple who had lost their only child in a tragic accident. He found that frequent prolonged periods of silence were painful, but also sometimes prayerful. The therapist was present to the clients, grieved with them, and silently prayed with them. Many of us have had what we might call prayerful or spiritual experiences. One client, in a discouraged frame of mind, waiting impatiently at a traffic light on a gray, snowy day, saw a young girl stop in front of his car, directly in his line of sight, lift her head back, open her mouth, and "receive communion" in the form of a large snowflake. The experience changed the client's day. He still talks about it warmly 30 years later.

It is clear that we can pray with more than words. A posture, a graceful movement can be worth a thousand words. We can and do pray with our bodies. Whatever makes us mindful of the sacred (see Chapter 2) is prayerful.

Bill Wilson (A.A., 1976, p. 55) says: "We found the Great Reality deep down within us. In the last analysis, it is only there that He may be found." We respect each person's belief system, whether it includes a personal God or not. Within these, the various and many types of prayer that our clients and we can experience seem deeply human and vital to us.

## Referring

When client issues are clearly spiritual or religious, we recommend referral to one of the "friendly clergy," or to a knowledgeable colleague. The friendly clergy are open to and appreciative of the process of counseling and nurturing of those in their care. Parenthetically, they can furnish counselors with helpful information on their particular faith system (Faiver, O'Brien, & McNally, 1998).

*Bea, age 77, approached a therapist for help with her grieving over the loss of her husband Frank, who had died the previous year. It had been her first marriage, a later-life marriage in her early fifties; but it had been Frank's second marriage. He had been widowed for several years previously. One of Bea's most disturbing and obsessive thoughts was this: In her religious belief system, Frank was now in Heaven with his first wife. Where did that leave her? Alone, with no one. Part of Bea's treatment included a referral to her minister, a trusted figure in her life. He assured her that, according to Christian faith based in scripture, she had nothing to worry about: her husband undoubtedly still loved her, and the rewards of the afterlife were beyond our understanding. The enduring quality of love became a much more healthy and positive theme for Bea in her recovery.*

## Relating

Gestalt psychologist Thomas Cutolo had occasion to tell one of us that "the essence of neurosis is lack of comfort." What a powerful statement, indeed. As we reflect on our myriad clinical experiences, we have come to appreciate how true Tom's wise words are. So many clients have had no one to provide a sense of security and comfort, whether as children or adults. Do we not as therapists endeavor to create a milieu of comfort? Does not every major religious system pose a central figure that humanizes the transcendent succor of the deity?

Our relationships with others and with that which is beyond us are key elements of this book. These relationships supply meaning and are infused with compassion, humor, and play. These relationships mandate that we honor those who seek our services. Stephan Gilligan (1997) talks about our touching the souls of others in therapy and their touching ours. (We note here that some body process therapies have a literal therapeutic touch, a form of "the laying on of hands.") In the end, the therapeutic relationship undergirds all other techniques and interventions and is the real "stuff" of counseling. Thus, in our opinion, the formation of the therapeutic alliance is key to a client's progress and a spiritual technique of sorts in the counseling process.

## Ritualizing

In his book *From Beginning to End: The Rituals of Our Lives* (1995), Robert Fulghum speaks of the importance of ritual as grounding and centering. Rituals can range from the mundane—brewing the morning coffee and reading the newspaper, or following the physical exercise routine—to the sacred—ritual washing prior to worship in the Islamic tradition or receiving Communion in Christian religions. (It is interesting to note how many of our religious rituals involve Jungian archetypes, such as fire [the use of candles], water [baptism], the Hero [Jesus, Buddha, Mohammed].) In fact, therapy itself may be viewed as a ritual in which the client's dysfunctional rituals are replaced with healthy ones. Myers (1997), positing that rituals are useful for accessing what is sacred, has proposed four stages of rituals. The first, setting off a sacred space, was mentioned in Chapter 2 as one of the themes that draws counseling and spirituality together. The second, liminality, is an anticipation of change or transformation during and at the conclusion of the ritual. Third, Myers also recommends the presence of a ritual elder to direct. Finally, he states an anticipation of transcendence as integral to the ritual. Fukuyama and Sevig (1999) found that rituals serve as a connection between the sacred and the concerns of everyday life. Those of us who work with children know how important the rituals and the "specialness" of therapy can be for them.

*Rodney, age 10, a boy whose parents were in bitter conflict and divorce proceedings, followed virtually the same ritual at every session. He would pull his chair very close to the therapist's and ask, "Can we tell stories?" He would then proceed to tell a long, detailed story featuring himself (thinly disguised) as a powerful superhero accompanied by a good friend, in control of events. Rodney was conducting his own therapy very creatively.*

## Supporting

Supporting clients in their spiritual quests and in their striving for well-being is elemental in counseling. This technique is complementary to disputing irrational and unhealthy beliefs.

*Mary, a cancer victim, experienced the emergence of various symbols of her faith during therapy sessions with a practitioner of hypnosis. The therapist encouraged Mary to use these comforting symbols, which she subsequently placed on an imaginary shield to combat her feelings of depression and nausea during chemotherapy.*

Kelly (1995) discusses supporting as "encouraging." He suggests that when a client's sustaining and supportive beliefs relate to his or her presenting concerns, it is appropriate to support these beliefs by encouraging activities related to the client's religious or spiritual path.

## Teaching

*A Buddhist monk came upon a traveler who asked, "The people in the next town, what are they like?" The monk paused and asked the traveler, "What were the people like where you are coming from?" The traveler said, "Mostly selfish and greedy, caring only for their own wants," to which the monk replied, "You'll find people in the next town pretty much the same." Days later the monk happened on a second traveler who also asked, "The people in the next town, what are they like?" The monk paused and asked the traveler, "What were the people like where you are coming from?" The traveler said, "A good people—loving, caring, and decent." The monk then said, "You'll find the people in the next town pretty much the same."*

We often talk of the *teaching* function of counseling—that is, the provision of information to the client. This may take the form of advice on college or career choice, information on testing, and so on. However, we look on the therapist's teaching in a broader sense. This teaching can involve exploring, interpreting, reframing, comparing and contrasting, confronting, and analyzing. Ideally, the therapist acts as a social model of congruence for the client as well. Teaching may include cognitive and/or behavioral interventions, role-plays, and psychodrama, too. (Relevant to our own training, we are reminded that the term *doctorate* is derived from the Latin *docere*, "to teach," and that the term *rabbi* denotes "teacher.")

The great teachers of past and present times, such as Jesus, Buddha, Confucius, Aesop, Martin Luther King, Jr., Ghandi, and Milton Erickson, for example, taught not only by modeling their beliefs but also by their use of storytelling. Others call these stories parables, fables, and metaphors. Whatever the case, stories often share a common denominator—use of narrative to illustrate a wise point. Both Coles (1989) and Guroian (1998) have written eloquently on the subject of healing through storytelling, noting ways in which stories well told may "call" us in a moral fashion, similar to a spiritual or religious inclination.

Consider the Christian parable of the mustard seed wherein Jesus relates that some seeds land on good soil where they may flourish while others, less fortunate, land on dry, hard ground where growth is impossible. We are in the business of not only planting therapeutic seeds but also of assisting the client in choosing a milieu of growth.

## CONSIDER THE CHILDREN

Many of the interventions discussed here may be accommodated to use with children, especially teaching through storytelling. We began this book with a quotation from a child and we end this chapter with the hope that the reader might go on to occasionally view the world with the wonder and awe of a child. Clinically, we have discovered that our work with adults often includes the blessing and affirming of their internal children. How many of our great historical figures echo respect for the wisdom of children!

## A CAUTIONARY NOTE

The application of spiritual interventions is a delicate matter replete with the potential for controversy. Our basic general guideline is this: We do not attack a person's beliefs nor we do not attempt to proselytize. We endeavor to honor the client and his or her beliefs and to work within the contexts of these beliefs whenever possible. We strive to refer the client when this is indicated.

There are some contraindications to using spiritual interventions. Obviously, one occurs when the client has made it clear that he or she has no interest in spiritual issues. Kelly (1995) wrote of another approach called "deferring," wherein the counselor temporarily "brackets off" spiritual issues when she or he believes there are other more pertinent tasks in need of attention. An extreme example would be a client who may be suffering from a severe mental and emotional disorder like schizophrenia and requires stabilization before issues of faith can be explored. Richards and Bergin (1997) have stated that spiritual interventions are contraindicated when spiritual issues are not relevant to the client's presenting problem. They also note the necessity of parent or caregiver permission when such interventions are utilized in the case of a minor.

## QUESTIONS FOR REFLECTION

1. Which of the techniques described in this chapter resonate with you? Why? Which do not? Why?
2. How might you apply the interventions delineated? Under what circumstances? Cite specific case examples in which you envision applying techniques.
3. What is it within the therapeutic encounter that has led you either to dispute or support a client's thoughts or actions? Do these divergent intervention techniques challenge you in similar ways as a practitioner, or do they call upon entirely different qualities? How do these qualities relate to your own experience of spirituality?

4. To what degree do you perceive forgiveness as a spiritual process? Can forgiveness be definitively accomplished without incorporation of some spiritual (i.e., transcendent) ethic?
5. To what degree does your own ability to be "present" to the client (in Rogerian fashion) involve potential qualities of spiritual awareness? Conversely, how might this awareness be affected by the potentially transcendent qualities of the therapeutic encounter?

# REFERENCES

Alcoholics Anonymous World Service. (1976). *The story of how many thousands of men and women have recovered from alcoholism* (3rd ed.). New York: Author.
Ball, R. A., & Goodyear, R. K. (1991). Self-reported professional practices of Christian psychologists. *Journal of Psychology and Christianity, 10*, 144–153.
Bullis, R. K. (1996). *Spirituality in social work practice*. Washington, DC: Taylor and Francis.
Coles, R. (1989). *Call of stories: Stories and the moral imagination*. Boston, MA: Houghton Mifflin.
Ellis, A. (1994). *Reason and emotion in psychotherapy*. New York: Birch Lane Press.
Faiver, C., O'Brien, E., & McNally, C. (1998). Characteristics of the friendly clergy. *Counseling and Values, 42*(3), 217–221.
Fukuyama, M. A., & Sevig, T. D. (1999). *Integrating spirituality into multicultural counseling*. London: Sage.
Fulghum, R. (1995). *From beginning to end: The rituals of our lives*. New York: Villard.
Gilligan, S. (1997). *The courage to love*. New York: Norton.
Guroian, V. (1998). *Tending the heart of virtue: How classic stories awaken a child's moral imagination*. New York: Oxford University Press.
Gyatso, T., (1999). *Ethics for the new millenium*. New York: Riverhead Books.
Jones, S. L., Watson, E. J., & Wolfram, T. J. (1992). Results of the Rech conference survey on religious faith and professional psychology. *Journal of Psychology and Theology, 20*, 147–158.
Kelly, E. W. (1995). *Spirituality and religion in counseling and psychotherapy*. Alexandria, VA: American Counseling Association.
Myers, B. K. (1997). *Young children and spirituality*. New York: Routledge.
Richards, P. S., & Bergin, A. E. (1997). *A spiritual strategy for counseling and psychotherapy*. Washington, DC: American Psychological Association.
Richards, P. S., & Potts, R. (1995). Using spiritual interventions in psychotherapy: Practices, successes, failures, and concerns of Mormon psychotherapists. *Association of Mormon Counselors and Psychotherapists Journal, 21*, 39–68.
Shafranske, E. P., & Malony, H. N. (1990). Clinical psychologists' religious and spiritual orientations and their practice of psychotherapy. *Psychotherapy, 27*, 72–78.
Yalom, I. (1995). *The theory and practice of group psychotherapy*. New York: Basic Books.

# THE SPIRITUALITY
# OF THE TWELVE STEPS

In a book about counseling and spirituality, the authors feel it is most appropriate to consider the spirituality of the twelve-step recovery programs. How many of our clients' lives and our own lives, directly or indirectly, have been damaged by alcoholism and addiction? Much of this damage—physical, emotional, and spiritual—is addressed in twelve-step programs. In the context of spiritual/religious interventions, it is important to take a closer look at a fellowship and a program that consists in great part, on the level of mutual support, of many interventions mentioned in the previous chapter: confessing, forgiving, giving, supporting, praying.

Every year, every day, across the world, alcoholism and addictions to drugs, gambling, sex, and many other abusive behaviors are ruining countless people's lives. Counselors and other psychotherapists often work with the sad human results: families torn apart, children born with neurological deficits or raised in abusive, neglectful settings, violence, post-traumatic stress, and personalities warped and disordered. Every day we see evidence of the erosion of personal standards and values caused by addiction. Alcoholism and other addictions are conditions with notoriously poor prognoses. Called by some a chronic, relapsing disease, alcoholism requires a lifelong course of treatment. The current writers have no desire to enter the dispute as to the exact nature of alcoholism. Bill Wilson, founder of Alcoholics Anonymous, himself avoided calling alcoholism a disease and stayed clear of the controversy. He sometimes used the expression "our malady" or similar terms to refer to alcoholism (Kurtz, 1991, p. 22).

To simplify our discussion and avoid confusion, we focus here primarily on alcoholism and on the Twelve-Step Fellowship from which other similar programs (such as Overeaters Anonymous, Narcotics Anonymous, et al.) borrow their structure and their programs: Alcoholics Anonymous (A.A.).

# A SPIRITUAL TREATMENT PROGRAM

Alcoholics Anonymous has been called a spiritual treatment program for a spiritual illness. Carl Jung said of alcoholics, in a now-famous letter to Bill Wilson, "The compulsion to use alcohol is so great that it is likely that only a spiritual experience could overwhelm that compulsion" (A.A., cited in Smith, 1994, p. 111). Father John Ford, a long-time friend and supporter of A.A., has said: "These steps are essentially spiritual exercises and, somehow or other, they work in rehabilitating alcoholics. If a program of spiritual and moral regeneration is the thing that helps alcoholics most and arrests their sickness, then that sickness must be at least partly of a moral and spiritual nature" (Darrah, 1992, p. x).

Many, both alcoholics and those who would help them professionally, have experienced some discomfort with the term *spiritual*. In this context, we like Booth's (1995) definition: "the relationship between body, mind, and emotions that allows people to be positively and creatively connected to others and the world around them. Spirituality is not 'out there' somewhere, on a higher level. Spiritual power is within us" (p. 6). The alcoholic recovering in A.A. is told not that spirituality is part of his or her recovery but that it is essential: "What we really have is a daily reprieve, contingent on the maintenance of our spiritual condition" (Alcoholics Anonymous World Services, 1976, p. 85.)

The purpose here is to examine this spiritual program—where it came from, what it consists of, what it means to thousands or millions of recovering people all over the world, and how counselors can understand it and make intelligent connections to it in their therapeutic work. In the following account, we see how those following the path of A.A. are encouraged to *assess* their own lives, to *confess* their faults, to *give* of themselves and to *support* one another.

Anyone familiar with twelve-step programs will recognize the importance of storytelling. The telling of personal stories—sharing experience, strength, and hope; "how it was, what happened, and how it is now"—is the meat and drink of the program. A.A. is a fellowship with an oral tradition, passed down through personal stories. As with any other society, the beginnings and early history of the group are enshrined and often recounted. We understand the reality by understanding its beginnings and its development. Many therapists will be familiar with much A.A. history. But we think that the spirituality of the A.A. Twelve-Step Program is too important a connection for counselors to pass by lightly. The physical, emotional, and spiritual destruction caused by addiction affects too many of our clients, and even ourselves. And so we ask the reader's indulgence in listening to some good and important stories: stories about recovery, on physical, emotional, and spiritual levels.

# BEGINNINGS OF ALCOHOLICS ANONYMOUS

In 1934, Bill Wilson, a man who had struggled for years with a terrible alcohol problem, received a visit from a friend named Ebby. This visit, well documented in early A.A. accounts (Alcoholics Anonymous World Services, 1976, pp. 8–12), came when Wilson was nearing the end of his options: He was broke, his health was ruined, he had been hospitalized numerous times. Ebby had been, if anything, a more severe case of alcoholism than Bill Wilson. But when he appeared this day, he was a new man. Bright-eyed, he told Wilson of a religious conversion, a spiritual experience that had changed him. He said he had "got religion." In his account of this very important visit, Kurtz (1991) makes the vital connection to an earlier contact: a mutual friend of Wilson's and Ebby's, a man known as Rowland H. (pp. 8–9). Rowland, a bright and highly successful young man, was also extremely troubled by alcoholism. He had decided, after many failures, to seek the best possible help, so he had entered treatment with none other than Dr. Carl Jung in Zurich. Rowland was in Zurich for over a year and left with great praise for the famous doctor and great hope for continued sobriety. Alas, he was soon drunk again. He returned to Dr. Jung, who spoke to him in the gravest terms: He was a hopeless alcoholic and would need to have himself confined. The discussion that ensued between Rowland and Dr. Jung was described by Wilson later, in a famous exchange of letters between himself and Jung, as "the first foundation stone upon which our society has since been built" (A.A., cited in Kurtz, 1991, p. 9). After making the point that it was hopeless for Rowland to seek further medical treatment for his alcoholism, and in response to Rowland's desperate query regarding any other possibility, Jung had responded in terms of a "spiritual or religious experience—in short, a genuine conversion," warning also that such experiences were comparatively rare (Kurtz, 1991, p. 9).

# IMPORTANCE OF THE OXFORD GROUP

In response to Jung's suggestion, Rowland returned home to the United States and involved himself with the Oxford Group, a religious movement begun in Britain after World War I in response to a general sense of disillusionment and dissatisfaction with religion and other institutions. Rowland found lasting sobriety and later rescued his friend Ebby from a jail sentence. Ebby too became an Oxford Group member, and though he died in active alcoholism, he found several years of sobriety through his religious involvement. Ebby was quoted by Wilson later as saying about his Oxford Group experience that he

> had to admit he was licked. . . . I learned that I ought to take stock of myself and confess my defects to another person in confidence; I learned that I needed to make restitution for the harm I had done to others. I was told that I had to practice

the kind of giving that has no price tag on it, the giving of yourself to somebody. . . .
They taught me I should try to pray to whatever God I thought there was for the
power to carry out these simple precepts. And if I did not believe there was any God,
then I had better try the experiment of praying to whatever God there might be.

(Alcoholics Anonymous World Services, 1957, pp. 58–59)

And, Ebby recounted, as soon as he decided he would try this with an open
mind, his drinking problem was lifted "right out of him" (Alcoholics Anonymous World Services, 1957, p. 59).

Not long after his visit from Ebby, Bill Wilson found himself in the Towns
Hospital again, at perhaps his lowest point—in A.A. terms, his "bottom."
In desperation, he prayed, "If there is a God, let Him show Himself! I am
ready to do anything, anything!" (Alcoholics Anonymous World Services, 1957,
p. 63). And Wilson recounts then a dramatic, life-altering experience of a brilliant, white light filling the room, accompanied by a great feeling of peace, a
feeling of Presence. Wilson never drank again. (The oral tradition of A.A. is full
of stories of transformation, of hieropanies.)

The importance of the "spiritual experience," whether dramatic and sudden
or of a more gradual nature, cannot be emphasized too much if one is to understand this twelve-step program. In later writings, Wilson recalled that Ebby
had brought him, in a subsequent visit, a copy of William James's *Varieties of
Religious Experience* (1929). Wilson wrote of this book, by one of America's
premier and original psychologists:

Spiritual experiences, James thought, could have objective reality; almost like gifts
from the blue, they could transform people. Some were sudden brilliant illumina-
tions; others came on very gradually. Some flowed out of religious channels; others
did not. But nearly all had the great common denominators of pain, suffering, and
calamity. Complete hopelessness and deflation at depth were almost always required to make the recipient ready. The significance of all this burst upon me.
*Deflation at depth*—yes, that was *it*. Exactly that had happened to me. Dr. Carl
Jung had told an Oxford Group friend of Ebby's how hopeless his alcoholism was
and Dr. Silkworth had passed the same sentence upon me. Then Ebby, also an
alcoholic, had handed me the identical dose. On Dr. Silkworth's say-so alone
maybe I would never have completely accepted the verdict, but when Ebby came
along and one alcoholic began to talk to another, that had clinched it.

My thoughts began to race as I envisioned a chain reaction among alcoholics,
one carrying this message and these principles to the next. More than I could ever
want anything else, I now knew that I wanted to work with other alcoholics.

(Alcoholics Anonymous World Services, 1957, p. 64)

As Kurtz points out in his scholarly history, these insights nearly completely
sum up all the meaning of Alcoholics Anonymous (Kurtz, 1991). Wilson would
later realize that he *needed* to work with other alcoholics to maintain his own
sobriety; and this giving away to another what one has found became part of
the spiritual program of recovery of A.A. In our discussion of the archetheme

of compassion in Chapter 2, we mentioned the Latin root, *cum patior* (to "suffer with"). This is literally borne out in the functioning of a support group such as A.A., made up of "fellow sufferers." And in Chapter 3, in discussing responses to evil, we saw that "support implies love and breeds strength" (p. 22). A.A. members would surely nod and say: "This is how it works!"

Like Ebby and Rowland, Bill Wilson also became a member of the Oxford Group. Here he sought the spiritual transformation or transcendence that had been recommended by Carl Jung. In Britain, the group's founding leader was Dr. Frank Buchman, a Lutheran pastor; in the United States, an Episcopal priest, Dr. Samuel Shoemaker, was the central figure in the early 1930s. The Oxford movement described itself as an "organism" rather than an organization and claimed no leadership except the Holy Spirit. "The movement had no board of directors, but relied instead on 'God-control' through men and women who had fully 'surrendered' to God's will" (*The Twelve Steps*, 1988, p. ix). Buchman and his group stressed the need to "surrender to God, for forgiveness and guidance," and to confess one's sins "to God and others." The members "made restitution for wrongs done, and witnessed about their changed lives in order to help change others" (*The Twelve Steps*, 1988, p. ix). The Oxford Group movement had six basic assumptions: (1) human beings are sinners; (2) human beings can be changed; (3) confession is a prerequisite to change; (4) the changed soul has direct access to God; (5) the age of miracles has returned; and (6) those who have changed are to change others (*The Twelve Steps*, 1988, p. x). The co-founders of A.A., Bill Wilson and Dr. Bob Smith, a physician, attended and were active participants in Oxford Group meetings in New York, led by Dr. Shoemaker, and in Akron. Wilson freely admitted: "It was from Sam Shoemaker that we absorbed most of the twelve steps of A.A., steps that express the heart of A.A.'s way of life. The early A.A. got its ideas of self-examination, acknowledgment of character defects, restitution for harm done, and working with others, straight from the Oxford Group and directly from Sam Shoemaker, their former leader in America, and from nowhere else" (Alcoholics Anonymous World Services, 1957, p. 199).

So the early members of A.A., before the fledgling society had any such name, were members of the Oxford Group. And these alcoholics struggling to remain sober adopted the assumptions and practices of the Oxford Group. (This group is in no way connected with the earlier Oxford Movement, at the end of the nineteenth century, in which Cardinal Newman and other prominent Anglicans changed their allegiance to the Roman Catholic Church.) Kurtz discusses specifically American religious traditions, the Pietist and the Humanist Liberal, and even the religious revival movement, within A.A. (Kurtz, 1991, pp. 178–179), which reach farther back than the Oxford Group experience.

# FOUNDING OF ALCOHOLICS ANONYMOUS AS A SEPARATE ORGANIZATION

Problems soon developed with the religious connection, however. Many alcoholics had had very negative experiences with religion, had heard more than their share of "shoulds" and "shouldn'ts," and had been labeled as sinners. The aggressive evangelical tone of many Oxford Group members was too much for many alcoholics in early recovery. By 1937, the alcoholic members of the Oxford Group in New York were feeling more and more pressure to form their own separate entity. There was dissatisfaction not only among the alcoholics but also from the nonalcoholic Oxford Group members (many of them members of the Episcopalian congregation of Calvary Church in New York). Things came to a crisis when alcoholic members were banned from a certain meeting and Bill Wilson and his wife Lois were encouraged to give up working with alcoholics. Wilson described the reasons for the break: "It was too authoritarian for [the alcoholics]. . . . The Oxford Groups' absolute concepts . . . were frequently too much for the drunks. . . . Our debt to them, nevertheless, was and is immense, and so the final breakaway was very painful" (Alcoholics Anonymous World Services, 1957, p. 74). By 1938, the Akron alcoholics were also meeting separately, after the regular Oxford Group meeting. Such separate meetings presaged the recovering alcoholics' moving out of the Oxford Group entirely as well as the later distinction between meetings that were "open" (for alcoholics and others, like spouses) and one that were "closed" (for recovering people only) (Kurtz, 1991, p. 77).

Bill Wilson consulted with the members of the organization and with friends in the clergy as well as the medical and psychiatric professions about the wording of the twelve steps and the book that became known as *Alcoholics Anonymous*. A draft copy was circulated to numerous individuals for their ideas and criticism (Kurtz, 1991, pp. 75–76). It became clear that connections with any religious group would not be helpful. The program was "spiritual," not religious. A.A. was a pioneering American institution in making this distinction.

# THE SPIRITUAL PROGRAM OF THE STEPS AND TRADITIONS OF ALCOHOLICS ANONYMOUS

Many scholarly treatises and heartfelt testimonials have been written about the meaning and purpose of the Twelve Steps of Alcoholics Anonymous. We approach these steps with respect for the Fellowship of A.A. and for these many distinguished authors. In addition to the Steps, we feel that at least a brief and selective look at the Traditions of A.A. is appropriate here too.

Starting with the principles they had learned from the Oxford Group, the founders of A.A. set out a program of admitting defeat, of surrender; of faith in a power greater than oneself; of turning one's life over to that power; of self-examination and confession of faults; of making restitution; and of giving oneself to help others. These are the steps suggested in this particular journey of transformation, a journey such as that described in Chapter 2 on the arche-theme of hope. The twelve steps are clearly aimed at achieving change in individual lives, as is the counseling process. (See Appendix B for the Twelve Steps and the Twelve Traditions of Alcoholics Anonymous).

## Twelve Steps of Alcoholics Anonymous

Steps 1, 2, and 3 can be called the "surrender" steps. We have seen previously Bill Wilson's language about "deflation at depth," or hitting bottom. In these steps, the alcoholic, having realized that he or she cannot keep going in the current direction, that "our lives had become unmanageable," ideally becomes willing to "give up" and put his or her life in the care of a higher power. Nothing is said about sin or sinners; such language had been shown to close doors for desperate alcoholics such as those the early A.A. movement was seeking out. Dr. Harry Tiebout, psychiatrist and early friend of A.A., wrote at length about "the infantile omnipotent ego" (Tiebout, cited in Hanna, 1992, p.171), and it is this unrealistic relationship with the world that Tiebout believed is here surrendered by the alcoholic. A "power greater than ourselves" is first mentioned in these steps, and then "God," but "God as we understood Him." The early withdrawal of A.A. from any specific religious ties is evident here. All theological disputes, so many problems real and false, so many prejudices are simply bypassed with this phrase, "God as we understood Him." Many recovering individuals come to their A.A. program with a lifelong faith in God; for others, the group, the fellowship is where God is found. One A.A. member was fond of using this lengthy but meaningful phrase: "by the grace of the higher power that I have come to know in Alcoholics Anonymous."

Steps 4 and 5 can be called the inventory and confessional steps. They are obviously meant to help overcome the shame and guilt that are usually a major part of the destructive cycle of alcoholism. Booth (1987) provides an interesting commentary on these steps. He remarks that step 4 is not meant to be merely a negative inventory or a list of faults. It is a "searching and fearless moral inventory of ourselves" and thus should include strengths, achievements, positive relationships, and personal qualities as well as failings, faults, and errors of the past (p. 271). Step 4 is obviously about the task of "facing oneself. Step 5 is the "confessional" step. Booth reminds us that it is made to God, to ourselves, and to another human being. Echoing Jourard (1964) and others, Booth comments: "The admission to another human being allows you to be known. There is something in the act of making yourself understood that allows you to know yourself" (Booth, 1987, p. 274). Especially because of his indirect but seminal role in the formation of A.A., we recall here with interest Carl Jung's comments on the need for confession, mentioned in Chapter 4. In a related manner, by telling and retelling her own story, by passing on her "experience, strength and hope" to others, the alcoholic's recovery is kept in her awareness, is deepened and maintained. "Alcoholism is a disease that flourished in secrecy, and it could so easily manipulate the admission to God and yourself as part of the continuing secret, but when you utter aloud the exact nature of your wrongs to another human being, the power of the disease is dissipated" (Booth, 1987, p. 274). In these steps, as in virtually all the others, the isolation and progressive withdrawal of the alcoholic is countered. What therapist does not know the power of confession and self-disclosure? As in many other instances, A.A. appeared to borrow what it needed from religion (as in sacramental confession) and psychotherapy.

Steps 6 and 7 can be called the character-change steps. They are meant to promote awareness of the character traits behind the faults mentioned in step 5, together with a willingness to seek God's help and to let go of these traits. In this sense, steps 6 and 7 are a continuation of the surrender of steps 1 through 3. The word *ready* is equivalent to *willing*, that magic concept in A.A. And the common experience shared by many recovering in A.A. is to see their defects, such as self-centeredness or impatience, slowly diminish over time. Many consider this gradual change an essential part of the "spiritual experience" they had been seeking.

Steps 8 and 9 are the relational steps. They help repair relationships often ruined or severely damaged by active alcoholism. The alcoholic needs to regain and renew social bonds and to overcome resentments, manipulative behavior, and blaming others for his or her problems. Many more quiet, withdrawn alcoholics have some difficulty with these steps at first because they have not acted out against others in any obvious way. Kinney and Close (1995) tell of a member of a religious community who felt she had harmed no one but herself. When asked if there was anyone she would avoid seeing, she replied affirmatively; and the suggestion was then made that she begin her list with this name (pp. 96–97).

Steps 10 and 11 are the maintenance steps. They encourage regular attention to one's spiritual health. It is spiritual health that is being maintained. Step 10 reviews and updates steps 4 through 9, and step 11 reviews and continues steps 1 through 3. At the beginning of this chapter, we commented on the nature of alcoholism as a chronic, recurring problem requiring lifelong attention. These steps make more evident the lifelong nature of this program of A.A. Many recovering women and men we know make a practice of asking for guidance from their higher power in the morning, and thank that power in the evening for another day of sobriety. Step 11 suggests regular "prayer and meditation"— expressing as well as listening, the active and the receptive mode, in opening oneself to a higher power.

Step 12 is the service step. "Having had a spiritual awakening as a result of these steps . . ." (Alcoholics Anonymous World Services, 1976, p. 60), this experience is elsewhere described as an "unsuspected inner resource" that recovering alcoholics become aware of gradually: "With few exceptions our members find that they have tapped an unsuspected inner resource which they presently identify with their own conception of a Power greater than themselves. Most of us think this awareness of a Power greater than ourselves is the essence of spiritual experience. Our more religious members call it 'God-consciousness' " (Alcoholics Anonymous World Services, 1976, pp. 569–570.) We are reminded that this is not meant to be just an overflowing of gratitude or kindness, but is an essential part of what makes A.A. work: what has kept thousands of women and men sober through these 60 years A.A. has existed. Again, it is a powerful example of a group response to evil, a mutual bonding in recovery. Bill Wilson used this striking image: "For a time [the alcoholic] may try to hug the treasure to himself. He may not see at once that he has barely scratched a limitless lode which will pay dividends only if he mines it for the rest of his life and insists on giving away the entire product" (Alcoholics Anonymous World Services, 1976, p. 129).

Passing the message of recovery one to another is essential to A.A. and its spirituality. For many in A.A., this personal contact is where the higher power is first found: between and among the recovering members. Berenson (1990) points out that the true beginning of A.A. was not the dramatic conversion experience of Bill Wilson but a process that came to completion in the six-hour dialogue that he and Dr. Bob Smith had in Akron, which soon brought about Smith's sobriety. (See also Kurtz, 1991, p. 33.) "Thus, Alcoholics Anonymous has avoided many of the traps and pitfalls that have beset other spiritual movements which place authority and leadership within a single individual rather than within a relationship that serves as a conduit for a transcendent power" (Berenson, 1990, p. 68).

## Twelve Traditions of Alcoholics Anonymous

The Traditions of A.A. (see Appendix B) represent a powerful statement of what the organization is and how it works. It is the closest thing to a "book of rules" that A.A. possesses. Our specific purpose and limits of space prevent us from a more extensive examination of the Traditions. We point out here only Traditions 2, 3, and 12. We see a direct descent from the Oxford Group's "God-direction" in Tradition 2 of A.A., which mentions "one ultimate authority: a loving God as he may express himself in our group conscience" (Alcoholics Anonymous World Services, 1952, p. 132). The individual surrender to a higher power, which is called for in the steps, is here applied to the working of the entire fellowship and of its many individual groups. Tradition 3 states that "the only requirement for membership is a desire to stop drinking" (Alcoholics Anonymous World Services, 1952, p. 139). Wilson recalls that this was not always so. In the early days of the fellowship, individual groups had many different rules and requirements. "Everybody was scared witless that something or somebody would capsize the boat and dump us all back into the drink. . . . If all those rules had been in effect everywhere, nobody could have possibly joined A.A. at all, so great was the sum of our anxiety and fear" (Alcoholics Anonymous World Services, 1952, pp. 139–140). One member expresses the current freedom of access to A.A. very starkly: "When I came to A.A., I could not accept myself, my alcoholism, or a Higher Power. If there had been any physical, mental, moral or religious requirements for membership, I would be dead today" (Alcoholics Anonymous World Services, 1990, p. 68).

Tradition 12 declares that "anonymity is the spiritual foundation of our traditions, ever reminding us to place principles before personalities" (Alcoholics Anonymous World Services, 1952, p. 184). While its insistence on personal anonymity can make A.A. seem shadowy or insubstantial to some, the remarkable fact for many is that this worldwide organization does actually maintain itself and grow, and serve the needs of millions of alcoholics in many countries, without any figureheads, notables, or spokespersons. It really does appear to place "principles before personalities" (Alcoholics Anonymous World Services, 1952, p. 184), living out its commitment to putting personal aspirations and notoriety aside for the good of the fellowship.

This brief look explains the essence of the twelve steps and some of the traditions of A.A., a spiritual program of recovery from a "spiritual illness." Royce (1995) shows in fine detail how an alcoholic typically loses whatever sense of values and spirituality he may have possessed, as he follows the downward progression of the illness. And in recovery, according to Royce's analysis, regaining and rebuilding spiritual values is also traceable and progressive in an upward direction. The drinking, progressively more addicted alcoholic tends to become more and more isolated and alienated; the recovering individual must reach out to others. In doing so, he begins to form and build new and positive relationships. Clearly, this spiritual, social, and emotional rebuilding is the purpose of the Twelve Steps of A.A.

# WOMEN IN THE EARLY GROWTH
# OF ALCOHOLICS ANONYMOUS

An often neglected part of the growth and development of the early A.A., especially pertaining to its spirituality, is the role of women. Darrah (1992) has written a moving and intimate portrait of Roman Catholic Sister Mary Ignatia, dubbed the "Angel of Alcoholics Anonymous." In it she details the important and vital roles women played in the birth and growth of A.A., which in its early literature and practice was aimed almost entirely at male alcoholics. Anne Smith, Dr. Bob's wife, was a long-suffering and deeply spiritual woman who received numerous alcoholics into her home in the early days. Along with breakfast, she fed them quotes from Scripture and periods of meditation and prayer. She almost single-handedly began the work with wives of alcoholic men that later became "Alanon." Kurtz recalls from early accounts that Anne Smith was a constant support to the early Akron A.A. members. One of her favorite scriptural quotes was "God is love," and it apparently had a mantra-like effect on these alcoholics: "How it worked, her visitors did not know, but hearing those words from that woman always brought calm—and confidence that they would not drink that day" (Kurtz, 1991, p. 55). As an interesting note, Darrah quotes from Anne Smith's early Oxford Group journal: "How am I to live? A day at a time," presaging the universally important component, in A.A. recovery, of approaching abstinence and sobriety one day at a time (Darrah, 1992, p. 116). Bill Wilson said of this staunch supporter of A.A.: "A.A. might never have been, without Anne Smith" (Darrah, 1992, p. 130).

In the early days of A.A., women alcoholics who approached the groups caused some consternation. Wives of alcoholic men viewed them with some suspicion. Dr. Bob Smith is described as being somewhat cold at first toward the women alcoholics who approached him. Undoubtedly, the early members were reflecting the double standard of the general society, which treated male and female alcoholics quite differently. While men who changed their ways and sobered up were forgiven and encouraged, women who sought and found sobriety were seen as somehow immoral and lesser creatures (Darrah, 1992, pp. 123–124). Eventually, as it became clearer to all that "the only requirement for membership" was a "desire to stop drinking," women were gradually accepted. Anne Smith and Sister Ignatia were very helpful to the early women in recovery.

Sister Ignatia became quite an A.A. legend. Her contribution appears to have been great, on both a practical and a spiritual level. Born Della Mary Gavin of Cleveland, she became a member of the Sisters of Charity of St. Augustine, a religious congregation of the Catholic Church. Sister Ignatia had a difficult early life as a nun, obsessively working in her field of music and in the practice of self-denial and the spiritual life encouraged by her vows. She suffered a severe physical and mental breakdown in 1927, and her life was radically changed. She was forced to "surrender" in her own way, to give up entirely her career in music, and with it, much of the obsessive perfectionism of her early years. Darrah compares her with Bill Wilson and Dr. Bob Smith. "As in the case of the two men, Ignatia's surrender to her own collapse had precipitated acceptance, but wholeheartedly extending herself to others guaranteed her recovery" (Darrah, 1992, pp. 77–78). After her career change to hospital work, Sister Ignatia made the acquaintance of Dr. Smith. Before he had met with Bill Wilson and started the path toward his own sobriety, he was not sympathetic to other alcoholics. Knowing this, Ignatia had been circumventing policy at St. Thomas, "hiding" alcoholic patients in out-of-the-way rooms and corridors. (Alcoholic patients were notoriously bad risks for payment and were also considered poor prospects for successful treatment.)

Thus, when the early band of recovering souls needed a hospital-based friend, Ignatia was there. Starting first with a bed here or there, and eventually moving to a special, set-aside unit, Ignatia worked for years, building with Dr. Smith the first A.A.-based hospital treatment program. And that treatment program was a spiritual one. (Sister Ignatia would give departing patients a badge with a religious inscription, a "Sacred Heart" badge, and extract from them a promise that they would return the badge to her before drinking, if they decided sobriety was not for them.) This diminutive nun was perhaps the *original practitioner* of the concept of "tough love" in alcoholism treatment. Ignatia was a tremendous support, apparently, to Smith and his wife Anne, talking with one or another of them daily about the growing pains of the group or of individual alcoholics (Darrah, 1992, p. 119). At Sister Ignatia's funeral in 1963, Cleveland's hotels were filled with thousands of visitors, most recovering alcoholics, many of whom were celebrities, who returned to pay tribute to the woman they called "the Angel of A.A." (Darrah, 1992, pp. 2–4). Bill Wilson said, "The ministry of Dr. Bob, his wife Anne, Sister Ignatia and Akron's early-timers sets an example for the practice of A.A.'s Twelve Steps that will remain for all time" (Darrah, 1992, p. 113).

## PROBLEMS FOR WOMEN AND MINORITIES IN A.A. RECOVERY

There are in A.A., as in the larger society, certain individuals and groups who will tend to have serious difficulties with the traditional language and structure of the Twelve Steps. Their difficulties arise from a history of oppression, mostly by white male authority figures (Kasl, 1992). Such groups include women, racial minorities, gays and lesbians, and those recovering from spousal or childhood sexual and physical abuse. For people who have struggled throughout life with issues of power and helplessness, "surrender," "letting go and letting God," and making a list of character defects may well be contraindicated. Kasl described her disappointment and frustration in her own recovery experience, and her felt need for an approach more appropriate for herself as a woman. She also describes a warm reception for her ideas from many women and minorities, for whom the Twelve Steps and the A.A.-style fellowship were inadequate, or a poor fit, or even a quite negative experience. She has published her own reworking of the Twelve Steps, called "Sixteen Steps to Discovery and Empowerment" (Kasl, 1992, pp. 338–339). The approach she suggests, while respectful and mindful of the deep value of traditional A.A. recovery, attempts to go beyond that recovery milieu to a broader and more positive, self-affirming position. Many will benefit from a reading of Kasl's material. She herself speaks positively about Bill Wilson, suggesting that if he were still alive and active, he would continue to be "open-minded" about the need of the recovery movement, including A.A., to keep changing and growing.

## Alternatives to Alcoholics Anonymous

Kasl describes several current programs that provide alternatives for A.A. and the A.A. approach to alcoholism and addiction (Kasl, 1992, p. 163). Women for Sobriety was founded by Jean Kirkpatrick in 1976 and provides an alternate Thirteen Steps particularly for women. James Christopher initiated the Secular Organization for Sobriety in 1985. Rational Recovery, also dating from 1985, is based on Albert Ellis's rational-emotive therapy. All these approaches have multiple groups operating in a number of locations. In addition, the Schick-Shadel aversion therapy treatment for alcoholism has been in use since 1935 and has apparently been successful with many alcoholics. Limitations of scope and purpose prevent us from detailing these other programs and approaches, but they are well described in sources such as Kasl.

Kasl herself takes a moderate approach, encouraging women and others who do not feel at home or feel uncomfortable with the A.A. approach to look at alternatives and go at their own pace (Kasl, 1992, p. 286). Kasl's Sixteen Steps, while rich in positive, empowering, and growth-oriented concepts, will be appropriate only for some (as an alternate to the Twelve-Step Program), or may be appropriate only later in recovery (or "uncovery" and "discovery," as Kasl prefers) for some. The Sixteen Steps may appear complex and confusing to some readers.

A.A. does not work for everyone. The founders state in the "big book" that they do not pretend to have the only answer. They are just detailing what "worked for them." The humility suggested often in A.A. shows itself frequently and clearly in these early writings: "Our book is meant to be suggestive only. We realize we know only a little. God will constantly disclose more to you and to us" (Alcoholics Anonymous World Services, 1976, p. 164). And again, they did not say, "These are the steps you must take," but "These are the steps we took, which are suggested as a program of recovery" (Alcoholics Anonymous World Services, 1976, p. 59). Alcoholics Anonymous is definitely not defined by a book or a set of steps, though these may be considered essential: It is a living tradition, passed from one alcoholic woman or man to another. The founders were wise enough to know that alcoholics are far too independent, and far too varied in their personalities and needs, to be fitted into an exact cookie-cutter mold. A favorite among countless A.A. slogans (part of that oral tradition) is "Take what you want and leave the rest." One of the first women to recover in A.A. was Ethel M. She recounts a conversation she had, early in her recovery, with Anne Smith: "I used to think I was cowardly when things came up pertaining to the program that troubled me. I said 'Annie, am I being a coward because I lay those things away on the shelf and skip them?' She said, 'No, you are just being wise. If it isn't anything that is going to help you or anybody else, why should you become involved in it and get all disturbed about it?'" (Darrah, 1992, p. 127).

A gay male client with a theological background found himself daily irritated by vague and overly pious sentiments he was reading in an A.A. meditation book. In his A.A. home group, an elderly woman, sober for many years, smiled and said: "Take what you want, and leave the rest." Another client found himself confused at first, by very open-ended talk in his group, of belief in a higher power, and then, at the end of the meeting, all standing to recite the Lord's Prayer, which for him was an uncomfortable reminder of bygone days. When he voiced his discomfort, he was relieved to see no shock; a group member assured him that he was welcome to return no matter what his beliefs about God happened to be.

Female clients, both heterosexual and lesbian, have at times been offended by the male, sexist language of the big book, composed in the 1930s. Some of these clients may need a "spiritual program" more specifically attuned to their needs, such as those described by Kasl. Others may be able to grow and flourish within A.A through the living tradition of A.A., which will include sponsorship, frequent contacts with other recovering women and men, and discovery of specific literature and practices that help them. Clark (1987), writing five years before Kasl, makes a still-valid point: "A.A. is a working system, and . . . we still do not have enough data to support abandoning or tinkering with these steps" (Hanna, 1992, p. 169).

## Success of Alcoholics Anonymous for Many

As counselors and therapists, we see solid evidence that the Twelve-Step Program is working for many women, many ethnic and racial minorities, many gay men and lesbians. The program was designed for alcoholics; it appears to work for many of them, and for many addicts of various other types. When a history of sexual abuse or extreme physical abuse and oppression is present, Kasl (1992) makes the case that something more may be required (pp. 238–259). Some individuals may need specialized services.

An anonymous HIV-positive gay male writer discusses his experience with A.A. in very positive terms ("Never too Late", 1995, p. 167). He mentions the many "special interest" A.A. groups that exist in many communities: "men's groups, women's groups, gay/lesbian groups, . . . beginners' groups . . . groups for people with special affiliations such as doctors, lawyers, judges." These special interest A.A. groups serve as safe starting places for many newcomers, allowing them to feel comfortable talking about the whole range of their lives and their problems. For many minorities in A.A., such groups are extremely important, not just at the beginning but often throughout their long-term physical, mental, and spiritual recovery. In any large community in America today, Latino groups will undoubtedly be available, as will African-American groups, men's and women's groups, and gay and lesbian groups. The central office of A.A. in the community has a schedule of all meetings available, with information on specialized meetings. Another indisputable advantage of A.A. as a resource for recovery is its omnipresence. A small handbook is now available, with phone numbers of central A.A. offices in virtually every city of the United States and communities in some 130 other countries (*The Anonymous Press*, 1993).

Alcoholics Anonymous members often remark that "everyone has her or his own program; what works for you may not work for me." In an early incident, an atheist member shocked and disturbed some others by talking in an aggressively negative way about faith in God. When some told him to get out, he reminded them of their Third Tradition: "The only requirement for membership is a desire to stop drinking" (Alcoholics Anonymous World Services, 1952, p. 139). He was allowed to remain, and, the story goes, changed his ways somewhat later. But the point is that he remained in the group (Alcoholics Anonymous World Services, 1952, pp. 143–145). As therapists, we may have firsthand information about this flexibility and openness in A.A. We may need to inform our clients of it. A.A. reflects the general culture in many ways. It professes "progress, not perfection" (Alcoholics Anonymous World Services, 1976, p. 60). And as an imperfect human society, A.A. will at times reflect the negative aspects of culture, like sexism and racism. In addition, individual A.A. groups have great autonomy. From time to time, groups may stray from purity of purpose and from an even-handed, loving reception to newcomers. If we hear of such things, we can help our clients with information about other groups, ways of accessing more appropriate A.A. contacts, or other forms of recovery. We hope this chapter will be an aid to counselors in such work. "Ultimately, what counts is that clinicians acknowledge the truth that there are many, many ways to find and define God/Higher Power and many, many paths to recovery" (Finnegan & McNally, 1995, pp. 47–48).

## CONCLUSIONS FOR COUNSELORS

"A.A. was developed as a series of clinical trials growing out of the failure of medicine, religion, psychiatry and psychology to provide effective long-term treatment for alcoholics" (Chappel, 1990, p. 482). Before A.A., there was little success on any large scale in treating those dependent on alcohol. And, while clearly there are many failures, there are more success stories in the twelve-step programs.

In the early days after A.A. came into being, "most psychiatrists and psychologists ignored it, discounted it or were baffled by it" (Keller, 1994, p. 109). Initially, psychotherapists were cold to the concepts of declaring defeat and invoking a higher power. They tended to view alcoholism as a symptom, not as an illness in itself. However, A.A. did not come about unnoticed and disregarded by mental health professionals or by the clergy, as we already know. Dr. Harry Tiebout offered early criticism and support. When Bill Wilson sent draft copies of the book that came to be titled *Alcoholics Anonymous* to numerous professionals for their comments, one source, a psychiatrist described only as Dr. Howard, had an extremely important impact on the final copy. Howard, according to Kurtz, suggested much of the softer, less imperative language (e.g., for "you must do," "this is what we did") (Kurtz, 1991, p. 75).

Keller (1994) shows that a turning point for professionals came in 1940, with the inception of the Yale Center for Alcohol Studies (later moved to Rutgers University). The Yale Center presented professionals with the thesis (largely unaccepted prior to that time) that alcoholism is a disease that needs treatment. The A.A. concept of alcoholism as a *spiritual* illness was foreign to most researchers, however. Yet, almost from the beginning, these scientists at Yale included on their staff an individual known as "Lefty," who was an alcoholic recovering in and familiar with A.A. While the professionals did not themselves deal with spiritual elements in recovery, Lefty did—with regularity. And Keller reminds us that today many scientific researchers, physicians, and therapists see that there can be an integration of the scientific and the spiritual in their own lives. "For some it has come in their own recovery through the spiritual program of Alcoholics Anonymous. One of the co-founders of Alcoholics Anonymous was a physician" (Keller, 1994, p. 111.)

There is strong support for the notion that only an experience of a spiritual nature is effective with most alcoholics and addicts in achieving any long-standing sobriety or abstinence (see Carl Jung's opinion, quoted earlier in this chapter). Important studies (Khantzian & Mack, 1994; Vaillant, 1983; Vaillant & Milofsky, 1982) have shown that A.A. involvement is in numerous cases more successful with alcoholics than psychotherapy and is related frequently to long-term abstinence and recovery. Carroll (1993) finds a strong correlation between the spiritual practices of step 11 in the A.A. program and both long-term sobriety and scores on the Purpose-In-Life (PIL) scale (Crumbaugh & Maholick, 1964), an instrument designed to measure a person's sense of meaning. For many addicts, the spiritual practices they may adopt in their recovery are a manifestation of growth. "For addicts, an integrated spirituality can be a continuing recognition of their limitations. . . . Part of this struggle is realizing that we are, at times, unable to do everything for ourselves; that maturation involves transcending our own thoughts, patterns, and feelings. It is this transcendence beyond the exclusive self that is most healing for the addict" (Clemmens, 1997, p. 58).

We have seen that the main thrust, the substance of the twelve steps, is a turning to a power greater than any individual, as a member of a community of recovering people ("*We* admitted we were powerless. . . . *We* came to believe . . .") in which the "only requirement for membership is a desire to stop drinking." Part of the process involves "cleaning house" and regaining personal values, repairing relationships damaged by abuse and selfishness. Many alcoholics and addicts, as we know, find themselves seeking psychotherapy, either before, or more often, after they begin to attempt a sober life. Some will find success through the twelve-step programs, others will not. All have a right to our objective support of their efforts to recover, on all levels. "Our task, as therapists, is to support this development and to provide our clients with behavioral observations" (Clemmens, 1997, p. 59). Green et al. (1998) take this a step further: "Discussing the ways in which an individual might find a Higher Power, as well as discussing past experiences that might interfere with such a task, can be an important part of therapy" (p. 331).

Because so much support for sobriety and so much relative success in sobriety is connected with maintaining A.A. contacts, it is no surprise that most treatment facilities make twelve-step meetings and contacts a major part of their programs. It is our hope that this chapter will provide some insight, information, and encouragement for counselors dealing with clients who are practicing the spirituality of the twelve steps. The references at the end of this chapter will provide much detail on A.A. recovery and alternative programs.

## A CASE STUDY

The following case study illustrates some of the links between counseling and the Twelve-Step Program of A.A., including some of the organization's spiritual practices and values.

*Bud is a 53-year-old white male, married to Andrea for 27 years. They have four adult children; the three older children, all male, are out of the home and married. Only one of the three is living in the immediate area near Bud and Andrea. The youngest child, female, is in her final year at a local college and living with her parents. (She is quite busy with work and school, and according to Bud, is rarely at home.) Bud is a recovering alcoholic, sober for 14 years. His sobriety time falls into three periods, with brief relapses at the two-year point and the 10-year point. He has been an active member of A.A. for nearly the whole 14-year period of his sobriety. He has a sponsor and has tried to work the twelve-step program to the best of his ability, particularly during the past four years. Bud is a chemical engineer with a large, international corporation. He has worked for this company for 23 years, has a graduate degree, a good position, and a good reputation with the company. During his drinking years (the first nine years with his employer) he almost lost his position on several occasions because of his frequent absences from work and other infractions of company policy. He was of such value to the company, however, that management was willing to overlook many of his problem behaviors for some time. His superiors at work eventually had an important role in Bud's becoming sober. According to his account, his immediate supervisor gave him an ultimatum, which resulted in Bud's seeking treatment for alcoholism 14 years ago. At that time, Bud and Andrea had four young children and their lives were increasingly* chaotic because of Bud's drinking. Andrea had taken the children and moved to an aunt's home on two occasions, the last of which lasted for several months. Bud was never violent, but he was deeply morose at some times and very irritable at others when he was drinking. He became verbally abusive during these periods. He had been a faithful husband and an attentive father in earlier years, but in his years of drinking he began staying out late into the evening, drinking with associates from work. Bud was very proud (and still is) of his accomplishments in his profession. (He was responsible for patented procedures that earned his company millions of dollars.) When confronted with a make-or-break ultimatum, he willingly entered treatment. He states now that he had known for some time that "things were out of hand," but he had been unable to gain control of his life. In the alcoholism treatment center, counselors helped Bud focus on several problems. He was first detoxified, helped medically in his withdrawal from dependence on alcohol (which had started as an occasional binge and progressed to frequent bouts of drunkenness and then to a daily abusive habit). Counselors required participation in Bud's treatment, first from Andrea, and then also from the children. Relationships in the family had suffered extensive damage, and there was a need to work with everyone, especially Andrea and the two older boys, then 11 and 10 years old, to begin reestablishing open communication and trust. For almost two years, periodic visits to a family therapist were necessary. This work apparently paid off very well, as Bud enjoys excellent relationships with Andrea and all his four children at present. Equally important to this ongoing family harmony is Bud's continued sobriety. Other issues that emerged in Bud's initial treatment were post-traumatic stress disorder and depression. Between high school and college, Bud was drafted into the U.S. Army and served one year in Vietnam in the infantry. He saw extensive combat and was slightly wounded in an ambush in which several of his friends were killed. Like many veterans of combat, Bud had talked very little about his experience and the terrible night when his friends died. He had frequent nightmares about that encounter and other very stressful experiences from the war. Later, he saw his progressive abuse of alcohol as a way of blocking out his feelings of anger, grief, and guilt over surviving the ambush. Bud came from a stable but emotionally repressed home. In his family, when members were disturbed about something, they kept it to themselves and "dealt with it." As a result, Bud's habit was to keep his feelings to himself, whether trivial (a minor irritation with Andrea or one of the children) or major (his burden of grief and self-blaming from wartime experiences). As a result, he often suffered from symptoms of depression: bouts of "the blues," sleep disorder, self-destructive feelings.

Bud was initially connected with A.A. through his treatment program and became a faithful participant in the fellowship thereafter. He found that peace was returning to his family life, and management was pleased with his renewed productivity at work. His religious beliefs, largely lost during his transition to adulthood, returned to a new, different, but important place in his life. He began a daily habit of self-examination, meditation, and prayer, encouraged by *his A.A. sponsor. Bud's first relapse was brief (under three days), and was trig-gered by a family argument between his mother (a controlling person with whom Bud had had a rocky relationship) and Andrea. He quickly saw the dis-astrous implications of his renewed drinking and returned to the A.A. program and sobriety.*

*While family tensions were adequately dealt with through family therapy in the early years of his sobriety, Bud's own tendency to repress his feelings and become depressed were not getting adequate treatment. He was clearly helped by discussing some things with his sponsor and some A.A. friends, but he found himself slipping further into depression as the years went by. His father and older brother died and all his sons left home within a four-year period—a traumatic time for Bud. He experienced a crisis of depression, which precipi-tated his most recent and most serious relapse, approximately four years ago. Bud reached a point of depression in which he felt quite hopeless, despite his sobriety and continued A.A. participation. He had strong suicidal feelings and began drinking again. The relapse lasted about 10 days. Through the interven-tion of Andrea and her aunt, also an A.A. member with many years of sobriety, Bud was persuaded to see his doctor, who prescribed a brief hospital stay and an antidepressant medication. Bud responded very well to these interventions and followed up his hospital stay with continued psychotherapy, with a psy-chiatrist and a licensed counselor. Bud found that some of his anger was directed at God, and much of it at himself. He was able to unburden himself in a fifth-step "confession" with an A.A. sponsor, who happened to be a member of the clergy. He has experienced progress in expressing his feelings more read-ily and feels more firmly entrenched in sobriety and in emotional health than ever before. One of his therapists encouraged Bud to make fuller use of the forum of A.A., participating regularly in discussion groups and talking more frequently with his sponsor. Bud is seen as a positive, contributing member of society in his family, in his workplace, and in A.A.*

## QUESTIONS FOR REFLECTION

1. How are counseling/psychotherapy and Twelve-Step Recovery mutually supportive? How might they clash?
2. Is A.A. spiritually neutral? Is A.A. "an enemy or a friend" to most religious beliefs and/or practices?
3. How might the Twelve-Step approach be applied to clients who are not chemically dependent? How might you utilize this approach in your per-sonal and professional life?
4. What might you recommend as an alternative for those addicted clients who have strong negative reactions to key parts of A.A. spirituality, such as total admission of defeat?

5. Some have accused Twelve-Step programs of symptom substitution—for example, pointing to caffeine in coffee, nicotine in cigarettes, and sugar in foods at meetings. Do you agree? Why or why not?

# REFERENCES

Alcoholics Anonymous World Services. (1952). *Twelve steps and twelve traditions.* New York: Author.

Alcoholics Anonymous World Services. (1957). *Alcoholics anonymous comes of age.* New York: Author.

Alcoholics Anonymous World Services. (1976). *Alcoholics anonymous: The story of how many thousands of men and women have recovered from alcoholism.* New York: Author.

Alcoholics Anonymous World Services. (1981). *Twelve steps and twelve traditions* (rev. ed.). New York: Author.

Alcoholics Anonymous World Services. (1985). *The Bill W.–Carl Jung letters: Best of the grapevine.* New York: Author.

Alcoholics Anonymous World Services. (1990). *Daily reflections.* New York: Author.

*The anonymous press mini-edition of Alcoholics Anonymous.* (1993). Croton Falls, NY: I.W.S.

Berenson, D. (1990). A systemic view of spirituality: God and twelve-step programs as resources in family therapy. *Journal of Strategic and Systemic Therapies, 9*(1), 59–70.

Booth, L. (1987). Alcoholism and the fourth and fifth steps of Alcoholics Anonymous. *Journal of Psychoactive Drugs, 19*(3), 260–274.

Booth, L. (1995). A new understanding of spirituality. In R. J. Kus (Ed.), *Spirituality and chemical dependency* (pp. 9–17). New York: Haworth.

Chappel, J. N. (1990). Spirituality is not necessarily religion: A commentary on "Divine intervention and the treatment of chemical dependency." *Journal of Substance Abuse, 2,* 481–483.

Clark, H. W. (1987). On professional therapists and Alcoholics Anonymous. *Journal of Psychoactive Drugs, 19*(3), 233–242.

Clemmens, M. C. (1997). *Getting beyond sobriety: Clinical approaches to long-term recovery.* San Francisco: Jossey-Bass.

Crumbaugh, J. C., & Maholick, L. T. (1964). An experimental study in existentialism: The psychometric approach to Frankl's concept of noogenic neurosis. *Journal of Clinical Psychology, 20,* 200–207.

Darrah, M. C. (1992). *Sister Ignatia: Angel of Alcoholics Anonymous.* Chicago: Loyola University Press.

Finnegan, D. G., & McNally, E. B. (1995). Defining God or a higher power. In R. J. Kus (Ed.), *Spirituality and chemical dependency* (pp. 39–48). New York: Haworth Press.

Green, L. L., Thompson-Fullilove, M., & Fullilove, R. E. (1998). Stories of spiritual awakening: The nature of spirituality in recovery. *Journal of Substance Abuse Treatment, 19*(4), 325–331.

Hanna, F. J. (1992). Reframing spirituality: Alcoholics Anonymous, the twelve steps, and the mental health counselor. *Journal of Mental Health Counseling, 14*(2), 166–179.

James, W. (1929). *The varieties of religious experience, a study in human nature: Being the Gifford lectures on natural religion delivered at Edinburgh in 1901–1902 by William James.* New York: Modern Library.

Jourard, S. (1964). *The transparent self: Self-disclosure and well-being*. New York: Van Nostrand.

Kasl, C. D.. (1992). *Many roads, one journey: Moving beyond the twelve steps*. New York: HarperPerennial.

Keller, J. E. (1994). Spirituality in treatment and recovery. In G. S. Howard & P. E. Nathan (Eds.), *Alcohol use and misuse by young adults* (pp. 109–132). Notre Dame, IN: University of Notre Dame Press.

Khantzian, E., & Mack, J. (1994). How AA works and why it's important for clinicians to understand. *Journal of Substance Abuse Treatment, 11*, 77–92.

Kinney, M. G., & Close, L. M. (1995). Steps eight and nine of Alcoholics Anonymous. In R. J. Kus (Ed.), *Spiritual and chemical dependency* (pp. 91–99). New York: Haworth.

Kurtz, E. (1991). *Not-God: A history of Alcoholics Anonymous*. Center City, MN: Hazelden Educational Materials.

Never too late: The spiritual recovery of an alcoholic with HIV. In R. J. Kus (Ed.), *Spiritual and chemical dependency* (pp. 167–168). New York: Haworth Press.

Royce, J. E. (1995). The effects of alcoholism and recovery on spirituality. In R. J. Kus (Ed.), *Spirituality and chemical dependency* (pp. 19–37). New York: Haworth.

Smith, D. E. (1994). A.A. recovery and spirituality: An addiction medicine perspective. *Journal of Substance Abuse Treatment, 11*(2), 111–112.

*The twelve steps: A spiritual journey*. (1988). San Diego: RPI Publishing.

Vaillant, G. (1983). *The natural history of alcoholism*. Cambridge, MA: Harvard University Press.

Vaillant, G., & Milofsky, E. (1982). Natural history of male alcoholism: Paths to recovery. *Archives General Psychiatry, 39*, 127–133.

# COUNSELOR BELIEF SYSTEM SELF-ASSESSMENT

We have discussed at length the need for a counselor to be astute in including the client's belief system in the assessment of the client, with the end goal being better clinical services. Additionally, the counselor needs to be cognizant of his or her belief system, not only to avoid issues of countertransference but to be present in an I-thou relationship during the course of therapy (see Buber, 1970). We believe that this relationship lies at the heart of the therapeutic process and is elemental to client improvement. Many have argued a similar humanistic-existential stance (Maslow, 1968; May, 1953, 1989; Rogers, 1942, 1951, 1957, 1961). Obviously, the counselor is as much a pilgrim as the client and, thus, must attend to her or his pilgrimage to be of the most help to clients. We should note that this counselor self-examination stance is supported by the spiritual competencies (see Appendix D) of the Association of Spiritual, Ethical, and Religious Values in Counseling (of the American Counseling Association).

What follows is our suggested outline for a counselor's self-assessment of personal beliefs. Certainly, we are aware that some counselors have no particular religious or spiritual orientation, but this structured exercise could nonetheless be of value to those individuals as well as the ones who believe in something beyond themselves. More generally, we believe that the "searching and fearless moral inventory of ourselves" suggested for alcoholics in the fourth step of A.A. (see Appendix B) is more or less essential to any thoughtful life.

We encourage those who choose to participate in this exercise to discuss any emerging archethemes that we described in Chapter 2. For instance, in the example that follows, the participant is concerned with mortality issues, balancing what he terms the scientist versus the artist in him, his psychotherapy and spiritual direction, his "life lessons," his search for meaning, his concern for what is sacred in life, his quest for understanding and compassion in various venues, his use of humor and play, and his attempts at finding meaning in relationships. These concerns illustrate several of the archethemes including finite and infinite, mythic and factual, lost and found, saying "yes," meaning, concern with the sacred, compassion, transcendence, and love.

We present a self-assessment format containing five areas of questioning: (1) My Introductory Statement; (2) Life Theme; (3) Life Influences; (4) Life's Lessons; and (5) Conclusions. (A copy of the form appears in Appendix E.) Some counselors benefit from having another therapist perform an extended interview to elicit a somewhat "free-associative" response; others prefer reacting to the questions in writing. There is no one way to complete the self-assessment. We encourage the respondent to intuit the method he or she prefers. We understand that the assessment is a "snapshot" of the counselor at a particular moment in time, subject to change. After all, we are teleological beings, in a process of becoming, as we continue our own pilgrimages.

## THE FORMAT

1. *Introductory Statement.* We view this section as an opportunity for the counselor to preface what follows. He or she may find it useful to state the purpose of participating in the assessment. Or the counselor may wish to tell a personal story, perhaps from childhood. We intentionally leave room for any and all types of responses.

2. *Life Theme.* What theme or themes run throughout my life? What common threads weave in and out? Perhaps I notice Jungian archetypes (Jung, 1980), such as my hero side or shadow side. Perhaps I see themes of anxiety or depression. Would I then agree with the poet Yeats, who wrote, "Fortunately, I have a prevailing sense of tragedy to sustain me through these brief moments of joy"? Or maybe I discern patterns of satisfaction, contentment, grounding, and centering that affect my self-esteem—what Branden (1994) refers to as "the reputation I have of myself."

3. *Life Influences.* As I review my personal developmental history, what masters have influenced me? Masters may include religious figures, prominent people in our field, and other major figures. Further, what mentors have had an impact on who I am? These people are personally known to me and have provided guidance and support to me during periods of my life. Finally, who are my friends who have nurtured me in my life's journey? We note here that family (both by birth and by choice) are included in this category. We suggest that the counselor act here in some sense as reporter, gleaning the who? what? when? where? and how? Review contacts and kind memories.

4. *Life's Lessons.* What, then, are the lessons I have learned from my years on earth? Try to be brief: Put the lessons in a short declaratory statement; include with this statement a story supporting each lesson.

5. *Personal Conclusions.* Finally, as I review this exercise in self-assessment, what conclusions can I draw? How shall I pass them on? Is there anything I haven't been asked in the assessment that would be important to know? (We suggest asking clients this same question; invariably, it generates additional pertinent information.)

# CASE STUDY: A LIFE IN PROCESS

What follows is one example of our suggested format for the counselor to use in assessing his or her belief system. There are many ways to do such an assessment. In this particular instance, the individual—a counselor educator—chose to express his views as if he were presenting his final lecture.

## *1. Introductory Statement*

*As a naïve and impressionistic undergraduate student in the late 60s, I was rather taken with the tradition of professors offering their "last lecture." Instructions were simple: Imagine that you were to give the very last lecture of your career. What would you say?*

*Following in the footsteps of those who attempted that task, I present here my last lecture, so to speak. What would I offer to those entering the field of counseling and therapy in the way of lessons, guidelines, and experience? How might I pass the torch to those beginning their professional journey? What have I gleaned from those master teachers and mentors and friends who have greatly impacted my life? How might I synthesize and share this knowledge with others? What seeds can I plant? What seeds have been planted in me?*

*I focus on the issue of breathing, to consider its actual and symbolic importance. I refer to a quote attributed to the essayist Emerson, which, for me, distills the essence of the helping professions: "To know even one life has breathed easier, because you have lived." This, Emerson states, is to have succeeded. From here, my therapeutic journey focuses on those who have been influential in my professional—and personal—life. Three categories of persons emerge: masters of the psychotherapeutic discipline, who usually have influenced me from a distance; mentors, who have subtly and not so subtly nurtured and guided me; and friends, who are there to dissuade and persuade. What, I ask, have those persons taught me? Years of conscious and unconscious thought result in some life guidelines for me as a professional and as a person.*

*My hope is to assess my professional journey, tracing it to the source, realizing others have their own unique journeys and paths. Moreover, I must trust myself, reflect, and pause as I continue in my quest for personal and professional wholeness. I view this process as balancing two inherent parts of me: the scientist, who skeptically demands tangible and verifiable evidence; and the artist, who accepts life intuitively, spiritually, and with a sense of awe and wonder. It is the artist in me who ponders Jung's (1933, p. 264) words:*

> Among all my patients in the second half of life—that is to say, over thirty-five—there has not been one whose problem in the last resort was not that of finding a religious outlook on life. It is safe to say that everyone of them feels ill because he lost that which the living religions of every age have given to their followers, and none of them have been really healed who did not regain his religious outlook.

*Conversely, it is the scientist in me who doubtingly dares to pray Cardinal Newman's prayer: "God, if there is a God, . . . Save my soul, if I have a soul." It is the very same scientist in me who cites Albert Ellis:*

> Although the probability is exceptionally low that any supernatural entities, such as a personal God, exist, this hypothesis cannot be clearly falsified, and therefore one may rationally believe in God's existence. But anyone who is absolutely convinced that God personally cares for him or her, has nothing to do in life than to spend tens of thousands of hours specifically spying on his or her activities and arranging for great rewards or severe penalties for these actions, is pretty damned crazy! (Ellis, 1995, p. 2)

## 2. Life Theme

*"What would I say to people if this were my last lecture?"*—*I've chosen to use that concept, and I've thought I'd talk about* breathing. *I got that idea a number of years ago when I gave a stress management class at a local university, and a guest lecturer, the wife of our department chair, discussed yoga and meditation. She began her talk by saying, "Practitioners of Eastern religions tell us that we are allocated a certain number of breaths, and that's that. These wise persons advise us to use these breaths wisely." That led me to think, ponder, about all of those people—ancient and modern—who remind us to "consider breathing."*

*For instance, in the Judeo-Christian tradition, the writer of the Creation story says: "The Lord God formed man of dust from the ground and breathed into his nostrils the breath of life, and man became a living being." This is certainly the inspiration for the hymn, "Breathe on Me, Breath of God." In a more modern context, the environmentalists describe the tropical rainforests as the "lungs of the world" and warn us against destroying them wantonly. They claim that the forests' destruction would lead to our demise. In our field, our own Abraham Maslow cites air as the most basic of human needs in his famous "Hierarchy of Needs." As a practitioner of clinical hypnosis, I have to put in a word for that modality here. In hypnotherapy and imagery, we ask clients to take a few long, slow, deep breaths to relax them, either as an induction technique or a deepening technique; it is also useful in anxiety and stress reduction.*

*Think of our expressions involving breathing: "It takes my breath away" or "It left me breathless." I think there was a movie named* Breathless. *Anthropologist Jacob Bronowski (1976) offers these words of wonderment: "Sooner or later, everyone of us breathes an atom that has been breathed before by anyone you can think of who has lived before: Michaelangelo, George Washington or Moses."*

*On December 7, 1992, about 6:45 in the evening, eastern standard time, on* NBC News *with Tom Brokaw, I watched as a small Somali girl painfully drew her last breaths in the arms of her father. She and the man's wife and his other children died from hunger and tuberculosis; in this case the father had no tears and the small girl died in front of me, in my living room.*

*Quite conversely, I joyously witnessed my two little nephews and my little grandson draw some of their first breaths. I felt a sense of communion at that point with the Universal. I was a participant in the great pageant of human history, and in holding them I held life itself, and I knew mystery. I was also privileged to be present and holding her hand as my mother breathed her last breaths and gave up her ghost. I, too, felt the warmth leave my father's body about an hour or two after he took his final breaths. Death became personal at that time, and yet I wasn't afraid.*

## 3. Life Influences

As I reflect on those who have assisted me in "breathing easier," I arrive at three categories of persons—the masters, my mentors, and my friends. There is some overlap among them, but I would like to consider these categories discretely.

### A. Masters

*These are the great historical and religious figures, such as Jesus Christ or Buddha, Gandhi, Martin Luther King, Jr.—those people who, according to Lawrence Kohlberg, operate on principles of conscience. In our own field, such figures are Freud, Adler, Jung, Erik Erikson, Rogers, and others. Usually, we aren't privileged to know these masters personally, but we come to appreciate them as they talk to us from their books, for example. However, they do impact our professional and personal lives, and often intimately. Fortuitously, I have been privileged to have met such masters as Bruno Bettelheim, Albert Ellis, R. D. Laing, Rollo May, Joseph Wolpe, and Virginia Satir, among others. In fact, I sat in a little workshop with Virginia Satir—she and I were both students in a hypnosis workshop for sports performance. During the workshop I gave her a mint and she thanked me profusely. About a week later I saw her in the Phoenix airport, and she thanked me again for the mint. The fact that Dr. Satir bothered to remember me, let alone thank me for a rather minor offering, has stuck with me to this day.*

*But I must admit it was Carl Rogers—his books, his workshops—that had the most profound impact upon my training and myself. Rogers reinforced the importance of the relationship with other people, especially in the counseling situation. More than techniques, it's the relationship the counselor establishes with the client that's most important. I had an opportunity to personally thank Carl Rogers for inspiring me professionally. I ran into him in an elevator—he was an old man at this point. It was a couple of years before he died—this was 1985—and I had a chance to thank him for the impact he had had upon me. I recall at that time being very impressed with the clarity of his eyes and how they appeared to see into me as a person. However, as a caveat to all this, I'm reminded to keep these people in the context of their times, both historical and personal; keep them in perspective and don't deify them.*

## B. Mentors

*The second category of people who have helped me breathe easier in my life are my mentors. This category includes many persons, such as teachers I've had, therapists, colleagues, and some very special friends. I can think of my therapist, my spiritual director, a couple of former bosses, and a couple of very special friends. Often I have not realized the impact they've had on me until later, even when it was a very powerful impact. Sometimes my mentors have been quite unexpected, such as clients, or students or someone with whom I've had casual but memorable contact. Some mentors may be internal, at least in my case, such as my "wise old man" figure and my "sprite," which have emerged during the course of my own psychotherapy.*

## C. Friends

*My final category would be my friends. According to one person, "Friends are the greatest gift of all." Two qualities emerge in the people whom I consider friends: loyalty and integrity. I'm so fortunate to have such wonderful friends! How many times these precious persons have helped me breathe easier!*

## 4. Life Lessons

*What does all this mean? As I reflect on the masters, mentors, and friends who have assisted me in breathing easier, a few simple lessons for living have emerged. These are my personal lessons, but I share them with you for your consideration. Let me remind you that I must put energy and work into these— they do not come easy for me. They take intensive effort at times, especially when I find I'm compromised. They represent my attempt to synthesize 20 years of formal education, 12 years of personal psychotherapy, 6 years of spiritual direction, 20 years of a regimen of physical exercise, and 52 years of living in this reality. Reality is what theologian Paul Tillich describes as "what we bump into from time to time."*

*These are my little lessons for living, which mean something to me. Number one is this:* **"Learn from all experiences."** *Be open to lessons from clients and students and anyone who has something to teach. Certainly, we're never too old to learn. I can think of my oldest student—75 years old—who always offered wonderful insights, asked good questions, and did very well in the course. I can also think of the older man who came up to me once after I'd given an hour-long talk on stress management. I had pontificated for an hour, but this man came up to me after the talk and gave me a wonderful, brief insight. He said, "You know, one thing that I've really learned in all of my living is that most of the things I worried about never happened." That certainly makes sense. I can also think of Milton Erickson—the father of hypnosis in this country—who reminds us to learn from our clients and stay out of the road. I am also aware that Ignatius Loyola, founder of the Jesuits, centuries earlier admonished his followers to "enter the others' door and exit through your door." Another lesson is to honor those with whom we're working. After all, are we not privileged to enter the I-thou relationship with these fellow human beings?*

*My second little lesson in life is this:* **"Life isn't fair, it just is."** *I'm not ready to give in to the negative dimension of life, as expressed by a former colleague, who said, "Life is nothing more than rearranging deck chairs on the Titanic." Nor do I dismiss the possibility of a higher power because of life's apparent cruelty at times, as Freud did. Freud said that if there were such a thing as God, he'd "hold up the cancerous bone of a child in front of God's face and ask, 'Why?'" I remind myself during trying times to read Rabbi Harold Kushner's (1981) book,* When Bad Things Happen to Good People. *Ragtime pianist Eubie Blake said, "Be grateful for luck, pay the thunder no mind, listen to the birds, and don't hate nobody." Blake was 100 years old when he spoke these words.*

*Lesson three:* **"Don't take life too seriously—have fun."** *View life from a child's point of reference, with awe, and wonder, and humor. I have a great love of fireworks—probably a Jungian archetype at work within me—and I recently watched a wonderful fireworks display after a baseball game downtown. When the game ended, I noticed many adults dragging their children out of the stadium, in a hurry, willing to skip the fireworks so they could avoid a traffic jam on their drive home. What a missed opportunity! I wanted to tell these people to have fun with life! Enjoy the present moment and don't worry so much about what's coming down the road. One question I ask myself in trying times is this: "In 50 years, will this matter?" In 50 years, what will matter?*

*Lesson four: I had a hectic time when I started my job. It was the first time I'd ever come into a job as the head of anything. I'd always started from the bottom and worked my way up; it was quite a different experience. I had students, faculty, and staff coming to me for information and forms of which I had no knowledge. Also, during that time my office was, literally, a former storage closet. My computer, containing 500 files, was stolen from this office.*

*These were disconcerting times for me, to say the least. During this period I was ready to check myself into the Cleveland Psychiatric Institute!*

*At a break during this hubbub, I checked my phone machine, and a good friend had left me a message. He said, "Chris, this is Gene calling, and I have a message for you. This is the message: 'One day at a time.'" It had a great impact on me then, and has subsequently. This message is nothing new. The twelve-step programs advocate it, and they certainly have a religious base. I'd also like to insert a corollary to "One day at a time;" that corollary is the philosopher Horace's admonition, "Carpe diem." Seize that day! Don't just take things one day at a time, but seize the day and work with it. This is the only arena you have for work—the present—not the past, and not the future.*

*Item five on my little list—"Don't be afraid to ask for help," from a friend or a mentor. I've been known to recall the presence of my "higher power" or ask for my archetypical "wise old man" or "sprite" to emerge, to assist me in my work.*

*Six—many of us have this one, I've noticed. I have some difficulty with it, so it's one I'm working on: "Don't be afraid to get mad." Life has maddening situations. Some people don't assist in others' breathing. They choke other people, or they smother them—neither one too helpful. These people need some yelling at. Appropriate yelling, certainly.*

*Seven is to "Say thanks." Say thanks to those mentors, masters, or friends. Tell them what they've meant to you. I find, personally, that this is very awkward to do. I find that I go around telling everybody else about how important somebody is, but never thank him or her personally. So, that is something that I have been working on as well.*

*Eight is to "Give beauty." Give beauty. Freud talks about Eros versus Thanatos. The life force versus the death force. I think about creators versus destroyers, and I think about all those who create. Don't underestimate your ability to give beauty, either. Recently, I went to a performance of the Cleveland Ballet. A subgroup within the ballet, "Dancing Wheels," is made up of wheelchair-bound persons who, in spite of their physical limitations, dance. During that performance of 15 persons in wheelchairs, I noticed a six-year-old girl in a wheelchair dancing with the help of other Cleveland Ballet dancers, who had full use of their abilities. She was lifted in her chair and moved about on the stage. This little girl had an absolutely awe-inspiring look on her face. I noticed people in the audience, many of whom who also had disabilities, being inspired by her. In our field I would say, "Give your therapy as a gift." It is a beautiful gift.*

*Nine is to "take care of yourself." Every time I get on a plane, the flight attendant says, and I quote, "If there's a drop in air pressure, an oxygen mask will drop from an overhead compartment. Place the mask on your face first, before assisting others." You can't help other people if you're compromised. Put that mask on and breathe in before you assist others in their breathing.*

*Ten—**"If you're compromised, get your therapy, if needed."** This is not a new argument. Most certainly, I think of the great commandment— "Love God, love your neighbor, as yourself." You can't love anybody else if you don't love yourself. When my mother died several years ago—I recall not much of that experience—I was in a line at the funeral home, during the wake, two nights for four hours, and I just recall a blur of people going by except for one old woman. I don't remember who she was, frankly. I'm sure she was one of my mother's friends. She came up to me and said, "You know, your Mom left the only thing you can leave in this life—a good name." Leave a good name. Be an inspiration to other people. In fact, did you know that the derivation of the word inspiration itself is from the Latin word inspirare, meaning "to breathe in"?*

*And, finally, **"share."** This includes sharing of yourself. Many years ago I worked with a family including several children. Both parents were alcoholics. The mother was dying in the hospital from cirrhosis of the liver. The father had lost his job and as a consequence was unable to take care of the children. The children were being removed by the local authorities, and necessarily so. It was a very sad time for all of us who were involved, but most especially for them. I drove out to the house on one bitterly cold November day and the house was in shambles. As I pulled into the driveway the littlest and youngest of the children came out to greet me. This five-year-old emerged in tattered clothes and said, " I got a present for you." I said, "What is it?" He removed his little torn tennis shoe and pulled out a stick of Juicy Fruit gum and gave me half of it.*

## 5. Personal Conclusions

*I guess I'm not asking us to share to that extent, but to share our gifts, and talents, and skills. To pass the torch to others. To share of ourselves. To not play the counselor role so much as to be a counselor. Tangentially, somebody once asked me, "How can I tell if a student is going to be a good counselor?" One way I tell is by how they treat the secretary—that makes a big difference. I end as I began: focusing on breathing. I ask myself: How many breaths have I breathed since beginning this exercise, and how am I going to use those remaining?*

# In Sum

We encourage the counselor to examine himself or herself with care, honesty, and kindness. It is our firm belief that only by such an examination can we come to prize the client in Rogers's sense. Only then can we participate in the present I-thou relationship, which is the essence of psychotherapy.

## Questions for Reflection

1. Should therapists perform self-examinations regarding their beliefs? Some training schools require therapists to undergo therapy as part of their training. Should a belief assessment on the part of the counseling professional be mandated?
2. When and where do you think therapists should pray with their clients (if at all)?
3. Does the source for meaning in life come from within? Or is the source for meaning found elsewhere, as in a particular philosophy or theology? Or is it a combination?
4. How does one interface his or her spirituality with professional practice?
5. What does the therapist do when his or her beliefs clash with those of a client? Give possible case examples. How do the professional ethics codes address this issue?

## References

Branden, N. (1994). *Six pillars of self-esteem*. New York: Bantam.

Bronowski, J. (1976). *The ascent of man*. Boston : Little, Brown.

Buber, M. (1970). *I and thou* (W. Kaufman, Trans.). New York: Scribner's.

Ellis, A. (1995). Corrections and clarifications. *M. H. Erickson Foundation Newsletter* 15(2), 2.

Jung, C. (1933). *Modern man in search of a soul*. New York: Harcourt, Brace.

Jung, C. (1980). *The archetypes and the collective unconscious* (R. Hull, Trans.). Princeton, NJ: Princeton University Press. (Original work published 1902)

Kushner, H. (1981). *When bad things happen to good people*. New York: Schocken.

Maslow, A. (1968). *Toward a psychology of being* (rev. ed.). New York: Van Nostrand Reinhold.

May, R. (1953). *Man's search for himself*. New York: Dell.

May, R. (1989). *The art of counseling*. New York: Gardner.

Rogers, C. (1942). *Counseling and psychotherapy*. Boston: Houghton Mifflin.

Rogers, C. (1951). *Client-centered therapy*. Boston: Houghton Mifflin.

Rogers, C. (1957). The necessary and sufficient conditions of therapeutic personality change. *Journal of Counseling Psychology, 21*(2), 95–103.

Rogers, C. (1961). *On becoming a person*. Boston: Houghton Mifflin.

## Additional Reading

Bradshaw, J. (1992). *Homecoming: Reclaiming and championing your inner child*. New York: Bantam.

Cameron, J. (1992). *The artist's way: A spiritual path to higher creativity*. New York: Putnam.

Cliness, D. (1996). *The journey of life*. Poland, OH: Banausic.

Corey, G., & Corey, M. (1997). *I never knew I had a choice* (6th ed.). Pacific Grove, CA: Brooks/Cole.

Corey, M., & Corey, J. (1998). *Becoming a helper* (3rd ed.). Pacific Grove, CA: Brooks/Cole.

Day, L. (1996). *Practical intuition: How to harness the power of your instinct and make it work for you*. Scranton, PA: Harper Audio.

Emery, M. (1994). *Intuition workbook*. Englewood Cliffs, NJ: Prentice Hall.

Frankl, V. (1992). *Man's search for meaning: An introduction to logotherapy*. Boston: Beacon Press. (Original work published 1963)

Fulghum, R. (1993). *All I really need to know I learned in kindergarten: Uncommon thoughts on uncommon things*. Westminster, MD: Faucet.

Fulghum, R. (1996). *From beginning to end: The rituals of our lives*. Westminster, MD: Faucet.

Moore, T. (1994). *Care of the soul: A guide to cultivating depth and sacredness in everyday life*. New York: HarperPerennial.

Moore, T. (1994). *Soul mates: Honoring the mysteries of love and relationship*. New York: HarperPerennial.

Moore, T. (1995). *Meditations: On the monk who dwells in daily life*. New York: HarperPerennial.

Peck, M. (1978). *The road less traveled*. New York: Simon & Schuster.

Peck, M. (1997). *The road less traveled and beyond: Spiritual growth in an age of anxiety*. Old Tappan, NJ: Thorndike.

Sussman, M. (1992). *A curious calling: Unconscious motivations for practicing psychotherapy*. Northvale, NJ: Jason Aronson.

# THE JOURNEY CONTINUES

## *Some Final Thoughts*

As we complete this book, we come to a way station in our never-ending journey. At this point, let's assess not only where we've come from, but also where we now head on our pilgrimage. Notice our intentional use of the first person plural. We authors have made a diligent attempt to involve you in our personal and professional journeys, trusting and hoping that you come to assess your own journey, to make changes as you find them necessary, and to continue in your current path or, perhaps, choose another. We realize that our paths may not be yours; however, in the end, we all share life's journey.

## UNSPOKEN AND *VERBOTEN*:
## THE LIMITATIONS OF VENUES AND OF WORDS

As we have noted elsewhere, there are venues, especially public ones, in which discussion of beliefs is avoided because of the separation of church and state. While we agree that we are not to proselytize, we fail to see how a client can be divorced from his or her belief system. Such separation is unhealthy because it artificially removes the person from an important dimension of his or her personhood. It artificially breaks a whole down into parts. Also, as we approach the end of this book, we are keenly aware of the limitations of words themselves. Words are not adequate to describe spiritual and religious experiences. In fact, words may actually limit the experiences by placing boundaries on them. Nonetheless, words may communicate a semblance of our collective experience to a larger population. Hence, the production of this book.

# FROM WHENCE WE COME

In Chapter 1 we offered definitions and reasons to consider counseling within the context of spirituality. In Chapters 2 through 5 we provided basic philosophical, theological, and psychological foundations, illustrated with case examples, for what was to follow. We did this with the understanding that such grounding can be beneficial in the same sense that our profession demands knowledge of theory before an application of techniques. To offer this grounding, we looked at the interconnections and issues among counseling and spirituality and religion. We examined common patterns or archethemes, to illustrate our basic premise of interconnection and universality. We did not shrink from investigating the negative: evil, suffering, guilt and their relation to counseling. Further, we posited in Chapters 6 and 9 that we must assess not only our clients but also ourselves in this dimension. To this end, we furnished instruments and illustrations for counselor self-examination and client examination. Chapter 7 summarized and augmented the interventions that we described throughout this book. In Chapter 8 we took a look at perhaps the most powerful impression that spirituality has had on our profession: the founding of the twelve-step movement. We outlined its development, impact, and meaning in the lives of our clients and ourselves. Finally, our appendices offer personal exercises, competencies, web sites, and forms for experimentation and exploration.

# WHAT NOW?

We recall the classic Stanley Kubrick film, *2001: A Space Odyssey* (1968), in which a far-advanced civilization plants the seeds of evolution and growth in humankind through contact with a mysterious black monolith. Were we only to be thus inspired! There are no such monoliths that can unite the billions of people in our postmodern world, with diverse languages, cultural backgrounds, and temperaments. However much common spiritual qualities may unite humanity, the human spiritual journey is always one of ambiguity: Each person must choose his or her own best path.

Each one of us, client and counselor, has a personal history that involves or *is* a spiritual journey. We may be fortunate enough to have such memories of the newness and wonder of things, from childhood, that we can still see our journey as a magical one, punctuated with wonder and awe. Or perhaps we have much work to do to regain the roots of our creativity. The task is worth the effort! (If we shrink from it, how can we expect more from our clients?) We can examine the path we have taken so far and change course if needed. We can and do take stock, take inventory of ourselves and our lives, engaging in spiritual practices such as prayer and meditation that can expand our spiritual awareness. We can grow to goodness, grow into our full potential, truly ourselves.

In Chapter 7 we described various spiritual interventions that were aimed at centering or grounding either the client or the counselor, or both. In the case of our own personal lives, we can speak simply of spiritual practices. All the words we have set forth here are most useful if reflected on within the context of personal spiritual practice, a practice that tills the soil of our soul so as to increase the probability of growth to goodness. Each person must choose a form for himself or herself—whether simply a quiet time early in the day, a form of meditation or prayer, a quiet walk in the open air, journaling, yoga, or attendance at a religious devotion. Certainly many people who engage in a regular spiritual practice would say that the practice chose them. Also, there is the possibility that we may not know what our spiritual practices are until we engage in some reflection on the course of our lives. Either way, there is no substitute for engaging in a practice aimed at the farther reaches of human growth.

## "STAR CHILDREN"

Finally, we wish for you an age regression for the purpose of growing to greater goodness—re-connecting with the wondrous and wonderful child that you were, full of amazement, curiosity, laughter, and the capability of being fully present in the moment. No matter what quirks, circumstances, or even trauma may have come later, at one time you were this "star child" (again, borrowing from the novel and Kubrick film). On some level, you still are. The capability of returning to this state of wonderment is to tap into your innate spirituality and is itself a spiritual practice. Once accessed, this centering and grounding experience can help to serve you as you serve your clients as persons. In bringing out the best in yourself, you are advancing one more step toward bringing out the best in the world.

## THANKS

Thank you for participating in our journey throughout this book. While we may not have met you personally, we do hope that we have touched you personally. We have humbly endeavored to present in this book our approach to counseling and spirituality: that is, that one cannot divorce a client—or a counselor—from his or her belief system.

Admittedly, we authors have our biases: We teach that one cannot divorce the theory from the theorist! Moreover, we focus in part on aspects and/or results of spirituality and religion that counselors may find themselves wrestling with day-to-day in their offices. This may be tough, dark stuff (such as excessive guilt, evil, and suffering)—hence, our need to discuss these negative issues in this book. However, we are also very aware of the support, sustenance, healing, and affirmation that spirituality and religion may serve in clients' lives. Our support for nurturance of this functional and positive aspect of existence cannot be overemphasized. At varying levels of awareness, it is this spirituality that we work daily to achieve.

## QUESTIONS FOR REFLECTION

1. What themes emerge for you as you finish this book? How might they be applied in your life? What would you add to the material in this book to make it more relevant to you? To your clients?
2. Consider your own experience as well as the experience of your clients. In moving through the developmental stages of life, how has spirituality either helped or hindered this process? Has your reading of this text altered your outlook on this subject? What sections of the book stand out for you, as particularly useful in your counseling practice?
3. What, in your opinion, is missing from this book? How might you incorporate this missing material into your personal and professional life?
4. What are the spiritual practices that have helped you become grounded and maintain spiritual growth? What have you seen, in these pages or elsewhere, that you might consider adding?
5. What comes next in your journey or pilgrimage?

## REFERENCE

Clarke, A., & Kubrick, S. (1993). *2001: A space odyssey*. New York: New American Library.

# Mantras and Meditations for Counselors and Other Therapists

Here we present several mantras (which we define as succinct, personal I statements) and meditations for counselors to use as they see fit. They are derived from our years of spiritual direction, meditation, and prayers. We view them as only a "jumping off" point, a start for those counselors and others wishing to travel down this path.

## Mantras

- "Not no, but know."
- "I recall the deep sleep of my childhood."
- "I am whole."
- "God in Me."
- "Thank you, God."
- "God, I love You, and I love my life."
- "My unconscious is my friend."
- "I focus on peace."
- "I breathe in the spirit of life and breathe out the spirit of life."
- "I focus on being present."
- "Peace in me and in my world."
- "I am centered and grounded."
- "I am with energy."
- "I learn from all persons and all things."
- "I am at peace."
- "I honor my clients."
- "I place my burdens on the altar."
- "I turn over what I have no control over."
- "I hear and I listen."
- "I look and I see."
- "I touch and I feel."

- "I discern direction from all sources."
- "I endeavor to be a person for others."
- "I attend to my inner child."
- "I am grateful for my life."
- "I am grateful for those in my life."
- "I recall the presence of my higher power."
- "Guide me."
- "I am intrigued with life."
- "I am open to my experiences."
- "I wonder."
- "I am my own hero."
- "I enter the pool of being."
- "I enter the river of life."
- "I am increasingly knowing myself."
- "I seek wisdom."
- "I comfort when able."
- "I am envious and creative."
- "I face myself with courage and dignity."
- "My mind travels beyond words."
- "I am a link to all that was and to all that is to come."
- "I am and I am becoming."
- "I am in constant creation."
- "I learn from my dreams."
- "I am nourished by nourishing others."
- "I laugh and I giggle."
- "I try not to take life too seriously."
- "I do something for fun each day."
- "I call upon my wise old man/wise old woman."
- "My spirit contains my sprite, my internal child."
- "I pray for others."
- "I learn from all experiences, both good and bad."
- " I can control how I handle life's experiences."
- "I am a colorful thread in the majestic tapestry of history."
- "I pray to pray better."
- "I face and finish my unfinished business."
- "I can re-parent myself as I need to."
- "How important is it?"
- "Be here now."
- "I am a thousand stories."
- "Life goes on."
- "All in the fullness of time."
- "This, too, shall pass."
- "If I'm not growing, I'm going."

- "Awake, awake."
- "Reality is complex; complexity is my friend."
- "Uncertainty is uncomfortable; certainty is ridiculous." (Chinese proverb)
- "In every day, in every way, I am getting better and better."
- "Be sincere, not serious."
- "Laugh a little; laugh a lot."
- "I can parent myself."

# MEDITATIONS

- I make an internal list of the things that I am grateful for:_____
- I focus on consolation (and those things that console me) versus desolation (and those things that "de-soul" me).
- I meditate on the pool. Being and becoming. River, pool.
- I spend time with the scientist in me. I list the things that my analytical, skeptical side tells me: _____ I spend time with the artist in me. I list the things that my creative, intuitive side tells me:_____
- I recall instances of wonderment from my childhood. I remember in detail a special holiday, a show, an event, a toy, a dream, a special person.
- I recall a person or persons with whom I share "unfinished business." I meditate on ways to settle this business with them, even though they may not now be accessible to me. I endeavor to set the scene in detail: the place, the person, and exactly what I might say or do. I focus on a positive outcome to my work. I focus on letting go. I place on the altar what may remain unsettled, if anything.
- I meet one of the masters of psychotherapy (such as Freud, Jung, Adler, Rogers, Horney, Satir, Erickson, etc.).
  1. What would I say to her or him?
  2. What specific learning, insights would I thank him or her for?
- I travel back in time to the center of the "Big Bang." I experience the formation of the universe. The immense power, energy, creativity. I project myself into the future and experience the wonder of things to come. I realize that I am unique, a part of all that was, is, and shall be. My matter and energy have been and shall be forever.
- A Counselor's Meal Blessing: As we gather for this meal, let us be thankful for the food that is placed before us, remembering also those who have no food, who will go hungry on this night. . . . Let us also be thankful for the opportunities that have been afforded us, remembering those less fortunate, those who struggle. . . . Let us be thankful as well for the friends, family, and colleagues that we gather together with here, remembering those who are alone, who have no one . . . those who need our

help. . . . With these things in our mind, let us ask the Lord to bless this meal and this evening that we spend together. . . . Amen.

- I practice a centering prayer for at least 20 minutes daily. I choose a word or a few words (my mantra) to focus on that reminds me of my potential to be a person who leaves the world better than I have found it.

## GUIDED MEDITATIONS

- Start by taking a couple of long, slow, deep breaths and close your eyes if you want to . . . or perhaps you'll choose to keep your eyes open, it doesn't really matter. What matters is that you're able to get comfortable and that you can get more and more relaxed as you choose with every breath you take. But going only to comfortable positions, comfortable places, comfortable stances . . . and imagining if you want to . . . imagine at this point, that you're taking a walk on a path . . . and this is a path that's a very special path. Perhaps it goes through the woods or forest . . . perhaps it is along the beach . . . perhaps it's in the mountains . . . perhaps it's a familiar path or an unfamiliar but friendly one . . . nonetheless, it's a path and a very special path because it leads you on your life's journey. . . . And . . . as you go through this little meditation exercise perhaps you will notice special things about this very special path that your life is on. As you wander down the path, perhaps there are hills, perhaps it's flat, perhaps there're curves, or perhaps there're forks in the road. It doesn't really matter. What matters most is what you envision . . . what you feel . . . what you think this path needs to be as you move down this very, very special path . . . and as you wander down this path, you can notice any special sounds that make sense to you . . . you may notice special feelings, the warm of the coolness, the breeze of the day, whether the sun is out or the moon or the stars . . . noticing if there are animals near by or if you're with somebody else as you move down this path . . . focus-ing on the special sounds, feelings, and special sights . . . taking a moment to breathe in the colors, the sounds, and the feelings . . . noticing as you move down the path that you may have choices to make as to direction, but always following your creativity and intuition to where they lead you on this life's journey. Realizing that at the end of the path, or along the path, you'll find some treasure . . . some special item . . . some special person . . . some special animal . . . something of meaning to you on this life's journey. You can stop and pay attention to this item and take in the life lesson it has for you. . . . Perhaps it's a sound, a feeling, or a sight . . . it doesn't really matter . . . what matters is what matters to you. . . . Notice how you can walk down the path or run down the path or skip or what-ever way you want to do . . . and you can find other items of value, other treasures, other things of importance to you of knowledge professional and personal, spiritual, mental, physical, which make sense to you as you wander down this path, taking in the sights, the sounds, the smells and the feelings . . . enjoying the pleasure, the invigoration, the comfort, the relaxation . . . that this path brings to you . . . taking a moment to breathe in . . . to breathe out and to enjoy the feeling of comfort and relaxation as you continue to wander the path, gaining perhaps insight, health, invigoration and comfort and relaxation as you move along . . . and realizing that, of course, when it is safe and appropriate to do so, either at home or at work, simply sit back and follow this path gaining new insights from treasures you come across on the path . . . noticing now how you can in your own way either turn around and come back or exit any way you want to, realizing that you're able to come back when you choose . . . when it's safe and appropriate to do so . . . to go on the path . . . but right now exiting the path anyway you choose.

- I would like you to imagine in whatever way you would like to imagine a house . . . and this house has special qualities. I don't know how big it is . . . I don't know how small it is . . . I don't know what colors or color it may be . . . I don't know if it's built with bricks or wood. I don't know if it looks like a castle or a cottage . . . I don't know if it has gardens . . . I don't know what kind of lawns it has or on what landscaping it is . . . I don't know if it's in the hills, or the forests, or the mountains or along water . . . but a house nonetheless, so imagine if you will this house in whatever way you'd like, whatever consistency it's made of, whatever it brings to mind to you. . . . And further, if you would, imagine that this house becomes a home . . . in whatever ways home means to you, perhaps comfort, perhaps good memories, perhaps other things that I'm not privy to, but imagine if you would, this special house that is your home . . . imagine if you would that you now walk up a path of some sort. Perhaps its brick, perhaps it's cement, perhaps it's gravel, perhaps it's dirt, I don't know, but a path that leads to the front door of your special house, your home. In your own way, however you'd like, reach for the knob, hook, or the item that allows you to open the door to your special home. And open that door, and step inside, and look around, see what you see, notice any special sounds perhaps or feelings that you have in addition . . . notice that this home and this room have very special qualities that as you enter and move through this, the first room you can gain in confidence, gain in strength and health, you can gain in well-being and relaxation. Perhaps in one location in this room there is a special item . . . perhaps it is a vase, perhaps it is a knick-knack, a chest, a statue, who knows, but some special item that may have some meaning to you and paying particular attention to that item . . . it's OK to take it with you as you move through the house, or leave it there, it doesn't really matter. Then if you would, find an entrance, a doorway, an archway that leads into the second room of your house, your home, and take special notice of this room and any additional special qualities that it may have . . . meaning . . . comfort . . . relaxation for you. And as with the other room, the first room, you may want to pick out a special item, a special package, a special book, something special in that room that may have some meaning to you . . . and you can take it with you or you can leave it there, whichever is fine . . . and now, if you would, move into the third room of this special house which is your home doing the same exploration, the same noticing, the same paying attention to an item that you've done in the first two rooms . . . gleaning any and all lessons, feelings, thoughts that may bubble to the surface . . . and if you'd like to, continue for a few moments to wander about through your home, paying attention to what needs cleaning, to what needs straightening up, perhaps to what is just in it's right place . . . to any special lessons you may learn from your items . . . to anything that makes sense to you as you wander though your home. . . . And when you have finished wandering through your home, come back to this room with any learning and with anything that makes sense to you to come back with . . . taking your time.

- Allow yourself to relax by taking in a couple of long, slow, deep breaths . . . if you tend to be into your head a little right now, just take your mind, take your thoughts out into your body . . . explore perhaps the feelings in your toes, or the feelings in your fingers, or the actual heartbeat, or your breathing, or taking any particular notice of any kind of activity going on in your body and experiencing that and enjoying it for a moment if you'd like to. So why don't we take a little trip now, if you'd like, part of your mind, if you'd like, and go along with this trip and park and wander, think about other things, if you would like to as well. I'm recalling, as a child, I really enjoyed the story of Peter Pan . . . how I could get really involved in that story about a flying boy who never aged, and who was always having fun and . . . about the little fairy Tinkerbell, who flew with him and protected him and was very sprightly . . . and about, of course, the themes of good and bad . . . Captain Hook, the pirates, and how Peter Pan and his friends, who were called the Lost Boys, would fight against the forces of evil and win out . . . and how they would look out after one another . . . and I'm recalling the wonderment that I had in those times of the idea of never growing old . . . of always being young . . . always being happy . . . always enjoying the idea of flying above everything . . . of fully experiencing a full perspective of what's below . . . of moving into domains that were beyond the physical . . . beyond the mental . . . and perhaps even into the spiritual. The idea of floating above and beyond . . . the idea of discerning what is really important here . . . what is important for me . . . what decisions do I need to make about my life and where I'm headed . . .

personally . . . professionally . . . where am I going here . . . over what lands am I flying. Is it Neverland or is it a forever land . . . what kinds of lands . . . a whateverland . . . perhaps even a never land . . . who knows. As I fly above it all trying to discern my path, my way and focusing, too, on consolation, such an important word. Some of us, some of our clients tend to involve themselves in desolation, but we can choose consolation and discernment. Above it all, gaining new experience . . . free floating . . . gaining new insights and meanings to our lives and taking a moment to quietly, internally enjoy the journey and then allowing myself to come back to this place.

# The Twelve Steps and Twelve Traditions of Alcoholics Anonymous

## The Twelve Steps

1. We admitted we were powerless over alcohol—that our lives had become unmanageable.
2. Came to believe that a Power greater than ourselves could restore us to sanity.
3. Made a decision to turn our will and our lives over to the care of *God as we understood Him.*
4. Made a searching and fearless moral inventory of ourselves.
5. Admitted to God, to ourselves, and to another human being the exact nature of our wrongs.
6. Were entirely ready to have God remove all these defects of character.
7. Humbly asked Him to remove our shortcomings.
8. Made a list of all persons we had harmed, and became willing to make amends to them all.
9. Made direct amends to such people wherever possible, except when to do so would injure them or others.
10. Continued to take personal inventory and when we were wrong promptly admitted it.
11. Sought through prayer and meditation to improve our conscious contact with *God as we understood Him*, praying only for knowledge of His will for us and the power to carry that out.
12. Having had a spiritual awakening as a result of these steps, we tried to carry this message to alcoholics, and to practice these principles in all our affairs.

---

Alcoholics Anonymous World Services. (1976). *Alcoholics Anonymous: The story of how many thousands of men and women have recovered from alcoholism.* New York: Author, pp. 59–60.

# THE TWELVE TRADITIONS

1. Our common welfare should come first; personal recovery depends upon A.A. unity.
2. For our group purpose there is but one ultimate authority—a loving God as He may express Himself in our group conscience. Our leaders are but trusted servants; they do not govern.
3. The only requirement for A.A. membership is a desire to stop drinking.
4. Each group should be autonomous except in matters affecting other groups or A.A. as a whole.
5. Each group has but one primary purpose—to carry its message to the alcoholic who still suffers.
6. An A.A. group ought never endorse, finance, or lend the A.A. name to any related facility or outside enterprise, lest problems of property, money, and prestige divert us from our primary purpose.
7. Every A.A. group ought to be fully self-supporting, declining outside contributions.
8. Alcoholics Anonymous should remain forever nonprofessional, but our service centers may employ special workers.
9. A.A., as such, ought never be organized; but we may create service boards or committees directly responsible to those they serve.
10. Alcoholics Anonymous has no opinion on outside issues; hence the A.A. name ought never be drawn into public controversy.
11. Our public relations policy is based on attraction rather than promotion; we need always maintain personal anonymity at the level of press, radio, and films.
12. Anonymity is the spiritual foundation of all our traditions, ever reminding us to place principles before personalities.

## Sample Intake Form (Incorporating Belief System Assessment)

Client Name _____     Counselor Name _____

Date _____     Length of Interview _____

I.  Client and Concern Description: (often the formula denoting age, race, gender, marital status in adults, followed by the words "complaining of . . ." or "reporting . . ."—for example, a 54-year-old Caucasian male, married complaining of . . . or reporting . . . )

II.  Psychosocial History: (note here relevant historical data on the client, exploring such areas as childhood and adolescence, current and family of origin history [including children], legal history, medical history, employment history, educational history, military history, history of mental health contacts, etc.) *Religious and spiritual belief and practice history, denomination/faith of origin, current denomination/faith, role of faith in client's life, religious conflicts/ supports, etc.*

III.  Mental Status: Client appeared alert (y, n) and oriented (y, n)

Cognition: (the counselor explores current functioning in the cognitive arena, including memory, intellectual level, concrete versus abstract thinking abilities, evidence of hallucinations, delusions, etc.) *Excessive and appropriate guilt may be assessed here.*

Affect: (here the counselor notes current type, level, and intensity of emotions, including depression, anxiety, mania, etc.)

Behaviors: (in this area of mental status, the counselor takes special notice of any behavioral anomalies, including tics, psychomotor agitation or retardation, pressured speech, unusual gestures, etc.)

Risk of Harm to Self or Others: (this area of current functioning is of special import and, thus, is listed separately. The counselor needs to determine level of lethality and any and all ideation, plans, and means. We strongly suggest that the intern become familiar with agency and ethical policies in this area.)

IV.  Diagnostic Impression (DSM-IV)

Axis I      Clinical Syndromes
            Other Conditions That May Be a Focus of Clinical Attention
Axis II     Personality Disorders
            Mental Retardation
Axis III    General Medical Conditions
Axis IV     Psychosocial and Environmental Problems
Axis V      Global Assessment of Functioning

V. Treatment Recommendations: (as with the diagnostic impression, treatment recommendations are conclusional data resulting from the process of the interview. And as with the diagnostic IMPRESSION, these recommendations are tentative and subject to modification as needed. They may include recommendations for psychological testing; psychiatric referral for medication assessment; referral to another professional [*including one of the "friendly clergy"*]; a specific type of therapy, such as marital, family, individual, group; a specific modality, such as hypnosis, biofeedback, cognitive/ behavioral; hospitalization; or even no treatment. A treatment plan usually follows. We suggest that the client be as involved in the process as possible.)

VI.  Additional Remarks:

# SPIRITUAL COMPETENCIES OF THE ASSOCIATION FOR SPIRITUAL, ETHICAL, AND RELIGIOUS VALUES IN COUNSELING

Revised 05/96

I. Believing that a general understanding of religious, spiritual, and transpersonal (r/s/t/) phenomena (experiences, beliefs, practices) is important to the counseling process, the professional counselor can

   A. Discuss possible relationships between religious, spiritual, and transpersonal phenomena, including similarities and differences between the three types of phenomena.

   B. Describe religious, spiritual, and transpersonal phenomena from the perspective of diversity.

   C. Explain one or two models of human religious, spiritual, and transpersonal development across the life span. (Chandler, Holden, & Kolander; Fowler; Grof; Hettler; Maslow; Osler; Sweeney & Wittmer; Washburn; Westerhoff; Wilber)

   D. Describe research, theory, and clinical evidence that indicates the relationships between religion, spiritual, and transpersonal phenomena on the one hand and mental health on the other.

II. Believing that awareness of one's own r/s/t/ belief system is important to the counseling process, the professional counselor can

   A. Describe one's r/s/t belief system.

   B. Identify key events in one's life that contributed to the development of one's own r/s/t belief system and explain how those events contributed.

   C. Identify specific attitudes, beliefs, and values from one's own r/s/t belief system both that support and that impede or hinder respect and valuing of different r/s/t belief systems.

   D. Actively engage in an ongoing process of challenging one's own attitudes and beliefs that do not support respecting and valuing of different r/s/t belief systems.

   E. Describe the extent to which one's own r/s/t belief system is held in relative favor or disfavor by individuals subscribing to other r/s/t belief systems.

   F. Develop appropriate responses to criticism of one's own r/st belief system.

   G. Conceptualize oneself from the perspective of at least two models of human r/s/t development across the life span.

   H. Conceptualize oneself in terms of research, theory, and clinical evidence that indicate the relationships between r/s/t phenomena and mental wellness.

   I. Identify limits to one's tolerance of religious, spiritual, and/or transpersonal phenomena that differ from one's own r/s/t belief system.

III. Believing that an understanding of the client's r/s/t worldview is important to the counseling process, the professional counselor can

   A. demonstrate openness to, empathy with, and an acceptance of a variety of r/s/t phenomena.

   B. Describe the role of the client's r/s/t worldview in an understanding of the client as a whole.

   C. Engage in the acquisition of knowledge needed to better understand a client's r/s/t worldview by requesting information from the clients themselves and/or acquiring it through outside resources.

   D. Use r/s/t terms and concepts that are meaningful to the client.

   E. Identify when one's understanding and/or tolerance of the client's r/s/t worldview is insufficient to adequately serve the client.

IV. Believing that appropriate intervention strategies and techniques are important to the counseling process, the professional counselor can

   A. Assess the relevance of the r/s/t domain in a client's therapeutic issues.

   B. Use a client's r/s/t phenomena in pursuit of the client's therapeutic goals as befits the client's expressed preferences.

   C. When relevant to the client's therapeutic issues and preferences, conceptualize the client

   1. From the perspective of at least two models of human r/s/t development across the life span.

2.  In terms of research, theory, and clinical evidence that indicates the relationships between r/s/t phenomena and mental wellness.

D.  Demonstrate competent use of techniques for remediation of problems with psychological integration of, facilitation of, and enhancement of r/s/t phenomena.

E.  Consult with r/s/t professionals including those to whom a client looks as a r/s/t authority when such consultation would significantly enhance service to the client.

F.  Having identified limits to one's tolerance and competence,

1.  Seek consultation

2.  Seek further training or education

3.  Demonstrate appropriate referral skills, or

4.  Engage in a combination of 1–3 above.

Source: ASERVIC, Association for Spiritual, Ethical, and Religious Values in Counseling, a division of the American Counseling Association.

# COUNSELOR SELF-ASSESSMENT EXERCISE

1. *Introductory Statement.* We view this section as an opportunity for the counselor to preface what follows. He or she may find it useful to state the purpose of participating in the assessment. Or the counselor may wish to tell a personal story, perhaps from childhood. We intentionally leave room for any and all variety of responses.

2. *Life Theme.* What theme or themes run throughout my life? What common threads weave in and out of the tapestry that is my life? Perhaps I notice Jungian archetypes (Jung, 1980), such as my hero side or shadow side. Perhaps I see themes of anxiety or depression. Would I then agree with the poet Yeats, who wrote, "Fortunately, I have a prevailing sense of tragedy to sustain me through these brief moments of joy"? Or maybe I discern patterns of satisfaction, contentment, grounding, and centering, affecting my self-esteem, what Branden (1994) refers to as "the reputation I have of myself."

3. *Life Influences.* As I review my personal developmental history, what masters have influenced me? Masters may include religious figures, prominent people in our field, and other major figures. Further, what mentors have had an impact on who I am? These people are personally known to me and have provided guidance and support to me during periods of my life. Finally, who are my friends who have nurtured me in my life's journey? We note here that family (both by birth and by choice) are included in this category. We suggest that the counselor act here in some senses as reporter, gleaning the who? what? when? where? and how? Review contacts and kind memories.

---

Branden, N. (1994). *Six pillars of self-esteem.* New York: Bantam.

Jung, C. (1980). *The archetypes and the collective unconscious* (R. Hull, Trans.). Princeton, NJ: Princeton University Press. (Original work published 1902)

4. *Life's Lessons.* What, then, may I conclude are the lessons I have learned from my years on earth? Try to be brief: Put the lessons in a short declaratory statement; include with this statement a story supporting each lesson.

5. *Personal Conclusions.* Finally, as I review this exercise in self-assessment, what conclusions can I draw? How shall I pass them on? Is there anything I haven't been asked in the assessment that would be important to know? (We suggest asking clients this same question; invariably, it generates additional pertinent information.)

# RELATED WEB SITES

**America Magazine**
*http://www.americapress.org*

**American Counseling Association**
*http://www.counseling.org*

**American Psychological Association**
*http://www.apa.org*

**Association for Transpersonal Psychology**
*http://www.igc.apc.org/atp/*

**G. K. Chesterton Home Page**
*http://www.dur.ac.uk/~dcs0mpw/gkc/*

**Grof Transpersonal Training Program**
*http://www.infoasis.com/people/grof/HBinternet.html*

**Holotropic Breathwork Homepage**
*http://www.breathwork.com*

**The Milton Erickson Foundation**
*http://www.erickson-foundation.org*

**The PL Ken Wilber Website**
*http://www.concentric.net/~Lemckay/wilber/*

**Psychotherapy and Spirituality Institute**
*http://www.mindspirit.org/*

**Sister Spirituality**
*www.teleport.com/nonprofit/sister-spirit/*

**Spirituality**
*www.gnv.fdt.net/~nother/spirit_index.html*

**Spirituality and Health**
*www.spiritualityhealth.com/*

**Spirituality and Humor**
*www.spiritslaughing.com*

**Spirituality, Yoga, Hinduism**
*www.geocities.com/RodeoDrive/1415/index1.html*

**Spirituality in the Workplace**
*www.spiritweb.org/Spirit/workplace-l.html*

**Spiritweb**
*www.spirweb.org*

**The World of Ken Wilber**
*http://people.a2000.nl/fvisser/wilber/frameeng.html*

# THE SPIRITUAL WELLNESS INVENTORY

## Elliott Ingersoll

## THE CREATION OF THE SPIRITUAL WELLNESS INVENTORY

The spiritual wellness inventory began as my doctoral dissertation (Ingersoll, 1995). At the time, I was very interested in developing a vocabulary that wasn't necessarily religious but that counselors could use to talk about spirituality with clients. Throughout my career I have been inspired by figures like Joseph Campbell, Huston Smith, Ken Wilber, and Stanislav Grof, all of whom have set forth the proposition that there are core spiritual values and experiences that transcend and unite religious expressions. I believed that a vocabulary that relied on such core values and experiences would facilitate an integration of spirituality into counseling sessions and counseling literature. This goal of infusion rested on the premise that, as Vaughan (1995) and others have stated, spirituality is a part of the human organism that may be nurtured in particular social institutions but, as such, does not derive from those institutions. As far as studying spirituality, there were some difficulties in operationalizing the term. As I noted in Ingersoll (1994), the etymological roots of the word *spirit* (including *ruach* in Hebrew, *pneuma* in Greek, and *spiritus* in Latin) all referred more to metaphors like courage, breath, wind, vigor, and life. Other researchers (Ellison, 1983; Moberg, 1971) resolved the problem through the construct *spiritual well-being*. Ellison noted that just as measures of physical well-being may be indices of underlying physical health, measures of spiritual well-being could serve as indices of underlying spiritual health. One challenge then was to identify dimensions of spiritual well-being or what I have called spiritual wellness. Previous spiritual well-being scales (Elkins, 1986; Ellison & Paloutzian, 1982; Kass et al., 1991; Moberg, 1984) suffered from various shortcomings, so I tried to address these in the construction of the Spiritual Wellness Inventory (SWI). I described in a journal article (Ingersoll, 1998) how I refined my own initial dimensions of spiritual wellness. This phase of research made use of qualitative interviews with people who were, to some extent, leaders in 11 different spiritual traditions or paths. These interviews explored with each person how spiritual wellness would manifest in someone practicing that particular path. After summarizing the dimensions that came out in the interviews, I had panelists rate the dimensions and then help design items for each dimension. The result was a 10-dimensional, 88-item inventory that was given to 515 subjects and then explored through factor analysis. Based on the factor analysis, weaker items were dropped to shorten the scale that is now a 55-item scale. There are 10 dimensions of spiritual wellness and a small fake-good scale derived from Reynolds (1982).

## The Dimensions of Spiritual Wellness

The dimensions of spiritual wellness addressed in the inventory are these:

- **Conception of the Absolute/Divine:** This may fit into the categories described as monotheistic ( Judaism, Islam, Christianity), deistic (belief in God on evidence of reason and nature only), atheistic, pantheistic (God in everything), or panentheistic (God in all things and transcending all things). An individual's conception of the divine is expressed as that person's image or experience of divinity. With spiritual maturity, one also tends to view one's images as finite—more as symbols that point to the reality of the divine. In esoteric practices, this conception may come second to experiences with what one considers being divine. Always be alert to psychological contamination of the conception that is more related to the person's issues than God per se.
- **Meaning:** This is the individual sense that life is worth living. This can become an overwhelming question in times of crisis but is not limited to crisis. Meaning can be an explicit sense of what it is that makes life meaningful or having a sense of purpose. Meaning does not have to be explicit. It may be simply a sense that pervades one's experiences. Many times meaning is expressed in being at peace with the question of meaning.
- **Connectedness:** Connectedness can occur with other people, with God or what is considered Divine, and with elements in the environment. Relationships could be thought of as a recognizing and celebrating connectedness, as could religious ritual or ecological awareness. Connectedness should not be stereotyped as extraversion or liking to socialize. It is a deeper sense, a sense of belonging. This sense of belonging may be to a community, to the universe, or as an integrated, whole person.
- **Mystery:** This dimension relates to how a person deals with ambiguity, the unexplained, and the uncertainty of life. This may be thought of as a person's capacity for awe and wonder. In addition, this dimension should reflect a person's comfort level with awe and wonder. It is certainly a

function of spiritual maturity too and may be a direct result of esoteric practices. Some exoteric paths may actually discourage mystery in practitioners.

- **Spiritual Freedom:** This dimension is related to one's capacity for play, experience of life and the world as "safe," a sense of freedom from fear and desire in living, and one's willingness to make a commitment. It includes the ability to "forget oneself" and all types of play like sexual play. Play and freedom are sincere but not serious. They are meaningful but not necessarily purposeful.

- **Experience/Ritual:** This includes rituals that are a healthy part of a person's life and the experiences that accompany the behavior of carrying out the ritual. A healthy ritual requires that the energy involved be directed toward an experience or activity. It is proactive, not passive. Meditation must be differentiated from something like watching television. The ritual often helps the person become present-centered, reconnect with others or the divine, and forge meaning in relation to life circumstances.

- **Forgiveness:** This dimension reflects one's attitudes toward giving and receiving forgiveness. Forgiveness is here described as a journey one embarks on with no guaranteed products/results. In total, it is a willful process engaged in from both the giving and receiving ends combined with the "magic" that heals. In this sense, the process may require considerable time.

- **Hope:** This is the experience that one's suffering is not in vain or going to last forever. Like one's sense of freedom, it too is an experience of, ultimately, feeling "safe" in life. Hope is also expressed as faith that there is some reality to life that allows one to endure experiences of suffering. Some people have said that loss of hope implies loss of faith in God in that hopeless people are feigning omniscience by assuming they *know* that things will be bad forever and always.

- **Knowledge/Learning:** A person possessing spiritual well-being has an interest in increasing both knowledge of self and knowledge of things perceived as external to self. This learning need not be defined by academic standards. Learning and acquiring knowledge are welcomed despite the trials that may be experienced in the process.

- **Present-centeredness:** Being able to be present in passing moments. This is not a state that you could be in all the time. When you are in this state, you can see what is going on around you. Ritual usually helps cultivate this. In the end, it is the ability to experience what is, to experience life (as Huston Smith says) point-blank. In contemplative traditions it is experienced as the only reality. The past is a thought, a memory, and the future is a thought, an anticipation. The eternal present is always, everywhere, everywhen.

# THE INTENDED USE FOR THE SPIRITUAL WELLNESS INVENTORY

One dynamic I am acutely aware of is the temptation to misuse numerically scored inventories. Students are always asking me how "spiritually well" they are based on their score, tempting me to say something like, "Ooh, you're a 23, that's bad. If only you were a 30 or a 32 there might be hope." Obviously such an answer would be my attempt at humor but we must be careful with such humor since, in our society, people ascribe power to numerical ratings that, in many cases, the ratings simply don't have. Although I recognize that I fueled this problem by using numbers in the subscales, I want to emphasize that the scale is designed to be a starting point for dialogue around spiritual issues. I encourage people using the scale to look at the relationships between the dimensions. As with any scale, the first step is to ask yourself how well the ratings match your sense of yourself. If you are using the inventory with a client, you may find the results deviate a great deal from the client's sense of her own spiritual wellness. If that is the case, it is far more productive to begin the discussion along the lines of the client's sense of self rather than how the inventory reflected that sense of self. When I have used the SWI with clients, I usually ask them, "What stands out the most for you?" Most of the time they will comment on a dimension where their score is particularly low. We are usually able to talk a bit about what that means to them. If the client doesn't mention the dimensions where his score is high, I will bring those up. Typically they reflect significant aspects of the client's support system that can be used throughout the counseling relationship. Following is a case summary using the SWI dimensions so readers can get a sense of how these could be used in their own explorations and, if the reader is a clinician, in exploration with clients.

*Ed was a 29-year-old, single, Caucasian male seeking counseling for what appeared to be dysthymia. Ed seems to recall always having a low-grade depression that he was more aware of since his last relationship ended with his partner calling him "a constant downer." Ed visited his primary care physician who prescribed a regimen of antidepressant medication (Paroxetine, 20 mg a day) and recommended that he supplement the medication with counseling. In our initial sessions Ed described his life as feeling like "cardboard" and said he rarely felt any enthusiasm. During our first three sessions, Ed revealed that in college he had abandoned an early interest in philosophy for "a more pragmatic" major in business. Although Ed held a good job (managing marketing for an industrial supply firm), his heart wasn't in it (but as noted, he felt his heart wasn't in anything). Ed was also interested in theology and comparative religion. He said he had been questioning the meaning of life pretty intensely since his girlfriend left him early that year. He said if he were a religious person, he might be said to be having a crisis of faith. I recalled Scott Peck's (1978) suggestion that therapists should find out their client's religion—even if the client said he didn't have one. I asked Ed if he would take the SWI. He actually showed enthusiasm for the idea and took the inventory. The first thing Ed noticed about his results was that the "meaning" and "mystery" dimensions were quite low while the others hovered around 20 points. In exploring the inventory, Ed conspicuously avoided discussing the mystery dimension and kept directing the dialogue to the meaning dimension. Toward the end of the session, I commented that I was curious about this dynamic since he had also commented on the "mystery" dimension as a low score. To this Ed became perturbed and asked if I had any expert insights he should be privy to. Sensing I had "touched a nerve," I backed off and said, "No, I was just curious." In our next session Ed noted that he really was upset by the low score on "mystery." He told me that all the fights with his ex-girlfriend had been because she thought he didn't take enough risks in life. He was beginning to think she was right. The next two months were spent exploring various periods of Ed's life when he had "taken the safe route," including his college major. Key to the events were the irrational thoughts Ed cultivated about himself because of the choices he had made. We realized that a great deal of his mood disturbance was fueled by these thoughts ("I'm a loser," "I'm not an alpha male—I'm an omega male"). Since Ed was experiencing some relief from the antidepressant, he had more energy to begin re-making his self-concept through learning how to dispute his irrational thoughts and reexamining the role of mystery and ambiguity in taking risks.*

Following is the actual SWI. You may take it if you wish and self-score it with the materials provided here. The demographics and descriptive statistics are included toward the end of the appendix if you wish to compare your scores to scores of a sample. Remember that the main goal of the inventory is to begin dialogue around spiritual issues with a trans-traditional vocabulary. There is still much research that needs to be done on the reliability and validity of the inventory in order to make it psychometrically sound.

## *The Spiritual Wellness Inventory*
### *Elliott Ingersoll, Ph.D., PCC*

Please respond to the following items, choosing a number from the scale provided that indicates the degree to which you agree or disagree with each item. Mark the number you select in the blank beside each item number.

## RESPONSE SCALE

| Strongly Disagree | | Disagree | | Agree | | Strongly Agree | |
|---|---|---|---|---|---|---|---|
| 1 | 2 | 3 | 4 | 5 | 6 | 7 | 8 |

1. I don't ever experience God's presence in my life. \_\_\_\_ 1
2. The meaning of life is a question I am at peace with. \_\_\_\_ 2
3. I never feel compassion for other people. \_\_\_\_ 3
4. I often feel a deep appreciation of every moment. \_\_\_\_ 4
5. I never experience a sense of awe about life. \_\_\_\_ 5
6. I have things I do to help me feel connected to life. \_\_\_\_ 6
7. There are reasons to give up hope. \_\_\_\_ 7
8. I feel called on to forgive others as God forgives me. \_\_\_\_ 8
9. I reject most challenges to my beliefs. \_\_\_\_ 9
10. I believe all people have a role in the web of life. \_\_\_\_ 10
11. I feel unsafe in the world. \_\_\_\_ 11
12. My sense of the divine increases my sense of connectedness to other people. \_\_\_\_ 12
13. I never experience my everyday life as meaningful. \_\_\_\_ 13
14. I feel part of at least one healthy community that is important to me and greatly affects my life. \_\_\_\_ 14
15. I don't enjoy being absorbed in physical sensations. \_\_\_\_ 15
16. Life is about growth and change. \_\_\_\_ 16
17. I don't know what to do to feel God's presence. \_\_\_\_ 17
18. Even when situations seem hopeless, I have faith they can change for the better. \_\_\_\_ 18
19. If I forgive others, it really doesn't help me. \_\_\_\_ 19
20. The way I live brings me to a greater knowledge of who I really am. \_\_\_\_ 20
21. I am a strict person insisting on doing things as correctly as possible. \_\_\_\_ 21
22. I experience playful moments daily. \_\_\_\_ 22
23. I never experience a strong inner sense of God's presence. \_\_\_\_ 23
24. I always reflect on the meaning of my life experiences. \_\_\_\_ 24
25. I don't feel a part of any real community. \_\_\_\_ 25
26. I often feel fully present in each passing moment. \_\_\_\_ 26
27. I am afraid to question my spiritual beliefs. \_\_\_\_ 27
28. I see everyday life as sacred. \_\_\_\_ 28
29. I have little faith that on some level my life will work out. \_\_\_\_ 29
30. I have often been forgiven by others in my life. \_\_\_\_ 30
31. I don't investigate questions that arise in my life. \_\_\_\_ 31
32. I have periods when it is hard to stop self-pity. \_\_\_\_ 32

33. I feel coerced by images of what life should be about. ____ 33
34. I am conscious of the divine in my daily activities. ____ 34
35. I don't get much meaning out of my life experiences. ____ 35
36. I often notice things in nature while I am riding or
    walking from place to place. ____ 36
37. When I attain a goal I don't savor it before moving on to
    the next goal. ____ 37
38. Ambiguity and uncertainty are healthy parts of life. ____ 38
39. I have not developed new spiritual rituals as I have grown. ____ 39
40. Every moment offers potential for hope. ____ 40
41. I have resentments about past injuries. ____ 41
42. The more I learn about myself the more I have to give. ____ 42
43. I would rather mix with polite people than rebellious types. ____ 43
44. I feel free to make strong commitments to things. ____ 44
45. My sense of God decreases my sense of connectedness
    to nature. ____ 45
46. My spirituality is very meaningful to me. ____ 46
47. My spiritual community isn't much help in celebrating life. ____ 47
48. I don't get tense thinking of things that lie ahead. ____ 48
49. It is important to be in control of the situations in which
    I find myself. ____ 49
50. I have rituals that help me integrate the spiritual into
    my life. ____ 50
51. I have not had difficult situations change for the better. ____ 51
52. I am able to forgive anything a person may do. ____ 52
53. I value knowledge except when it conflicts with my beliefs. ____ 53
54. I wait until I am sure that my views are correct before
    speaking up. ____ 54
55. I feel great pressure to live up to a social image. ____ 55

## Scoring the SWI

1. Reverse the ratings for all odd-numbered items so the new numerals
   match the following key: 8=1, 7=2, 6=3, 5=4, 4=5, 3=6, 2=7, 1=8

   *Example*: Your rating for an odd-numbered item is a "4." According to
   the key, the rating would be transformed to a "5."

2. Enter corrected odd-numbered values on the blanks next to each item on
   the inventory.

3. Enter all response values, even-numbered and corrected odd-numbered,
   on the response grid below. Next, total the numbers across each row for
   the dimension totals.

| | | | | | | |
|---|---|---|---|---|---|---|
| 1. ___ | 12. ___ | 23. ___ | 34. ___ | 45. ___ | TOTAL ___ | Conception of Divinity |
| 2. ___ | 13. ___ | 24. ___ | 35. ___ | 46. ___ | TOTAL ___ | Meaning |
| 3. ___ | 14. ___ | 25. ___ | 36. ___ | 47. ___ | TOTAL ___ | Connectedness |
| 4. ___ | 15. ___ | 26. ___ | 37. ___ | 48. ___ | TOTAL ___ | Present-Centeredness |
| 5. ___ | 16. ___ | 27. ___ | 38. ___ | 49. ___ | TOTAL ___ | Mystery |
| 6. ___ | 17. ___ | 28. ___ | 39. ___ | 50. ___ | TOTAL ___ | Ritual |
| 7. ___ | 18. ___ | 29. ___ | 40. ___ | 51. ___ | TOTAL ___ | Hope |
| 8. ___ | 19. ___ | 30. ___ | 41. ___ | 52. ___ | TOTAL ___ | Forgiveness |
| 9. ___ | 20. ___ | 31. ___ | 42. ___ | 53. ___ | TOTAL ___ | Knowledge/Learning |
| 10. ___ | 21. ___ | 32. ___ | 43. ___ | 54. ___ | TOTAL ___ | Fake Good |
| 11. ___ | 22. ___ | 33. ___ | 44. ___ | 55. ___ | TOTAL ___ | Spiritual Freedom |

Now, using the SWI profile sheet, enter the dimension totals (row totals) on the profile sheet line matching the dimension total you are recording. There is no "total" score since the dimensions overlap quite a bit.

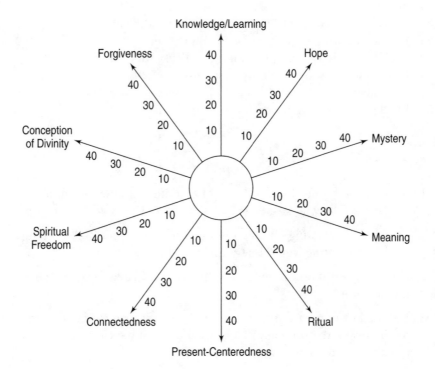

**Spiritual Wellness Inventory**
**Profile Sheet**
**Elliott Ingersoll, Ph.D., PCC**

## Spiritual Wellness Inventory Means & Demographics (Revised)

N = 515

AGE:

| | | | |
|---|---|---|---|
| 18–21 = 12% | | 50–59 = 12% | |
| 22–26 = 18% | | 60–65 = 2% | |
| 27–33 = 15% | | 70–75 = 2% | |
| 34–40 = 13% | | 76 and over = 1% | |
| 41–49 = 20% | | | |

## SPIRITUAL TRADITION

| | | | |
|---|---|---|---|
| Reform Jewish | 2% | Latter Day Saints | 2% |
| Orthodox Jewish | 1% | Transpersonal | 10% |
| Catholic Christian | 32% | Yoga practitioner | 3% |
| Protestant Christian | 34% | Martial artist | 3% |
| Other Christian | 1% | Dead Head | 3% |
| Pagan | 0% | Sufi/Muslim | 1% |
| Buddhist | 4% | Native American | 1% |
| Baha'i' | 1% | | |

## CULTURAL BACKGROUND

| | | | |
|---|---|---|---|
| African-American | 4% | Latino/Latina | 1% |
| Asian-American | 1% | Native-American | 2% |
| European-American | 90% | | |

## EDUCATION: Highest Level Attained

| | | | |
|---|---|---|---|
| High school | 5% | master's degree | 28% |
| 2-year college | 2% | doctoral degree | 3% |
| some college | 18% | post-doctoral degree | 1% |
| bachelor's degree | 40% | | |

## Weekly Estimated Hours of TV Watched:

| | | | |
|---|---|---|---|
| 0–5 | 37% | 21–25 | 2% |
| 6–10 | 28% | 26–30 | 2% |
| 11–15 | 14% | 31–35 | 2% |
| 16–20 | 7% | 36+ | 1% |

| Dimension | Revised Mean (Rounded) |
|---|---|
| Conception of Divinity | 17 |
| Meaning | 20 |
| Connectedness | 19 |
| Present-Centeredness | 18 |
| Mystery | 22 |
| Ritual | 18 |
| Hope | 20 |
| Forgiveness | 21 |
| Knowledge/Learning | 21 |
| Spiritual Freedom | 16 |

# REFERENCES

Elkins, D. N. (1986). *Spiritual Orientation Inventory*. Unpublished work. Irvine, CA: Pepperdine University Center.

Ellison, C. W. (1983). Spiritual well-being: Conceptualization and measurement. *Journal of Psychology and Theology, 11*, 330–340.

Ellison, C. W., & Paloutzian, R. F. (1982). Loneliness, spiritual well-being, and quality of life. In L. A. Peplar & D. Perlman (Eds.), *Loneliness: A sourcebook of current theory, research, and therapy.* New York: Wiley.

Ingersoll, R. E. (1994). Spirituality, religion, and counseling: Dimensions and relationships. *Counseling and Values, 38*, 98–112.

Ingersoll, R. E. (1995). *Construction and initial validation of the spiritual wellness inventory.* Unpublished doctoral dissertation, Kent State University.

Ingersoll, R. E. (1998). Refining dimensions of spiritual wellness: A cross-traditional approach. *Counseling and Values, 42*, 156–165.

Kass, J., Friedman, R., Leserman, J., Zuttermeister, P., & Benson, H. (1991). Health outcomes and a new index of spiritual experience. *Journal for the Scientific Study of Religion, 30*, 203–211.

Moberg, D. O. (1971). *Spiritual well-being: Background.* Washington, DC: University Press of America.

Moberg, D. O. (1984). Subjective measures of spiritual well-being. *Review of Religious Research, 25*, 351–364.

Peck, M. (1978). *The road less traveled.* New York: Simon & Schuster.

Reynolds, W. M. (1982). Development of reliable and valid short forms of the Marlowe-Crown social desirability scale. *Journal of Clinical Psychology, 38*, 119–125.

Vaughan, F. (1995). *Shadows of the sacred: Seeing through spiritual illusions.* Wheaton, IL: Quest.

# Index

Abel, C., 26
Activity
  balancing receptivity and, 69–70
  polarity of, 27–28
Addiction
  defined, 71
  and story of Job, 71
  *See also* Alcoholics Anonymous (A.A.)
Adler, A., "The Question" of, 92
Alcoholics Anonymous (A.A.), 130–148
  alternatives to, 142–143
  case study of, 146–148
  counselors and, 144–146
  founding of, 135
  origins of, 132
  Oxford Group as predecessor of,
    132–134
  as spiritual treatment program, 131,
    139
  Twelve Steps of, 136–138, 174
  Twelve Traditions of, 138–139, 175
  women in early development of,
    139–141
  women and minorities in, 141–144
Allport, G., 76
Ambiguity, honoring, 70
American cultural beliefs
  Americans as chosen people, 71–72
  scientific method, 5–6, 68
  suffering/wickedness link, 62–63
Anders, T., 49
Archethemes, 18–38
  defined, 18
  in departure stage of hero's journey,
    20–25

as essence of support groups, 133–134
in initiation stage of hero's journey,
  25–34
in return stage of hero's journey,
  34–38
used in responding to evil, 56–59
*See also specific archethemes*
Arendt, H., 53, 57
Armstrong, K., 7, 8, 10, 25, 102–103
Arterburn, S., 98
Assagioli, R., 103
Assessment
  of client's spirituality, 93–94, 176–177
  form for, 176–177
  including religion/spirituality in, 91–94
  questions for, 92–93
  as spiritual intervention technique,
    119–120
  spirituality-related inventories for,
    113, 185–194
  *See also* Self-assessment
Association for Spiritual, Ethical, and
    Religious Values in Counseling
    (ASERVIC), spiritual
    competencies of, 178–180
Atheists, 4, 12
Augustine, Saint, 47
Automazation, 28

Barnhouse, R. T., 96, 97
Baumeister, R. F., 44, 50
Bechtel, L., 63
Beliefs
  American cultural, 5–6, 62–63, 68,
    71–72

TO THE OWNER OF THIS BOOK:

We hope that you have found *Explorations in Counseling and Spirituality* useful. So that this book can be improved in a future edition, would you take the time to complete this sheet and return it? Thank you.

School and address: _____

_____

Department: _____

Instructor's name: _____

1. What I like most about this book is: _____

_____

_____

2. What I like least about this book is: _____

_____

_____

3. My general reaction to this book is: _____

_____

_____

4. The name of the course in which I used this book is: _____

_____

5. Were all of the chapters of the book assigned for you to read?_____

   If not, which ones weren't? _____

6. In the space below, or on a separate sheet of paper, please write specific suggestions for improving this book and anything else you'd care to share about your experience in using this book.

_____

_____

_____

_____

OPTIONAL:

Your name: _____ Date: _____

Address: _____

Phone: _____ Email: _____

May we quote you, either in promotion for *Explorations in Counseling and Spirituality*, or in future publishing ventures?

Yes: _____ No: _____

Sincerely yours,

Christopher Faiver          Eugene O'Brien
R. Elliott Ingersoll        Christopher McNally

FOLD HERE

----------------------------------------

FOLD HERE